The Civil War In America

The Civil War In America

The Observations of One of Britain's Most
Famous Special Correspondents

William Howard Russell

LEONAUR

The Civil War In America
The Observations of One of Britain's Most Famous Special Correspondents
by William Howard Russell

First published under the title
The Civil War In America

Leonaur is an imprint of Oakpast Ltd

Copyright in this form © 2012 Oakpast Ltd

ISBN: 978-1-78282-032-1 (hardcover)
ISBN: 978-1-78282-033-8 (softcover)

http://www.leonaur.com

Publisher's Notes

Contents

Letter 1	7
Letter 2	16
Letter 3	28
Letter 4	32
Letter 5	37
Letter 6	47
Letter 7	57
Letter 8	66
Letter 9	77
Letter 10	87
Letter 11	105
Letter 12	117
Letter 13	150
Letter 14	176

Letter 1

Washington, March 29, 1861

If the intelligent foreigner who is supposed to make so many interesting and novel observations on the aspect of the countries he visits, and on the manners of the people among whom he travels, were to visit the United States at this juncture, he would fail to detect any marked indication of the extraordinary crisis which agitates the members of the Great Republic, either at the principal emporium of its commerce, or at the city which claims to be the sole seat of its government. Accustomed to the manifestation of violent animosity and great excitement among the nations of Europe during political convulsions, he would be struck with astonishment, if not moved to doubt, when, casting his eyes on the columns of the multitudinous journals which swarm from every printing-press in the land, he read that the United States were in such throes of mortal agony, that those who knew the constitution of the patient best, were scarce able to prophesy any result except final dissolution.

It would require such special acquaintance as only those well versed in the various signs and forms of the dangerous influences which are at work can possess, to appreciate from anything to be seen at New York or Washington, the fact that the vast body politic which sprang forth with the thews and sinews of a giant from the womb of rebellion and revolution; which claimed half the New World as its heritage, and reserved the other as the certain reward of future victory; which extended its commerce over every sea, and affronted the antiquity of international law by bold innovations and defiant enumerations of new principles; which seemed to revel in success of doctrines that the experience of the Old World had proved to be untenable, or had rejected as unsuited to the government of mankind; which had developed all the resources of the physical agencies in manufactures, machinery, electricity, and steam, that could give strength, and wealth, and vigour to its frame;—that this mighty Confederation should suddenly be smitten with a desire to tear its limbs asunder, and was only restrained by the palsy that had smitten some of its members.

Certainly no notion of the kind could be formed from actual observation of the words and deeds of men in the cities I have visited, or from any source of information, except the casual conversations of fellow travellers, or the startling headings in the newspapers, which have, however, reduced "sensation" paragraphs and lines to such every-day routine, that the American is no more affected by them than the workman in the proof-house is moved by the constant explosion of cannon. We are accustomed to think the Americans a very excitable people; their personal conflicts, their rapid transitions of feeling, the accounts of their public demonstrations, their energetic expressions, their love of popular assemblies, and the cultivation of the arts, which excite their passions, are favourable to that notion. But New York seems full of divine calm and human phlegm.

A panic in Wall Street would, doubtless, create greater external disturbance than seemed to me to exist in its streets and pleasant mansions. No doubt there is, and must be, very great agitation of feeling, and much apprehension; but to the stranger they are not very patent or visible. An elegant refinement, which almost assumes the airs of pococuranteism, reigns in society, only broken by the vehement voices of female patriotism, or the denunciations addressed against the provisions of a tariff, which New York seems unanimous in regarding with hostility and dismay. If Rome be burning, there are hundreds of noble Romans fiddling away in the Fifth Avenue, and in its dependencies, quite satisfied that they cannot join any of the fire companies, and that they are not responsible for the deeds of the "Nero" or "anti-Nero" who applied the torch. They marry, and are given in marriage; they attend their favourite theatres, dramatic or devotional, as the case may be, in the very best coats or bonnets; they eat the largest oysters, drink the best wines, and enjoy the many goods the gods provide them, unmoved by the daily announcement that Fort Sumter is evacuated, that the South is arming, and the Morrill tariff is ruining the trade of the country.

And, as they say, "What can we do?" They insinuate:

We are powerless to avert the march of events. We think everybody is wrong. Things were going on very pleasantly when

8

these abolitionists disturbed the course of trade, and commerce, and speculation with their furious fantasies; and now the South, availing themselves of the opportunity which the blindness of their enemies has afforded them to do what they have wished in their hearts for many a year, start in business for themselves, and will not be readily brought back by the lure of any concession till they find they are unable to get money to pay their way, and resort to measures which may be ruinous to capital, or lead to reconstruction of the Confederation on both sides.

If, pursuing the researches which such remarks suggest, an investigation is made in the same stratum of thought by careful exploration, it will not be long before the miner comes upon matters which he never could have expected to find in that particular gallery. What are the most cherished institutions of the Great Republic? If the intelligent foreigner were asked what were the fundamental principles which, guaranteed by, and guaranteeing, their constitution, the people of the United States admired the most, he would probably reply, "Universal suffrage (with its incidental exercise of vote by ballot), free citizenship, a free press." Probably he would answer correctly in the main, for he would know more of the matter than I do; but if he visited New York for a few days, what would be his amazement to see his best friends shake their heads at the very mention of these grand Shibboleths!

How would his faith be disturbed when he learnt from some merchant prince that universal suffrage, in its practical working in that city, had handed over the municipal government to the most ignorant, if not the most unprincipled men; that it flooded and submerged the landmarks of respectability and station by a tide of barbarous immigrant foreigners; that the press had substituted licentiousness for liberty; and that the evils done in New York by these agencies afflicted the whole State! Ingenious theorists might attempt to convince him that the effect of these mischievous elements had been felt at the very centre of the social system, and had led to the separation which, be it temporary or permanent, all Northern Americans deplore. Few, however, would admit that the failure of Republican institutions is by any means involved in the disasters which have fallen on the Commonwealth, even when they freely confess that they desire to modify the constitution, while they lament the impossibility of doing so in consequence of the very condition of things it has created.

It is my firm conviction, forced on my mind by the words of many men of note with whom I have spoken, that they would gladly, if they could, place some limits to their own liberties as far as their fellow-men are concerned, and that they begin to doubt whether a constitution founded on abstract principles of the equality of mankind can be worked out in huge cities—veritable *cloacæ gentium*—however successful it was in the earlier days of the Republic, and as it is in the sparsely inhabited rural districts where every inhabitant represents property. These men may be a small minority, but they certainly represent great wealth, much ability, and high intelligence in the State of which I speak. They assert there is no recuperative power in the constitution.

The sick physician cannot heal himself, for he has caused his own illness, and a convention, the great nostrum of the fathers of the Republic, is only an appeal from Philip drunk to Philip mad. "*Volumus leges Americæ mutari*," is their despairing aspiration, and they justify the wish by contrasts between the state of things which existed when the Constitution was prepared for the thirteen Confederated States and that which prevails at the present time, when thirty-four States, some two or three of which are equal to the original Republic, and many of which declare they are absolute sovereignties; which have absorbed all the nomads of the Old World, with a fair proportion of Genghis Khans, Attilas, and Timours in embryo, present a spectacle which the most sagacious of the framers of the original compact never could have imagined.

They are impatient of the ills they have, and are somewhat indifferent to the wondrous and magnificent results in material prosperity and intellectual development which the old system either promoted or caused. New York, however, would do anything rather than fight; her delight is to eat her bread and honey, and count her dollars, in peace. The vigorous, determined hostility of the South to her commercial eminence, is met by a sort of maudlin sympathy without any action, or intention to act. The only matter in which the great commercial aristocracy take any interest is the Morrill tariff, which threatens to inflict on them the most serious losses and calamity. There is a general expectation that an extra session of Congress will be called to amend the obnoxious measure; and it is asserted that the necessity for such a session is imperious; but, so far as I can judge, all such hopes will be disappointed.

There is no desire at Washington to complicate matters by stormy debates, and the statesmen so recently elevated to power are sufficiently well read in general and in national history to know that extraordinary parliaments are generally the executioners of those who call them.

The representatives of the great protected interests at the capital deny that the tariff will have the injurious effects attributed to it, or that it augments to any very grievous extent the burdens of the New Yorkers or of the foreign manufacturers. Even if it does, they declare that protection is necessary. The ingenious proposals to evade the operation of the tariff by a jugglery of cargoes between the Southern and Northern ports will, they say, be frustrated by the more rigid application of the Revenue and Customs' system, out of which most serious complications must inevitably arise at no distant period. While at New York all is calm doubtfulness or indolent anticipation, at Washington there is excitement and activity. The aristocracy of New York has yielded itself unresistingly to a tyranny it hates; it cannot wield at will the fierce democracy, and it abandons all efforts to control it, forgetting the abundant proofs in every history of the power of genius, wealth, and superior intelligence to control the heavier masses, however wild and difficult of approach.

At Washington there is at this moment such a ferment as no other part of the world could exhibit—a spectacle which makes one wonder that any man can be induced to seek for office, or that any government can be conducted under such a system. The storm which rolled over the capital has, I am told, subsided; but the stranger, unaccustomed to such tempestuous zones, thinks the gale is quite strong enough even in its diminished intensity. All the hotels are full of keen gray-eyed men, who fondly believe their destiny is to fill for four years some pet appointment under government. The streets are crowded with them; the steamers and the railway carriages, the public departments, the steps of the senators' dwellings, the lobbies of houses, the President's mansion, are crowded with them. From all parts of the vast Union, not even excepting the South, they have come fast as steam or wind and waves could bear them to concentrate in one focus on the devoted head of the President all the myriad influences which, by letter, testimonial, personal application, unceasing canvass, and sleepless solicitation, they can collect together.

Willard's Hotel, a huge caravanserai, is a curious study of character and institutions. Every form of speech and every accent under which the English tongue can be recognized, rings through the long corridors in tones of expostulation, anger, or gratification. Crowds of

11

long-limbed, nervous, eager-looking men, in loose black garments, undulating shirt collars, vast conceptions in hatting and booting, angular with documents and pregnant with demand, throng every avenue, in spite of the printed notices directing them "to move on from front of the cigar-stand." They are "senator hunters," and every senator has a *clientelle* more numerous than the most popular young Roman noble who ever sauntered down the Via Sacra. If one of them ventures out of cover, the cry is raised, and he is immediately run to earth. The printing-presses are busy with endless copies of testimonials, which are hurled at everybody with reckless profusion.

The writing-room of the hotel is full of people preparing statements or writing for "more testimonials," demanding more places, or submitting "extra certificates." The bar-room is full of people inspiring themselves with fresh confidence, or engaged in plots to surprise some place or find one out; and the ladies who are connected with members of the party in power find themselves the centres of irresistible attraction. "Sir," said a gentleman to whom I had letters of introduction, "I know you must be a stranger, because you did not stop me to present these letters in the street."

At the head of the list of persecuted men is the President himself. Ever one has a right to walk into the White House, which is the President's private as well as his official residence. Mr. Lincoln is actuated by the highest motives in the distribution of office. All the vast patronage of tens of thousands of places, from the highest to the lowest, is his; and, instead of submitting the various claims to the heads of departments, the President seeks to investigate them, and to see all the candidates. Even his iron frame and robust constitution are affected by the process, which lasts all day, and is not over in the night or in the morning. The particular *formula* which he has adopted to show the impossibility of satisfying everybody is by no means accepted by anybody who is disappointed. What is the use of telling a man he can't have a place because a hundred others are asking for it, if that man thinks he is the only one who has a right to get it?

At the very moment when the President and his Cabinet should be left undisturbed to deal with the tremendous questions which have arisen for their action, the roar of office seekers dins every sense, and almost annihilates them. The Senate, which is now sitting merely to confirm appointments, relieving the monotony of executive reviews with odd skirmishes between old political antagonists now and then, will, it is said, rise this week. Around their chamber is the ever-recurring question heard, "Who has got what?" and the answer is never satisfactory to all. This hunting after office, which destroys self-respect when it is the moving motive of any considerable section of a great party, is an innovation which was introduced by General Jackson; but it is likely to be as permanent as the Republic, inasmuch as no candidate dares declare his intention of reverting to the old system. These "spoils," as they are called, are now being distributed by two governments—the *de jure* and *de facto* government of Washington, and the government erected by the Southern States at Montgomery.

It is difficult for one who has arrived so recently in this country, and who has been subjected to such a variety of statements to come to any very definite conclusion in reference to the great questions which agitate it. But as far as I can I shall form my opinions from what I see, and not from what I hear; and as I shall proceed South in a few days, there is a probability of my being able to ascertain what is the real state of affairs in that direction. As far as I can judge—my conclusion, let it be understood, being drawn from the prevailing opinions of others— "the South will never go back into the Union." On the same day I heard a gentleman of position among the Southern party say, "No concession, no compromise, nothing that can be done or suggested, shall induce us to join any confederation of which the New England States are members;" and by another gentleman, well known as one of the ablest of the abolitionists, I was told, "If I could bring back the Southern States by holding up my little finger, I should consider it criminal to do so."

The friends of the Union sometimes endeavour to disguise their sorrow and their humiliation at the prospect presented by the Great Republic under the garb of pride in the peculiar excellence of institutions which have permitted such a revolution as secession without the loss of one drop of blood. But concession averts bloodshed. If I give up my purse to the footpad who presents a pistol at my head I satisfy all his demands, and he must be a sanguinary miscreant if he pulls trigger afterwards. The policeman has, surely, no business to boast of the peculiar excellence, in such a transaction, of the state of things which allows the transfer to take place without bloodshed. A government may be so elastic as, like an overstretched india-rubber band, to have no compressive force whatever; and that very quality is claimed for the Federal Government as excellence by some eminent men whom I have met, and who maintained the thesis, that the United States Government has no right whatever to assert its authority by force over the people of any State whatever; that, based on the consent of all, it ceases to exist whenever there is dissent,—a doctrine which no one need analyze who understands what are the real uses and ends of government.

The friends of the existing administration, on the whole, regard the secession as a temporary aberration, which a "masterly inactivity," the effects of time, inherent weakness, and a strong reaction, of which, they flatter themselves, they see many proofs in the Southern States, will correct. "Let us," they say, "deal with this matter in our own way. Do not interfere. A recognition of the secession would be an interference amounting to hostility. In good time the violent men down South will come to their senses, and the treason will die out." They ignore the difficulties which European States may feel in refusing to recognize the principles on which the United States were founded when they find them embodied in a new Confederation, which, so far as we know, may be to all intents and purposes constituted in an entire independence, and present itself to the world with claims to recognition to which England, at least, having regard to precedents of *de facto* governments, could only present an illogical refusal.

The hopes of other sections of the Northerners are founded on the want of capital in the Slave States; on the pressure which will come upon them when they have to guard their own frontiers against the wild tribes who have been hitherto repelled at the expense of the whole Union by the Federal troops; on the exigencies of trade, which will compel them to deal with the North, and thereby to enter into friendly relations and ultimate re-alliance. But most impartial people, at least in New York, are of opinion that the South has shaken the dust off her feet, and will never enter the portals of the Union again. She is confident in her own destiny. She feels strong enough to stand alone. She believes her mission is one of extension and conquest—her leaders are men of singular political ability and undaunted resolution.

She has but to stretch forth her hand, as she believes, and the Gulf becomes an American lake closed by Cuba. The reality of these visions the South is ready to test, and she would not now forego the trial, which may, indeed, be the work of years, but which she will certainly make. All the considerations which can be urged against her resolves are as nothing in the way of her passionate will, and the world may soon see under its eyes the conflict of two republics founded on the same principles, but subjected to influences that produce repulsion as great as exists in two bodies charged with the same electricity. If ever

14

the explosion come it will be tremendous in its results, and distant Europe must feel the shock.

The authorities seem resolved to make a stand at Fort Pickens, notwithstanding the advice of Mr. Douglass to give it up. They regard it as an important Federal fortress, as indisputably essential for national purposes as Tortugas or Key West. Although United States property has been "occupied," the store vessels of the State seized, and the sovereignty of the seceding States successfully asserted by the appropriation of arsenals, and money, and war materials, on the part of the local authorities, the Government of Washington are content by non-recognition to reserve their own rights in face of the exercise of *force majeure.*

The Chevalier Bertinnati, who has been *Chargé d'Affaires* for the government of King Victor Emmanuel, has been raised to the rank of Minister, and in that capacity delivered his letters of credence to the President on Wednesday. The letter addressed to the President by the King of Piedmont was couched in terms of much friendliness and sympathy, and Mr. Lincoln's reply was equally warm. There is no display of military preparation to meet the eye either at Washington or along the road to it. General Scott, who was to have dined at the President's Cabinet dinner last night, and who was actually in the White House for that purpose, was compelled to leave by indisposition. Any attempt to relieve Fort Sumter would unquestionably be attended with great loss of life; but most Americans readily admit that if they had a foreign force to deal with, no consideration of that kind would stay the hands of the government. The fort stands on a sandbank in shallow water, and batteries have been cast up on both shores effectually commanding the whole of the channels for several miles.

The military activity and enterprise—I hear the skill as well—of the South have been displayed in the readiness and completeness of their preparations. In Galveston, Texas, Governor Houston, who has resigned, or been deposed, protests, it is said, against the acts of the new government, and is likely to give them trouble. The telegraph will, however, anticipate any news of this sort which I can send you, though its intelligence should be received with many grains of salt. Some people assert that "the telegraph has caused the secession," and there is a strong feeling that some restrictions should be placed upon the misuse of it in disseminating false reports.

Letter 2

Washington, April 1, 1861.

From all I have seen and heard, my belief is that the Southern States have gone from the Union, if not forever, at least for such time as will secure for their government an absolute independence till it be terminated by war, or, if their opponents be right, by the certain processes of internal decay arising from inherent vices in their system, faulty organization, and want of population, vigour, and wealth. That the causes which have led to their secession now agitate the Border States most powerfully with a tendency to follow them is not to be denied by those who watch the course of events, and as these powerful neutrals oscillate to and fro, under the pressure of contending parties and passions, the government at Washington and the authorities of the revolting States regard every motion with anxiety; the former fearful lest by word or deed they may repel them forever, the latter more disposed by active demonstrations to determine the ultimate decision in their own favour, and to attach them permanently to the slave States by resolute declarations of principle.

Whatever the results of the Morrill tariff may be, it is probable they must be endured on both sides of the Atlantic, for there is no power in the government or in the President, as I understand, to modify its provisions, and there is a strong feeling in Mr. Lincoln's Cabinet against the extra session, so loudly demanded in New York, and so confidently expected in some parts of the Union. Nothing but some overwhelming State necessity will overcome that opposition, and, as the magnitude of such an occasion will have to be estimated by those who are vehemently opposed to an extra Congress, it is not likely that anything can occur which will be considered of sufficient gravity by the government at Washington to induce them to encounter the difficulties and dangers they anticipate in consequence of the convocation of an extraordinary assemblage of both Houses.

Until next December, then, in all probability, the President and his Cabinet will have such control of affairs as is possible in the system of this government, or in the circumstances, together with the far more than co-ordinate responsibility attached to their position as a Federal Government. It is scarcely possible for an Englishman, far less for the native of any State possessing a powerful executive, to comprehend the limits which are assigned to the powers of the State in this country, or to the extent to which resistance to its authority can be carried by the action of the States supposed to be consenting parties to its constitution and supporters of its jurisdiction. Take, for instance, what is occurring within a few miles of the seat of the central government, across the Potomac. At a certain iron-foundry guns have been cast for the United States Government, which are about to be removed to Fort Monroe, in the State of Virginia, one of the fortresses for the defence of the United States.

The Legislature of Virginia sat all night last Saturday, and authorized the governor of that State to call out the public guard in order to prevent by force, if necessary, the removal of those guns, at the same time offering to the contractor the price which he was to have received for them from the Federal Government. Again, at Mobile, where a writ of *habeas corpus* is sued out on behalf of the master of a vessel, who was seized because he had a cargo of small stores which he intended to sell to the United States men-of-war on observation off Pensacola, the counsel for the State of Florida resists the application on the ground that the prisoner was carrying supplies to an enemy, and that a state of war exists in consequence of the acts of the Federal Government; and the Court, without deciding on the point, discharge the prisoner, in order that it may be freed from responsibility.

On the other hand, the Federal Government remits the penalties of forfeiture and fines on the vessel seized by the Custom House at New York for want of proper clearances from Southern ports. The stereotype plates with the words "Evacuation of Fort Sumter" have apparently been worn out, but it is believed on all sides that it will be abandoned by Major Anderson this week, although I heard a member of the Cabinet declare last week that no orders had been issued to that officer to evacuate it. If the opinions of some of the Northern people prevailed, the fort would be retained until it was taken by assault. The Southern Confederation, secure of Fort Sumter, are now preparing for active operations against Fort Pickens, which protects the entrance

17

to the quondam United States Navy Yard at Pensacola, now in the possession of the troops of Florida; and certain organs of the extreme party in the South have already demanded that the forts at Tortugas and Key West, which are situated far out at sea from the coast, should be surrendered.

The Cabinet of Mr. Lincoln is understood to contain the representatives of three different courses of policy—that trinity of action which generally produces torpid and uncertain motion or complete rest. First, there are those who would, at any risk, vindicate the rights they claim for the Federal Government, and use force, even though it could only, in its most successful application, overrun the States of the South, and compel a temporary submission, without leading to the reestablishment of Federal authority, or the reincorporation of the States with the Union. Secondly, there are those, men of intellect and capacity, who, dissenting altogether from the doctrines propounded by the leaders of the revolution, and convinced that the separation will not be permanent, see the surest and safest mode of action in the total abstinence from all aggressive assertion of rights, and in a policy of *laissez aller* of indeterminate longitude and latitude. These statesmen believe that, like most revolutions, the secession is the work of the minority, and that a strong party of reaction exists, which will come to the front by and by, "expel the traitors," and return triumphantly with their repentant States into the bosom of the Union.

The gentlemen who hold these views have either a more accurate knowledge than the public, are better read in the signs of the times, or have more faith in the efficacy of inaction on the love of Americans for the Union, than is possessed by most of the outer world. The third party is formed of those who are inclined to take the South at their word; to cut the cord at once, believing that the loss would be a gain, and that the Southern Confederation would inflict on itself a most signal retribution for what they consider as the crime of breaking up the Union. Practically, so far as I have gone, I have failed to meet many people who really exhibited any passionate attachment to the Union for its own sake, or who pretended to be animated by any strong feelings of regard or admiration for the Government of the United States in itself. The word "Constitution" is forever ringing in one's ears, its "principles" and its authority are continually appealed to, but the end is no nearer.

The other day I bought the whole *Constitution of the United States,* neatly printed, for three halfpence. But the only conclusion I could draw was, that it was better for States not to have constitutions which could be bought at such very moderate prices. It is rather an inopportune moment for the professor of the Harvard Law School to send forth his lecture on the Constitution of the United States, and on the differences between it and that of Great Britain. Just as the learned gentleman is glorying in the supremacy of the Judicial body of the United States over Congress, Presidents, and Legislatures, the course of events exhibits that Supreme Court as a mere nullity in the body politic, unable to take cognizance, or unwilling to act in regard to matters which are tearing the constitution into atoms. No one thinks of appealing to it, or invoking its decision.

And, after all, if the court were to decide, what would be the use of its judgment, if one or other of the two great parties resisted it? The *ultima ratio* would be the only means by which the decision could be enforced. In the very midst of the hymns which are offered up around the shrines of the constitution, whether old or mended, all celebrating the powers of the great priestess of the mysteries, there are heretic voices to be heard, which, in addition to other matters, deny that the Supreme Court was ever intended by the constitution to exercise the sole and signal right of interpreting the constitution, that it is competent to do so, or that it would be safe to give it the power. Its powers are judicial, not political, and Mr. Calhoun on that very point said:

> Let it never be forgotten, that if we should absurdly attribute to the Supreme Court the exclusive right of construing the constitution, there would be, in fact, between the sovereign and subject under such a government no constitution, or at least nothing deserving the name, or serving the legitimate object of so sacred an instrument.

The argument revolves in a circle; it ends nowhere, and there seems no solution except such as concession or a sword cut may give.

There are at present in Washington two of the three unrecognized Ministers Plenipotentiary of the Southern Government, Mr. Roman and Mr. Crawford. Judging from the tone of these gentlemen, all idea of returning to the Union, under any circumstances whatever, has been utterly abandoned. Mr. Forsyth, the third of the commissioners, who is at present engaged in adjusting certain business of a very important character at New York, is expected back in a few days, and it will then be seen whether the commissioners consent to walk up and down in the *salles des pas perdus* any longer. They are armed with full powers on all questions which can come up for settlement.

The government has refused to receive them, or to take any official notice of them whatever; but there is reason to believe that certain propositions and negotiations have been laid before Mr. Seward in a private and unofficial manner, to which no reply of a definite character has been given. Before this letter reaches you, Mr. Yancey, Mr. Mann, and Mr. Rort will have arrived in Europe to try the temper of the Governments of England and France in reference to the recognition of the Southern States. Both parties have been somewhat startled by the intelligence of an active movement of Spain to gain political ascendancy in St. Domingo; and the news that France and England are sending a combined fleet to these shores, though coming in a very questionable shape, has excited uneasy feeling and some recrimination.

If the Congress is reassembled, there is much reason to fear an open rupture; if not, another solution may be arrived at. It is unfortunate for the government that General Scott is suffering at this moment from the infirmities of age, and the effect of the great demands made upon his strength. Mr. Lincoln gave a dinner to his Cabinet on Thursday last, the first of the season, in honour principally of General Scott; but the veteran general, who had entered the White House, was obliged to leave before dinner was served. There has been a great emigration of candidates and office-hunters from this since I last wrote, some contented, many more grumbling. It is asserted that there never has been such a clean sweep of office-holders since the practice was introduced by General Jackson. If I am rightly informed, the President has the patronage of one hundred and forty thousand places, great and small—some very small.

Night.—The influence of England and of France on the destinies of the Republic is greater than any American patriot would like to admit. It must not be expected, therefore, that there will be any proof of excessive anxiety afforded by the leaders of either party in reference to the course which may be taken by the European Governments in the present crisis; but it is not the less to be apprehended, that an immediate recognition of the confederated independence of the South, or of the doctrine of absolute individual sovereignty on the part of those States, may precipitate the hostile action which, in the event of absolute final separation, seems to be inevitable. To the North it would be a heavy blow and great discouragement, the consequences of which could only be averted by some very violent remedies. Separation without war is scarcely to be expected.

The establishment of an independent Republic in the South may, indeed, be effected peaceably; but it is not, humanly speaking, within the limits of any probability that the diverse questions which will arise out of conflicting interests in regard to revenue and State and Federal rights can be settled without an appeal to arms. At the present minute there is nothing to induce a stranger to believe that an effectual resistance could be offered to a vigorous aggressive movement from the South, supposing the means to make it existed either in the adhesion or permission of the Border States. The North, however, is strong in its population, in its wealth, and in its calm. In the hands of the Border States are all the arbitraments of revolution or union, of war or peace. By an unmeaning euphemism the revolution of the South has been called "Secession;" but the confusion and mischief caused by the euphemistic timidity of statesmen disappear, when the acts of the South are tested by the standard applicable to revolutionary crises; and by that standard alone are those acts intelligible and coherent.

Measured in that way, the seizure of property, the deeds and the language of the leaders of the movement, and the acts of the masses, can be properly estimated. Mr. Douglass, whose mental capacity is a splendid justification of his enormous political activity, and of a high political rank—unattached—is understood to be engaged on a vast system for establishing duties all over the North American continent in the nature of a Zollverein. It is his opinion that the North, in case of separation, must fight the South on the arena of free trade; that the tariff must be completely altered; and that the duties must be lowered from point to point, in proportion as the South bids against the North for the commerce of Europe, till the reduction reaches such a point that the South, forced to raise revenue for the actual expenses of government, and unable to struggle against the superior wealth of the North in such a contest, is obliged to come to an understanding with its powerful competitor, and to submit to a treaty of commerce which shall include all the States of the North American continent, from the Isthmus of Panama to the ice of the Arctic Seas.

The Canadas are, of course, included in such a project; indeed, it is difficult to say where the means of escaping from their present embarrassment will not be sought by the leading statesmen of America. But on one point all are agreed. Whatever may happen, the North will insist on a Free Mississippi. It is the very current of life for the trade of myriads of people hundreds of miles from New Orleans. If Louisiana, either as sovereign State or representative agent of the Southern Confederation, attempts to control the navigation of that river, we shall see a most terrible and ruinous war. Let England look to the contingencies.

April, 5.—One month and one day have elapsed since Mr. Lincoln and his Cabinet were installed at Washington. Long previous to their accession to power or rather to office, the revolution of the South had assumed the aspect of an independent government. When the new administration tried to direct the horses' heads, they found the reins were cut, and all they could do was to sit on the State coach, and take their chance of falling in a soft place, or of the fiery steeds coming to a standstill from exhaustion. A month ago and the State Treasury was nearly exhausted; only some £370,000 was forthcoming to meet demands and requirements four times as large. The navy was scattered all over the world at stations by no means readily accessible, the army posted along frontier lines, between which and the Northern States was interposed the expanse of the Southern Confederation; the officers disaffected to the government, or at all events so well affected to their individual sovereign States as to feel indisposed to serve the United States; the whole machinery of government in the hands of the revolutionary leaders, every trace of Federal existence erased in the South, wiped away by acts which, unless justified by successful revolt, would be called treasonable, or by force or stratagem, and only two forts held on the seaboard, weekly garrisoned, and unhappily situated with reference to operations of relief.

In addition to these sources of weakness, came the confusion and apprehension caused by divided counsels, want of cohesion, the disorders of a violent national contest, mistrust of adequate support, and above all the imperious necessities of the place-seekers, whose importunate requisitions distracted the attention of the government from the more important business which presented itself for adjustment. It was, of course, necessary to fill the posts which were occupied by enemies with men devoted to the interests of a government which could little brook any indifference or treacherous tendencies on the part of its subordinates. But had the administration been as strong in all respects as any United States Government ever could or can hope to be, in reference to such emergencies as the present, it really could have done little except precipitate a civil war, in which the Border States would have arranged themselves by the side of the Cotton States.

A considerable portion of the North would have been hostile to coercion, and the theories which have been propounded with much apparent approbation respecting the actual uses of government, its powers and jurisdiction, show that European doctrines on such points are not at all accepted by statesmen, politicians and jurists in North America. Without the means of enforcing an authority which many of its own adherents, and most of the neutral parties denied to it, Mr. Lincoln's administration finds itself called upon to propound a policy and to proceed to vigorous action. The demand is scarcely reasonable. The policy of such men suddenly lifted to the head of affairs, which they cannot attempt to guide, must be to wait and watch, and their action must be simply tentative as they have no power to put forth with moderate hope of success any aggressive force.

Be satisfied of this—the United States Government will give up no power or possession which it has at present got. By its voluntary act it will surrender nothing whatever. No matter what reports may appear in the papers or in letters, distrust them if they would lead you to believe that Mr. Lincoln is preparing either to abandon what he has now, or to recover that which he has not.

The United States Government is in an attitude of protest; it cannot strike an offensive blow. But, if any attack is made upon it, the government hopes that it will be strengthened by the indignation of the North and West, to such an extent that it cannot only repel the aggression, but possibly give a stimulus to a great reaction in its favour.

On these principles Fort Sumter and Fort Pickens are held. They are claimed as Federal fortresses. The Stars and Stripes still float over them. Whatever may be said to the contrary, they will remain there till they are removed by the action of the Confederate States. The commissioners of Mr. Jefferson Davis's government "have reason to say that if any attempt be made to throw re-enforcements into Fort Pickens, unless they receive previous notice of it as promised, it will be a breach of good faith." From all I can learn, no intention of strengthening the fort is at present entertained; but it may be doubted if the attempt would not be made should any favourable opportunity of doing so present itself.

All "the movements of troops," of which you will see accounts, are preparations against—not for—aggression. At most they amount to the march of a few companies and guns to various forts, now all but undefended. Fort Washington, of which I shall have a few words to say hereafter, was till lately held by a very inadequate force. As a member of the Cabinet said to me, "I could have taken it last week with a little whisky," that potent artillery being applied to the weak defences of the aged Irish artilleryman who constituted "the garrison."

The "formidable military force concentrated in Washington," of which you may read in the American journals, consists of about 700 men of all arms, as far as I can see, and four brass field guns. There is a good deal of drumming, fifing, marching, and music going on daily. I look on and see a small band in gay uniforms, a small body of men in sombre uniforms, varying from fifteen to thirty rank and file, armed, however, with excellent rifles, and a very large standard, pass by; and next day I read that such and such a company had a parade, and "attracted much admiration by their efficient and soldierly appearance, and the manner in which," &c.

But these military companies have no intention of fighting for the government. Their sympathies are quite undetermined. Formidable as they would be in skirmishing in the open country, they would be of comparatively little use against regular troops at the outset of the contest, as they have never learnt to act together, and do not aspire to form even battalions. But their existence indicates the strong military tendencies of the people, and the danger of doing anything which might turn them against the government. Mr. Lincoln has no power to make war against the South: the Congress alone could give it to him; and that is not likely to be given, because Congress will not be assembled before the usual time, unless under the pressure of and imperious necessity.

Why, then, hold these forts at all? Why not give them up? Why not withdraw the garrison, strike the flag, and cease to keep up a useless source of irritation in the midst of the Southern Confederation? The answer to these questions is: These forts are Federal property. The government does not acknowledge the existence of any right on the part of the people of the States to seize them as appertaining to individual States. The forts are protests against the acts of violence to which the Federal authority has yielded elsewhere. They are, moreover, the *points d'appui,* small as they are, on which the Federal Government can rest its resistance to the claims of the Southern Confederation to be acknowledged as an independent republic. If they were surrendered without attack, or without the existence of any pressure arising from the refusal of the Southern authorities to permit them to get supplies, which is an act of war, the case of the United States Government would be, they consider, materially weakened.

If it be observed that these forts have no strategic value, it may readily be replied that their political value is very great. But, serious as these considerations may be, or may be thought to be, with respect to foreign relations, there are in reference to domestic politics still more weighty inducements to hold them. The effect produced in the North and Northwest by an attack on the forts while the United States flag is floating over them, would be as useful to the government at Washington as the effect of abandoning the forts or tamely surrendering them would be hurtful to them in the estimation of the extreme Republicans. A desperate attack, a gallant defence, the shedding of the blood of gallant men, whose duty it was to defend that intrusted to their keeping, and who yielded only to numbers—the outrage on the United States flag—would create an excitement in the Union which the South, with all its determination and courage, is unwilling to provoke, but which the government would be forced to use in its own service. Such an event must lead to war, a very terrible and merciless war, and both parties pause before they resort to that court of arms.

Unless the Border States join the South, Mr. Jefferson Davis could scarcely hope to carry out the grand projects which are attributed to his military genius of marching northward, and dictating terms on their own soil to the Republicans. He could scarcely venture to leave the negro population unguarded in his rear, and his flanks menaced by the sea-born northerners on the one side, and by such operations as the water-sheds significantly indicate on the other. It is idle to speculate on the incidents of that which may never occur, and which, occurring, may assume the insignificant aspect of border skirmishes, or the tremendous proportions of a war of races and creeds, intensified by the worst elements of servile and civil conflict.

The government of Mr. Lincoln hope and believe that the contest may be averted. The commissioners of the South are inclined to think, also, there will be a peaceful solution, obtained, of course, by full concession and recognition. But inaction cannot last on the part of the South. Already they have begun the system of coercion. The supplies of the garrison at Sumter will be cut off henceforth, if they are not already forbidden. They do not fear the moral effect of this act, for some of their leading men actually believe that nothing can stop the progress of a movement which will, they fondly think, absorb all the other States of the Union, and leave the New England States to form an insignificant republic of its own, with a possible larger destiny in Canada. Their opponents in the North are as fully satisfied that the direst Nemesis will fall on the Montgomery Government in the utter ruin of all their States the moment they are left to themselves.

The government is elated at the success of the loan, and Mr. Chase has taken high ground in refusing offers made to him yesterday, and in resolving to issue government securities for the balance of the amount required to complete the amount. Mr. Forsyth, one of the Southern commissioners, who has just returned from New York here, is equally satisfied with the temper of parties in that city, and seems to think that the New Yorkers are preparing for a secession. But, though States may be sovereign, it has never been ascertained that cities or portions of States are so, and in the western and northern portions of the State of New York there is a large agricultural population, which, with the aid of government, would speedily suppress any attempt to secede on the part of the city, if men are to be believed who say they know the circumstances of the case. Virginia is claimed by both sides, but accounts this morning are to the effect that the secessionists have been defeated on a division by a vote of two to one in favour of the Union; and although General Houston appears to be forced to accept the situation for a time, there are many who think he will organize a strong reaction against the dominant secessionists.

Whatever may be these result of all the diverse actions, the Great Republic is gone! The shape of the fragments is not yet determined any more than their fate. They may reunite, but the cohesion can never be perfect. The ship of the State was built of too many "platforms," there were too many officers on board, perhaps the principles of construction were erroneous, the rigid cast-iron old constitution guns burst violently when tried with new projectiles—any way, those who adhere with most devotion to the vessel, admit that it is parted right amidships, and that its *prestige* has vanished. The more desperate of these would gladly see an enemy, or go out of their way to find one, in the hope of a common bond of union being discovered in a common animosity and danger.

The naval preparations, of which you will hear a good deal, are intended to make good existing deficiencies and to meet contingencies. At any other time the action of Spain in St. Domingo would create a cry for war. Now all the Federal Government can do is to demand and receive explanations. In reply to Mr. Seward's inquiries, the Spanish minister has possibly stated that the recent events in St. Domingo have been caused by the acts and threats of Hayti, which forced the

Dominicans to call in the aid and claim the protection of Spain. There have been several attempts from time to time to induce France to assume the dominion of its former possession, and it is not unlikely that an excellent understanding exists between the Court of Madrid and the Emperor Napoleon in reference to the subject. The report that the Mexicans have made, or contemplate making, an attack on Texas, is scarcely worthy of credence.

As to the Morrill tariff, I can only repeat what I have already said. It must be borne till results show that it cannot be persisted in. Then only will it be repealed or modified. The theory of the government is, that the United States always takes far more from Europe than it can pay for. "If the revenue is collected, there is no ground for complaint. The English and French manufacturer will be satisfied, as well as the northern population. If the revenue is not collected, then the tariff must be repealed, and that will be done within the year, if the mischief is serious." Birmingham, Wolverhampton, and Manchester must make the best they can out of the doctrine.

Letter 3

Washington, April 9, 1861.

The critical position of the Federal Government has compelled its members to preserve secrecy. Never before under any administration was so little of the councils of the Cabinet known to the public, or to those who are supposed to be acquainted with the opinions of the statesmen in office. Mr. Seward has issued the most stringent orders to the officers and clerks in his department to observe the rules, which heretofore have been much disregarded, in reference to the confidential character of State papers in their charge. The sources of the fountain of knowledge from which friendly journalists drew so freely are thus stopped without fear, favor, or affection, toward any. The result has been much irritation in quarters where such "interference" is regarded as unwarrantable, or, at least, as very injurious. The newspapers which enjoyed the privilege of free access to despatches are hatching *canards*, which they let fly along the telegraph wires with amazing productiveness and fertility of conception and incubation.

Hence the monstrous and ridiculous rumours which harden into type everyday—hence the clamours for "a policy," and hence the contending accusations that the government is doing nothing, and that it is also preparing to plunge the country into civil war. Each member of the Cabinet has become a Burleigh, every shake of whose head perplexes New York with a fear of change; every senator is watched by private reporters, who trace "the day's disasters in his morning's face." If a weak company of artillery is marched on board a ship, its movements are chronicled in columns of vivid description, and its footsteps are made to sound like the march of a vast army. The telegraph from Washington has learnt its daily message about Fort Sumter and Fort Pickens by heart, and the world has been soothed daily by the assurance that General Braxton Bragg is ready, and that the South Carolinians can no longer be restrained.

But there is always a secret understanding that Generals Bragg and Beauregard will be more ready still the next day, and that the people will be more unrestrainable by next telegram. When I landed in New York, the first news I learnt was that Fort Sumter would be evacuated next day; and if not, that the supplies would be cut off, and that the garrison would be starved out. I have learnt how to distrust prophecy, and I am going South in the hope that the end is not yet. The Southern commissioners state that the government here has promised them that no efforts shall be made to re-enforce Fort Pickens without previous notice to them—a very singular promise.

The government, however, denies that it has been in communication with them. Fort Sumter must be considered as gone, for there is no disposition, apparently, on the part of the government to hazard the loss of life and great risk which must inevitably attend any attempt to relieve or carry off the garrison, now that the channels are under the fire of numerous heavily armed batteries, which the people of South Carolina were permitted to throw up without molestation. The operations of a relieving force would have to be conducted on a very large scale by troops disembarking on the shores and taking the batteries in reverse, in conjunction with an attack from the sea; and, after all, such an expedition would be futile, unless it were intended to occupy Charleston, and try the fortune of war in South Carolina—an intention quite opposed to the expressions and, I believe, the feelings of the Cabinet of Washington, not to speak of the people of the Border States and of large remnants of the Union. From your correspondent at New York you will receive full particulars of the movements of troops, and of the naval preparations which are reported in the papers, which create more curiosity than excitement among the people I meet. My task must be to describe what I see around me.

It may be as well to state in the most positive terms that the reports which have appeared in the American papers of communications between the English minister and the American Government on the subject of a blockade of the Southern ports, are totally and entirely destitute of foundation. No communication of any kind has passed between Lord Lyons, on the part of the English Government, and Mr. Seward, or anyone else, on behalf of the government at Washington. It would be a most offensive proceeding to volunteer any intimation of the course to be pursued by a European Power respecting a contingency of action on the part of the United States; nor would it be necessary, in case a blockade were declared, to formulate a supere-rogatory notice that it must be such a blockade as the law of nations recognizes.

The importance of a distinct understanding on that point is all the greater in connection with the stories which are afloat that the naval preparations of the hour are intended to afford the Federal Government the means of blockading the mouths of the Mississippi and the Southern ports, with the object of collecting the Federal revenue. If anything is clearer than another, in the doubt and perplexity which prevail, it is that the government will do nothing whatever to precipitate a conflict. It would ill become me, in such a crisis, to hazard any authoritative statements as to the conduct of the administration under the very great variety of complications which may arise hereafter. Of this, however, be assured, not a ship, or a gun, or a man will be directed to make any attack, or to begin an offensive movement against the Confederate States.

If any promise was made by the Buchanan Administration to inform the members of the Southern government or its representatives of their course of action, it will not be considered binding on the consciences of Mr. Lincoln's Cabinet, composed as it is of men who look on their predecessors as guilty of treason to the State. An attempt may be made to re-enforce Fort Pickens, and neither that nor any position occupied by the Federal authorities will be voluntarily abandoned.

Once for all, let it be impressed on the minds of the English people that whatever reports they hear, and however they may come—no matter whence, or in what guise—there is no truth in them if they indicate the smallest intention on the part of Mr. Lincoln to depart from the policy indicated in his Inaugural Address. As strongly as words can do it, I repeat that the forces which have been assembled are only intended for the re-enforcement of the strong places at Tortugas and Key West, which have been left short of every necessary of occupation and defence, and for the establishment of posts of observation, which are essential in case of hostility and to guard against surprise or treachery. I have dwelt in previous letters on the obvious policy of the government of the United States, and I beg your readers to have firm faith that there will be no departure from it.

By concentrating forces at Key West and Tortugas very valuable political results are obtained in face of the present disputes, and material strategical advantages in case those disputes should lead to a rupture, which will not be initiated by the Cabinet at Washington.

These places are within a few hours' sail of the coast; they are healthy, and can be easily supplied, as long as the United States fleet can keep the sea and cover the movements of its transports. Their occupation in force cannot be taken as an act of open war, while it is undoubtedly an alarming menace, which will keep the Confederates in a state of constant apprehension and preparation, leading to much internal trouble and great expense. By a confusion of metaphor which events may justify, the eye to watch may be turned into an arm to strike.

The Southern commissioners are still here, but they are still unable to procure even a semi-official recognition of their existence, and all their correspondence has been carried on through one of their clerks.

It is, perhaps, not necessary to add that Mr. Seward has no intention of resigning, as has been stated, and that there is no dissention in the Cabinet.

Letter 4

Norfolk, Va., April, 15, 1861.

Sumter has fallen at last. So much may be accepted. Before many hours I hope to stand amid the ruins of a spot which will probably become historic, and has already made more noise in the world than its guns, gallant as the defence may have been. The news will produce an extraordinary impression at New York—it will disconcert stock-jobbers, and derange the most ingenious speculations. But, considerable as may be its results in any part of the Union, I venture to say that nowhere will the shock cause such painful convulsions as in the Cabinet at Washington, where there appeared to exist the most perfect conviction that the plan for the relief of Sumter could not fail to be successful, either through the force of the expedition provided for that object, or through the unwillingness of the leaders at Charleston to fire the first shot, and to compel the surrender of the place by actual hostilities.

The confidence of Mr. Seward in the strength of the name and of the resources of the United States Federal Government must have received a rude blow; but his confidences are by no means of a weakly constitution, and it will be long ere he can bring himself to think that all his prophecies must be given up one after another before the inexorable logic of facts, with which his vaticinations have been in "irrepressible conflict." It seems to me that Mr. Seward has all along undervalued the spirit and the resolution of the Southern Slave States, or that he has disguised from others the sense he entertains of their extent and vigour. The days assigned for the life of secession have been numbered over and over again, and secession has not yielded up the ghost. The "bravado" of the South has been sustained by deeds which render retreat from its advanced position impossible.

Mr. Seward will probably find himself hard pushed to maintain his views in the Cabinet in the face of recent events, which will, no doubt, be used with effect and skill by Mr. Chase, who is understood to be in favour of letting the South go as it lists without any more trouble, convinced as he is that it is an element of weakness in the body politic, while he would be prepared to treat as treason any attempts in the remaining States of the Union to act on the doctrine of secession. But the Union party must now prevail.

As yet I do not know whether the views I expressed relative to the destination of the greater part of the troops and stores sent from the North were correct, for it cannot be learned how many ships were off Sumter when it surrendered; but, notwithstanding what has occurred, I reiterate the assertion that the Washington Cabinet always said and say they had no intention to provoke a conflict there, and that had the authorities at Charleston continued their permission to the garrison to procure supplies in their markets, there would have been no immediate action on their part to precipitate the fight, though they were determined to hold it and Fort Pickens, as well as Tortugas and Key West, and to victual and strengthen the garrison of the former as soon as they were able. Fate was against them. The decision and power of their opponents were against them. But their defence will be that they could not do anything till they got troops, and ships, and munitions of war together, and that they did as much as they could in a month. Sumter, in fact, was a mouse in the jaws of the cat, and the moment an attempt was made to release the prey by external influence, the jaws were closed and the mouse disposed of.

The act will produce, I believe, in spite of what I see, a very deep impression throughout all the States, and will tend to bring about an immediate collision between the high-minded parties on both sides. When Mr. Lincoln came into office it was discovered that a promise had been made by outgoing members of the preceding government to surrender the Southern forts. The promise was ignored by the incoming ministry. The Southern commissioners insist on it that, apart from the compact of Mr. Buchanan's Cabinet, a pledge had been given to the South that no attempt would be made to re-enforce the forts without notice to the government at Montgomery; and so far as can be ascertained the authorities at Washington did cause to be conveyed to the Southern Confederation the expression of their intention to victual Sumter: but whether they do so in respect to their pledge, if it existed, or in consequence of the decision at Charleston to prevent the issuing of further supplies to the garrison, is uncertain.

The withdrawal of the permission to market was all but an act of war. If the United States Government would act on the hypothesis that the Southern Confederation was an independent power, it would surely have considered the proceeding as a prelude to immediate hostility. But the course thus adopted arose out of the preparations made by the United States Government in fitting out expeditions, the object of which was scarcely dubious. The commissioners of the Southern States at Washington, never acknowledged, at last met with a decisive rebuff just as Virginia saw her representatives from the convention on the way to ask Mr. Lincoln to explain his intentions. The commissioners were given to understand that their presence was useless, and that the forts would be re-enforced; and on the intelligence thus furnished to the government at Montgomery it was resolved to act by summoning Major Anderson to surrender before succour could arrive, and in event of refusal by compelling him to yield in the sight of the would-be relieving squadron.

As soon as the commissioners found that Mr. Lincoln had made his decision, they departed in no very yielding temper, and washed their hands in a valedictory paper of the results. It was my intention to have left Washington early in the week, and to have reached Charleston before these gentlemen had departed, but the heavy storms and floods which washed away part of the railway between Washington and Richmond at the other side of the Potomac prevented my departure, and not only arrested the mails from the South and the journey of the Virginian delegates for several days, but obliged the commissioners to take the round-about course by rail to Baltimore, thence by steamer to Norfolk, Virginia, and then on by rail to Charleston, which I am now pursuing one day later.

Although the ministers at the capital affected to discredit the existence of any design to seize upon the city, their acts indicated an apprehension of danger, or at least a desire to take all possible precautions against treachery. The district militia were called out and sworn for service, and the result showed that there were more citizens in the ranks ready to stand by the government than there were secessionists who would not defend it. Tuesday, Wednesday, and Thursday last were very busy days. The companies forming the battalions of the district militia were mustered and marched off from their various quarters to the inclosure in front of the War Department, where they took or refused the oath of service, as the humour moved them. It is scarcely possible to imagine a more heterogeneous-looking body of men; the variety of uniform, of clothing, and of accoutrements was as great as if a specimen squad had been taken from the battalions of the Grand Army of 1812.

The general effect of the men and of their habiliments is decidedly French, and there is even a small company of *Zouaves*, but I cannot understand how these little independent bodies are to be brought into line of battle, or depended on for united action. On the days above mentioned the monotony of the wide, lifeless streets was broken at intervals by the tap of the drum, beating a *pas* in the French fashion, and then came the crowd of idlers who are fond of cheap martial display. To a company of forty rank and file there are generally two drummers and six or seven officers or more, and the glory of epaulettes shines out bravely through the cloud of French gray, and light and dark blue capotes. The musters are not, I am told, as they should be. There are some pale faces, rounded shoulders, and weak frames in the ranks, but the majority are very fair specimens of a fine race of men, and some companies were composed of soldier-like, stout fellows, who only required active service to set them up for any military duty.

Not a fourth of those bound to serve were ready, however, to come forward and fight for the government at Washington; and it is probable that nothing short of a struggle for life or death would induce one-half to take the field. Not one-half of the militia is properly armed. It is a great army on paper; no army in the world is so magnificently officered, even in proportion to its numbers. The strength of the militia of the whole of the ex-United States is nearly 3,000,000 men of all ranks. Of those there are no less than 3,833 generals of all sorts, 9,800 colonels and field officers, 38,580 captains and subalterns. Kentucky boasts of 188 generals, New York has not less than 392, Michigan is rich in 383 generals, and so on. But, unless there were some popular passion to excite the country, the actual force available for the field would be a fractional part of these grand totals.

The American Minerva which sprang from the womb of the great Revolutionary War with panoply of proof, believes that she is invincible, and there is unquestionably a strong military spirit among the people, generated by the instances which attended their national birth, and developed by the subsequent small wars in which they have been engaged with rather impotent enemies. Whether this spirit will be called forth in the North and West as largely as it unquestionably has been in the South, remains to be seen. The evidences of the near approach of a civil war are now beyond all dispute, but the nature of the conflict will depend on the steps taken by the belligerents. If the Southern States await invasion they fight over a loaded mine. To avoid the horrors of a conflict on their own soil, they will probably seek to make good their boast of marching upon Washington; but whether they will reach it is quite another matter. The present means of defending it are very contemptible; but vast populations are close at hand which can furnish thousands of men for its protection.

The city contains no stragetical points, and in a military sense its possession is not so important that it would be worthwhile to risk all to gain it; but its political significance is enormous, and it is likely enough that the Capital will become the object of military demonstrations on both sides. With the Potomac and Chesapeake Bay strongly held by the Federal Government, Virginia, in case she casts in her lot with the South, will find herself menaced in the most formidable manner. Southern men have complained to me in terms of the strongest indignation, that Virginia secessionists have applied to South Carolina for five thousand men to enable them to seize the forts which command the rivers and the sea-coast. It proves that little active aid can be expected from that State if the Confederate party cannot do that little piece of business on their own account.

From the date of this letter it will be seen that I am on my way to the South; and, although I shall not arrive in time to give any account of the recent operations against Fort Sumter, I hope to gain some insight into the actual condition of the army of the Confederate States.

On Friday evening I bade goodbye to Washington, and none of the ministers had any idea that Sumter had been attacked, nor had Lord Lyons received any intelligence from Charleston.

Letter 5

Charleston, S. C., April 21, 1861.

I find some consolation for the disappointment of not arriving in time to witness the attack upon Fort Sumter in describing the condition of the work soon after Major Anderson surrendered it. Already I have upon my table a pamphlet entitled *The Battle of Fort Sumter and First Victory of the Southern Troops,* &c.; several "poems," and a variety of versicules, songs, and rhetorical exercitations upon this event, which, however important as a political demonstration, is of small value in a military sense, except in so far as the bloodless occupation of a position commanding Charleston Harbor is concerned. It may tend to prevent any false impressions founded on imperfect information to state a few facts connected with the fire in the work, and its effects, which will interest, at least, some military readers.

In the first place, it may be well to admit that the military preparations and positions of the South Carolinians were more formidable than one was prepared to expect on the part of a small State, without any considerable internal organization or resources. This comparative efficiency was due mainly to General Beauregard and his assistant engineer, Major Whiting, who are both professional engineer officers of the United States Army, and who had capacity and influence enough to direct the energies of the undisciplined masses in the proper direction, instead of allowing them to rush on their fate in the perilous essay of an escalade, as they intended.

The State of South Carolina had for a long time past been accumulating arms and munitions of war, and it may be said that ever since the nullification contest she had permitted herself to dwell on the idea of ultimate secession, to be effected by force, if necessary. When General Beauregard and Major Whiting came here, the works intended to resist the fleet and to crush the fort were in a very imperfect state. Major Anderson and his officers had a true professional contempt for the batteries of the civilians and militiamen, which was in some measure justifiable. One morning, however, as they took their survey of the enemy's labours for the previous night, they perceived a change had come over the design of their works. That "someone who knows his business is over there" was evident. Their strange relationship with those who were preparing to destroy them if possible, however, prevented their recourse to the obvious means which were then in abundance in their hands to avert the coming danger.

Had Major Anderson maintained a well-regulated fire on the enemy the moment they began to throw up their batteries and prepare Fort Moultrie against him, he could have made their progress very slow and exceedingly laborious, and have marked it at every step with blood. His command over the ground was very decided, but he had, it is to be supposed, no authority to defend himself in the only way in which it could be done. "Too late"—that fatal phrase—was the echo to every order which came from the seat of government at Washington. Meantime the South Carolinians worked at their batteries, and were soon able to obtain cover on the soft sandy plains on which they were planting their guns and mortars. They practised their men at the guns, stacked shot and shell, and furnished their magazines, and drilled their raw levies with impunity within fourteen hundred yards of the fort.

We all know what impunity is worth in offensive demonstrations. It is a powerful agent sometimes in creating enthusiasm. Every day more volunteers flocked to the various companies, or created new associations of armed men, and the heterogeneous and motley mass began to assume some resemblance to an army, however irregular. At the present moment Charleston is like a place in the neighbourhood of a camp where military and volunteer tailors are at work trying experiments in uniforms, and sending in their animated models for inspection. There is an endless variety—often of ugliness—in dress and equipment and nomenclature among these companies. The headdress is generally, however, a smart cap like the French *kepi*; the tunic is of different cuts, colours, facings, and materials—green with gray and yellow, gray with orange and black and white, blue with white, and yellow facings, roan, brown, burnt sienna, and olive—jackets, frocks, tunics, blouses, cloth, linen, tweed, flannel.

The officers are generally in blue frocks and brass buttons, with red sashes, the rank being indicated by gold lace parallelograms on the shoulder straps, which are like those in use in the Russian Army. The arms of the men seem tolerably well kept and in good order. Many, however, still shoulder "White Bess"—the old smooth-bore musket with unbrowned barrel. The following is an official return, which I am enabled to present to you through the courtesy of the authorities, showing the actual number of men under arms yesterday in and around Charleston:—

Morris Island.—17th Regiment, 700 men; 1st Regiment, 950 men; 2nd Regiment 975 men. Total, 2625.

Sullivan's Island.—5th Regiment, 1,075 men; detachment of 8th Regiment, 250 men; detachment of 6th Regiment, 200 men; cavalry and others, 225 men. Total, 1,750.

Stone and other points, 750 men; Charleston, 1,900 men; Columbia, 1,950 men.

	Men
Morris Island	2,625
Sullivan's Island	1,750
Stone and other points	750
Total	5,125
Columbia	1,950
Charleston	1,900
Total	8,975
In field at the time of report	3,027
Total	12,002

The regiments mentioned here are composed of the various companies raised in different localities with different names, but the State regulars are in expectation that they will soon be made portions of the regular army of the Confederate States, which is in course of formation. There are, I believe, only fifty-five thousand registered voters in South Carolina. The number of men furnished by them is a fair indication of the zeal for the cause which animates the population. The *physique* of the troops is undeniably good. Now and then undersized, weakly men may be met with, but the great majority of the companies consist of rank and file exceeding the average stature of Europeans, and very well built and muscular. The men run very large down here.

Nothing, indeed, can be more obvious when one looks at the full-grown, healthy, handsome race which develops itself in the streets, in the bar-rooms, and in the hotel halls, than the error of the argument, which is mainly used by the Carolinians themselves, that white men cannot thrive in their State. In limb, figure, height, weight, they are equal to any people I have ever seen, and their features are very regular and pronounced. They are, indeed, as unlike the ideal American of our caricaturists and our stage as is the *"milor"* of the Porte St. Martin to the English gentleman. Some of this superiority is due to the fact that the bulk of the white population here are in all but name aristocrats or rather oligarchs. The State is but a gigantic Sparta, in which the helotry are marked by an indelible difference of colour and race from the masters.

The white population, which is not land and slaveholding and agricultural, is very small and very insignificant. The masters enjoy every advantage which can conduce to the physical excellence of a people, and to the cultivation of the graces and accomplishments of life, even though they are rather disposed to neglect purely intellectual enjoyments and tastes. Many of those who serve in the ranks are men worth from £5,000 to £10,000 a year—at least, so I was told—and men were pointed out to me who were said to be worth far more. One private feeds his company on French *pâtés* and Madeira, another provides his comrades with unlimited champagne, most grateful on the arid sand-hill; a third, with a more soldierly view to their permanent rather than occasional efficiency, purchases for the men of his "guard" a complete equipment of Enfield rifles. How long the zeal and resources of these gentlemen will last it may not be easy to say. At present they would prove formidable to any enemy, except a regular army on the plain and in the open field, but they are not provided with field artillery or with adequate cavalry, and they are not accustomed to act in concert and in large bodies.

Yesterday morning I waited on General Beauregard, who is commanding the forces of South Carolina. His *aides-de-camp*, Mr. Manning, Mr. Chesnut, Mr. Porcher Miles, and Colonel Lucas, accompanied me. Of these, the former has been governor of this State, the next has been a senator, the third a member of Congress. They are all volunteers, and are gentlemen of position in the State, and the fact that they are not only content but gratified to act as *aides* to the professional soldier, is the best proof of the reality of the spirit which animates the class they represent. Mr. Lucas is a gentleman of the State, who is acting as *aide-de-camp* to Governor Pickens. Passing through the dense crowd which, talking, smoking, and reading newspapers, fills the large hall on Mills's house, we emerge on the dirty streets, sufficiently broad, and lined with trees protected by wooden sheathings at the base.

The houses, not very lofty, are clean and spacious, and provided with verandahs facing the South as far as possible. The trees give the streets the air of a boulevard, and the town has somehow or other a reminiscence of the Hague about it, which I cannot explain or account for satisfactorily. The headquarters are in a large, airy, public building, once devoted to an insurance company's operations, or to the accommodation of the public fire companies. There was no guard at the door; officers and privates were passing to and fro in the hall, part of which was cut off by canvass screens, so as to form rooms for departments of the Horse Guards of South Carolina.

Into one of these we turned, and found the desks occupied by officers in uniform, waiting despatches and copying documents with all the *abandon* which distinguishes the true soldier when he can get at printed forms and government stationery. In another moment we were ushered into a smaller room, and were presented to the general, who was also seated at his desk. Any one accustomed to soldiers can readily detect the "real article" from the counterfeit, and when General Beauregard stood up to welcome us, it was patent he was a man capable of greater things than taking Sumter.

He is a squarely-built, lean man, of about forty years of age, with broad shoulders, and legs "made to fit" a horse, of middle height, and his head is covered with thick hair, cropped close, and showing the bumps, which are reflective and combative, with a true Gallic air, at the back of the skull; the forehead, broad and well-developed, projects somewhat over the keen, eager, dark eyes; the face is very thin, with very high cheek-bones, a well-shaped nose, slightly aquiline, and a large, rigid, sharply cut mouth, set above a full fighting chin. In the event of any important operations taking place, the name of this officer will, I feel assured, be heard often enough to be my excuse for this little sketch of his outward man. He was good enough to detail his chief engineer officer to go with me over the works, and I found in Major Whiting a most able guide and agreeable companion.

It is scarcely worthwhile to waste time in describing the position of Charleston. It lies as low as Venice, the look of which it rather affects from a distance, with long, sandy islands stretching out as arms to close up the approaches, and lagunes cutting into the marshy shores. On a sandy island and spit on the left hand shore stands Fort Moultrie. On the southern side, on another sandy island, are the lines of the batteries which, probably, were most dangerous, from their proximity and position, to the unprotected face of Sumter. The fort itself is built in the tideway, on a rocky point, which has been increased by artificial deposits of granite chips. Embarked, with a few additions to our original party, on board a small steamer, called the *Lady Davis,* we first proceeded to Morris Island, about 3¾ miles from Charleston.

Our steamer was filled with commissariat stores for the troops, of whom 4,000 were said to be encamped among the sand-hills. Anyone who has ever been at Southport, or has seen the dunes about Dunkirk or Calais, will have a good idea of the place. Our landing was opposed by a guard of stout volunteers, with crossed firelocks; but they were satisfied by the general's authority, and we proceeded, ankle-deep in the soft, white sand, to visit the batteries which played on the landward face of Sumter. They are made of sand-bags for the most part, well placed in the sand-hills, with good traverses and well-protected magazines, the embrasures being faced with palmetto logs, which do not splinter when struck by shot.

It did not, however, require much investigation to show that these works would be greatly injured by a fire of vertical and horizontal shell from the fort, and that the distance of their armament would render it difficult to breach the solid walls which were opposed to them at upward of 1,200 yards away. However, there were two powerful mortar batteries, which could have done great damage if they were well served, and have made the *terreplein* and parade of the fort a complete "shell trap" unless the mortars were injured. The civilians and militiamen set greater store on the Iron Battery at Cummings' Point, which is the part of the island nearest to the fort, but the fire of heavy guns would have soon destroyed their confidence. It consists of yellow pine logs placed as vertical uprights. The roof, of the same material, slopes from the top of the uprights to the sand facing the enemy; over it are dovetailed bars of railroad iron, of the T pattern, from top to bottom, all riveted down in the most secure manner.

On the front the railroad iron roof and incline present an angle of about thirty degrees. There are three portholes with iron shutters. When opened by the action of a lever the muzzles of the columbiads fill up the space completely. The columbiad guns with which this battery is equipped bear on the south wall of Sumter at an angle. The inclined side of the battery has been struck by six shots, the effect of two of which is enough to demonstrate that the fire of the guns *en barbette* would have been destructive. The columbiad is a kind of Dahlgren— that is, a piece of ordinance very thick in the breech, and lightened off gradually from the trunnions to the muzzle. The platforms were rather light, but the carriages were solid and well made, and the elevating screws or hitches of the guns were in good order.

The mortars are of various calibres and descriptions, mostly 8-inch and 10-inch; and it is said there were seventeen of them in position and working against the fort, and that thirty-five guns were from time to time directed against it. Shot and shell appeared to be abundant enough. The works are all small detached batteries, with sand-bag merlons, and open at the gorge, and they extend for four miles along the shore of the island. The camps are pitched most irregularly between the sand-hills—tents of all shapes and sizes, in the fashion called higgledy-piggledy, here and there, in knots and groups, in a way that would drive an Indian quartermaster-general mad.

Bones of beef and mutton, champagne and wine bottles, obstructed the approaches, which were of a nature to afflict Dr. Sutherland and Sir John M'Neill most bitterly, and to suggest the reflection that the army which so utterly neglected sanitary regulations could not long exist as soon as the sun gained full power. They say, however, the men are not sickly, and that these sand-hills are the most healthy spots about Charleston. The men were occupied as soldiers generally are when they have nothing to do—lounging or lying on the straw and plank carpets, smoking, reading, sleeping. The owners of the tents give them various names, of which "The Lions' Den," "The Tigers' Lair," "The Eagles' Nest," "Mars' Delight," are fair specimens, and these are done in black on the white calico. In one which we visited, the hospitable inmates were busily engaged in brewing claret cup, and Bordeaux, lemons, sugar, ice, and Champagne, and salads were in abundance, and at the end of the tent was a bar, where anything else in reason could be had for the asking, though water was not so plentiful.

At one of the batteries the great object of attraction was a gun made on Captain Blakeley's principle, by Messrs. Fawcett, Preston & Co., of Liverpool, which was only put in battery the day before the fire opened, and the effect of which on the masonry is said to have been very powerful. It is a 12-pounder—the same which was tried last year, I think—and bears a brass plate with the inscription, "Presented to South Carolina by one of her citizens." It is remarkable enough that the vessel which carried it lay in the midst of the United States war vessels at the mouth of the harbour.

Having satisfied our curiosity as well as time and a sand-storm permitted, we got in a row-boat and proceeded to Sumter. At a distance, the fort bears some resemblance to Fort Paul at Sevastopol. It is a truncated pentagon, with three faces armed—that which is toward Morris Island being considered safe from attack, as the work was only intended to resist an approach from the sea. It is said to have cost altogether more than £200,000 sterling. The walls are of solid brick and concrete masonry, built close to the edge of the water, sixty feet high, and from eight to twelve feet in thickness, and carry three tiers of guns on the north, east, and west exterior sides. Its weakest point is on the south side, where the masonry is not protected by any flank fire to sweep the wharf. The work is designed for an armament of one hundred and forty pieces of ordnance of all calibres.

Two tiers are under bomb-proof casemates, and the third or upper tier is en *barbette*; the lower tier is intended for 42-pounders Paixhan guns; the second tier for eight and ten-inch columbiads, for throwing solid or hollow shot, and the upper tier for mortars and guns. But only seventy-five are now mounted. Eleven Paixhan guns are among that number, nine of them commanding Fort Moultrie. Some of the columbiads are not mounted. Four of the 32-pounder *barbette* guns are on pivot carriages, and others have a sweep of 180°. The walls are pierced everywhere for musketry. The magazine contains several hundred barrels of gunpowder, and a supply of shot, powder, and shells. The garrison was amply supplied with water from artificial wells. The war garrison of the fort ought to be at least six hundred men, but only seventy-nine were within its walls, with the labourers—one hundred and nine all told—at the time of the attack.

The walls of the fort are dented on all sides by shot marks, but in no instance was any approach made to a breach, and the greatest damage, at one of the angles on the south face, did not extend more than two feet into the masonry, which is of very fine brick. The parapet is, of course, damaged, but the casemate embrasures are uninjured. On landing at the wharf we perceived that the granite copings had suffered more than the brickwork, and that the stone had split up and splintered where it was struck. The ingenuity of the defenders was evident even here. They had no mortar with which to fasten up the stone slabs they had adapted as blinds to the windows of the unprotected south side; but Major Anderson, or his subordinate, Captain

Foster, had closed the slabs in with lead, which he procured from some water piping, and had rendered them proof against escalade, which he was prepared also to resent by extensive mines laid under the wharf and landing-place, to be fired by friction tubes and lines laid inside the work.

He had also prepared a number of shells for the same purpose, to act as hand-grenades, with friction tubes and lanyards, when hurled down from the parapet on his assailants. The entrance to the fort was blocked up by masses of masonry, which had been thrown down from the walls of the burnt barracks and officers' quarters, along the south side. A number of men were engaged in digging up the mines at the wharf, and others were busied in completing the ruin of the tottering walls, which were still so hot that it was necessary to keep a hose of water playing on part of the brickwork. To an uninitiated eye it would seem as if the fort was untenable, but, in reality, in spite of the destruction done to it, a stout garrison, properly supplied, would have been in no danger from anything, except the explosion of the magazine, of which the copper door was jammed by the heat at the time of the surrender.

Exclusive of the burning of the quarters and the intense heat, there was no reason for a properly handled and sufficient force to surrender the place. It is needless to say Major Anderson had neither one nor the other. He was in all respects most miserably equipped. His guns were without screws, scales, or tangents, so that his elevations were managed by rude wedges of deal, and his scales marked in chalk on the breech of the guns, and his distances and bearings scratched in the same way on the side of the embrasures. He had not a single fuse for his shells, and he tried in vain to improvise them by filling pieces of bored-out pine with caked gunpowder. His cartridges were out, and he was compelled to detail some few of his men to make them out of shirts, stockings, and jackets. He had not a single mortar, and he was compelled to the desperate expedient of planting long guns in the ground at an angle of 45 degrees, for which he could find no shell, as he had no fuses which could be fired with safety. He had no sheers to mount his guns, and chance alone enabled him to do so by drifting some large logs down with the tide against Sumter.

Finally, he had not even one engine to put out a fire in quarters. I walked carefully over the parade, and could detect the marks of only seven shells in the ground; but Major Whiting told me the orders were to burst the shells over the parapet, so as to frustrate any attempt to work the *barbette* guns. Two of these were injured by shot, and one was overturned, apparently by its own recoil; but there was no injury done inside any of the casemates to the guns or works. The shell splinters had all disappeared, carried off, I am told, as "trophies." Had Major Anderson been properly provided, so that he could have at once sent his men to the guns, opened fire from those in *barbette*, thrown shell and hot shot, kept relays to all his casemates, and put out fires as they arose from red-hot shot or shell, he must, I have no earthly doubt, have driven the troops off Morris Island, burnt out Fort Moultrie, and silenced the enemy's fire. His loss might have been considerable; that of the Confederates must have been very great. As it was, not a life was lost by actual fire on either side. A week hence and it will be impossible for a fleet to do anything except cover the descent of an army here, and they must lie off, at the least, four miles from the nearest available beach.

Letter 6

The State of South Carolina.
April 30, 1861.

Nothing I could say can be worth one fact which has forced itself upon my mind in reference to the sentiments which prevail among the gentlemen of this State. I have been among them several days. I have visited their plantations, I have conversed with them freely and fully, and I have enjoyed that frank, courteous, and graceful intercourse which constitutes an irresistible charm of their society. From all quarters have come to my ears the echoes of the same voice; it may be feigned, but there is no discord in the note, and it sounds in wonderful strength and monotony all over the country. Shades of George III., of North, of Johnson, of all who contended against the great rebellion which tore these colonies from England, can you hear the chorus which rings through the State of Marion, Sumter, and Pinckney, and not clap your ghostly hands in triumph? That voice says, "If we could only get one of the royal race of England to rule over us, we should be content."

Let there be no misconception on this point. That sentiment, varied in a hundred ways, has been repeated to me over and over again. There is a general admission that the means to such an end are wanting, and that the desire cannot be gratified. But the admiration for monarchical institutions on the English model, for privileged classes, and for a landed aristocracy and gentry, is undisguised and apparently genuine. With the pride of having achieved their independence is mingled in the South Carolinians' hearts a strange regret at the result and consequences, and many are they who "would go back tomorrow if we could."

An intense affection for the British connection, a love of British habits and customs, a respect for British sentiment, law, authority, order, civilization, and literature, pre-eminently distinguish the inhabitants of this State, who, glorying in their descent from ancient families on the three islands, whose fortunes they still follow, and with whose members they maintain not unfrequently familiar relations, regard with an aversion of which it is impossible to give an idea to one who has not seen its manifestations, the people of New England and the populations of the Northern States, whom they regard as tainted beyond cure by the venom of "Puritanism." Whatever may be the cause, this is the fact and the effect.

"The State of South Carolina was," I am told, "founded by gentlemen." It was not established by witch-burning Puritans, by cruel persecuting fanatics, who implanted in the North the standard of Torquemada, and breathed into the nostrils of their newly-born colonies all the ferocity of blood-thirstiness and rabid intolerance of the Inquisition. It is absolutely astounding to a stranger, who aims at the preservation of a decent neutrality, to mark the violence of these opinions.

"If that confounded ship had sunk with those —— Pilgrim Fathers on board," says one, "we never should have been driven to these extremities!"

"We could have got on with fanatics if they had been either Christians or gentlemen," says another; "for in the first case they would have acted with common charity, and in the second they would have fought when they insulted us; but there are neither Christians nor gentlemen among them!"

"Anything on the earth!" exclaims a third, "any form of government, any tyranny or despotism you will; but"—and here is an appeal more terrible than the adjuration of all the Gods—"nothing on earth shall ever induce us to submit to any union with the brutal, bigoted blackguards of the New England States, who neither comprehend nor regard the feelings of gentlemen! Man, woman, and child, we'll die first."

Imagine these and an infinite variety of similar sentiments uttered by courtly, well-educated men, who set great store on a nice observance of the usages of society, and who are only moved to extreme bitterness and anger when they speak of the North, and you will fail to conceive the intensity of the dislike of the South Carolinians for the Free States. There are national antipathies on our side of the Atlantic which are tolerably strong, and have been unfortunately pertinacious and long-lived. The hatred of the Italian for the Tedesco, of the Greek for the Turk, of the Turk for the Russ, is warm and fierce enough to satisfy the Prince of Darkness, not to speak of a few little pet aversions among the allied Powers and the atoms of composite empires; but they are all mere indifference and neutrality of feeling compared to the animosity evinced by the "gentry" of South Carolina for the "rabble of the North."

The contests of Cavalier and Roundhead, of Vendean and Republican, even of Orangeman and Croppy, have been elegant joustings, regulated by the finest rules of chivalry, compared with those which North and South will carry on if their deeds support their words. "Immortal hate, the study of revenge," will actuate every blow, and never in the history of the world, perhaps, will go forth such a dreadful *væ victis* as that which may be heard before the fight has begun. There is nothing in all the dark caves of human passion so cruel and deadly as the hatred the South Carolinians profess for the Yankees. That hatred has been swelling for years, till it is the very life-blood of the State. It has set South Carolina to work steadily to organize her resources for the struggle which she intended to provoke, if it did not come in the course of time.

"Incompatibility of temper" would have been sufficient ground for the divorce, and I am satisfied that there has been a deep-rooted design, conceived in some men's minds thirty years ago, and extended gradually year after year to others, to break away from the Union at the very first opportunity. The North is to South Carolina a corrupt and evil thing, to which for long years she has been bound by burning chains, while monopolists and manufacturers fed on her tender limbs. She has been bound in a Maxentian union to the object she loathes. New England is to her the incarnation of moral and political wickedness and social corruption. It is the source of everything which South Carolina hates, and of the torrents of free thought and taxed manufactures, of abolitionism and of filibustering, which have flooded the land.

Believe a Southern man as he believes himself, and you must regard New England and the kindred States as the birthplace of impurity of mind among men and of unchastity in women—the home of Free Love, of Fourierism, of Infidelity, of Abolitionism, of false teachings in political economy and in social life; a land saturated with the drippings of rotten philosophy, with the poisonous infections of a fanatic press; without honour or modesty; whose wisdom is paltry cunning, whose valour and manhood have been swallowed up in a corrupt, howling demagogy, and in the marts of a dishonest commerce.

It is the merchants of New York who fit out ships for the slave-trade, and carry it on in Yankee ships. It is the capital of the North which supports, and it is Northern men who concoct and execute, the filibustering expeditions which have brought discredit on the Slave-holding States. In the large cities people are corrupted by itinerant and ignorant lecturers—in the towns and in the country by an unprincipled press. The populations, indeed, know how to read and write, but they don't know how to think, and they are the easy victims of the wretched impostors on all the 'ologies and 'isms who swarm over the region, and subsist by lecturing on subjects which the innate vices of mankind induce them to accept with eagerness, while they assume the garb of philosophical abstractions to cover their nastiness in deference to a contemptible and universal hypocrisy.

Who fills the butchers' shops with large blue flies?

Assuredly the New England demon who has been persecuting the South until its intolerable cruelty and insolence forced her, in a spasm of agony, to rend her chains asunder. The New Englander must have something to persecute, and as he has hunted down all his Indians, burnt all his witches, and persecuted all his opponents to the death, he invented abolitionism as the sole resource left to him for the gratification of his favourite passion. Next to this motive principle is his desire to make money dishonestly, trickily, meanly, and shabbily. He has acted on it in all his relations with the South, and has cheated and plundered her in all his dealings by villainous tariffs. If one objects that the South must have been a party to this, because her boast is that her statesmen have ruled the government of the country, you are told that the South yielded out of pure good nature. Now, however, she will have free trade, and will open the coasting trade to foreign nations, and shut out from it the hated Yankees, who so long monopolized and made their fortunes by it.

Under all the varied burdens and miseries to which she was subjected, the South held fast to her sheet anchor. South Carolina was the mooring ground in which it found the surest hold. The doctrine of State Rights was her salvation, and the fiercer the storm raged against her—the more stoutly demagogy, immigrant preponderance, and the blasts of universal suffrage bore down on her, threatening to sweep away the vested interests of the South in her right to govern the States—the greater was her confidence and the more resolutely she held on her cable. The North attracted "hordes of ignorant Germans

50

and Irish," and the scum of Europe, while the South repelled them.

The industry, the capital of the North increased with enormous rapidity, under the influence of cheap labour and manufacturing ingenuity and enterprise, in the villages which swelled into towns, and the towns which became cities, under the unenvious eye of the South. She, on the contrary, toiled on slowly, clearing forests and draining swamps to find new cotton-grounds and rice-fields, for the employment of her only industry and for the development of her only capital—"involuntary labour." The tide of immigration waxed stronger, and by degrees she saw the districts into which she claimed the right to introduce that capital closed against her, and occupied by free labour. The doctrine of squatter "sovereignty," and the force of hostile tariffs, which placed a heavy duty on the very articles which the South most required, completed the measure of injuries to which she was subjected, and the spirit of discontent found vent in fiery debate, in personal insults, and in acrimonious speaking and writing, which increased in intensity in proportion as the Abolition movement, and the contest between the Federal principle and State Rights, became more vehement.

I am desirous of showing in a few words, for the information of English readers, how it is that the Confederacy which Europe knew simply as a political entity has succeeded in dividing itself. The Slave States held the doctrine, or say they did, that each State was independent as France or as England, but that for certain purposes they chose a common agent to deal with foreign nations, and to impose taxes for the purpose of paying the expenses of the agency. We, it appears, talked of American citizens when there were no such beings at all. There were, indeed, citizens of the Sovereign State of South Carolina, or of Georgia or Florida, who permitted themselves to pass under that designation, but it was merely as a matter of personal convenience. It will be difficult for Europeans to understand this doctrine, as nothing like it has been heard before, and no such Confederation of Sovereign States has ever existed in any country in the world.

The Northern men deny that it existed here, and claim for the Federal Government powers not compatible with such assumptions. *They* have lived for the Union, they served it, they laboured for and made money by it. A man as a New York man was nothing—as an American citizen he was a great deal. A South Carolinian objected to lose his identity in any description which included him and a "Yankee clockmaker" in the same category. The Union was against him; he remembered that he came from a race of English gentlemen who had been persecuted by the representatives—for he will not call them the ancestors—of the Puritans of New England, and he thought that they were animated by the same hostility to himself. He was proud of old names, and he felt pleasure in tracing his connection with old families in the old country.

His plantations were held by old charters, or had been in the hands of his fathers for several generations; and he delighted to remember that when the Stuarts were banished from their throne and their country, the burgesses of South Carolina had solemnly elected the wandering Charles king of their State, and had offered him an asylum and a kingdom. The philosophical historian may exercise his ingenuity in conjecturing what would have been the result if the fugitive had carried his fortunes to Charleston.

South Carolina contains 34,000 square miles and a population of 720,000 inhabitants, of whom 385,000 are black slaves. In the old rebellion it was distracted between revolutionary principles and the loyalist predilections, and at least one half of the planters were faithful to George III., nor did they yield till Washington sent an army to support their antagonists, and drove them from the colony.

In my next letter I shall give a brief account of a visit to some of the planters, as far as it can be made consistent with the obligations which the rites and rights of hospitality impose on the guest as well as upon the host. These gentlemen are well-bred, courteous, and hospitable. A genuine aristocracy, they have time to cultivate their minds, to apply themselves to politics and the guidance of public affairs. They travel and read, love field sports, racing, shooting, hunting and fishing, are bold horsemen, and good shots. But, after all, their State is a modern Sparta—an aristocracy resting on a helotry, and with nothing else to rest upon.

Although they profess (and I believe, indeed, sincerely) to hold opinions in opposition to the opening of the slave trade, it is nevertheless true that the clause in the Constitution of the Confederate States which prohibited the importation of negroes was especially and energetically resisted by them, because, as they say, it seemed to be an admission that slavery was in itself an evil and a wrong. Their whole system rests on slavery, and as such they defend it. They entertain very exaggerated ideas of the military strength of their little community, although one may do full justice to its military spirit.

Out of their whole population they cannot reckon more than

60,000 adult men by any arithmetic, and as there are nearly 30,000 plantations which must be, according to law, superintended by white men, a considerable number of these adults cannot be spared from the State for service in the open field. The planters boast that they can raise their crops without any inconvenience by the labour of their negroes, and they seem confident that the negroes will work without superintendence. But the experiment is rather dangerous, and it will only be tried in the last extremity

Savannah, Ga., May 1, 1861.

It is said that "*fools build houses for wise men to live in.*" Be that true or not, it is certain that "Uncle Sam" has built strong places for his enemies to occupy. Today I visited Fort Pulaski, which defends the mouth of the Savannah River and the approaches to the city. It was left to take care of itself, and the Georgians quietly stepped into it, and have been busied in completing its defences, so that it is now capable of stopping a fleet very effectually. Pulaski was a Pole who fell in the defence of Savannah against the British, and whose memory is perpetuated in the name of the fort, which is now under the Confederate flag, and garrisoned by bitter foes of the United States.

Among our party were Commodore Tattnall, whose name will be familiar to English ears in connection with the attack on the Peiho Forts, where the gallant American showed the world that "*blood was thicker than water,*" Brigadier-General Lawton, in command of the forces of Georgia, and a number of naval and military officers, of whom many had belonged to the United States regular service. It was strange to look at such a man as the commodore, who for forty-nine long years had served under the Stars and Stripes, quietly preparing to meet his old comrades and friends, if needs be, in the battle-field—his allegiance to the country and to the flag renounced, his long service flung away, his old ties and connections severed—and all this in defence of the sacred right of rebellion on the part of "his State." He is not now, nor has he been for years, a slave-owner; all his family and familiar associations connect him with the North.

There are no naval stations on the Southern coasts except one at Pensacola, and he knows almost no one in the South. He has no fortune whatever, his fleet consists of two small river or coasting steamers, without guns, and as he said, in talking over the resources of the South, "My bones will be bleached many a long year before the Confederate States can hope to have a navy." "State Rights!" To us the question is simply inexplicable or absurd. And yet thousands of Americans sacrifice all for it. The river at Savannah is as broad as the Thames at Gravesend, and resembles that stream very much in the colour of its waters and the level natures of its shores. Rice fields bound it on either side, as far down as the influence of the fresh water extends, and the eye wanders over a flat expanse of mud and water and green oziers and rushes, till its search is arrested on the horizon by the unfailing line of forest. In the fields here and there are the whitewashed, square, wooden huts in which the slaves dwell, looking very like the beginnings of the camp in the Crimea.

At one point a small fort, covering a creek by which gunboats could get up behind Savannah, displayed its "garrison" on the walls, and lowered its flag to salute the small blue ensign at the fore, which proclaimed the presence of the commodore of the naval forces of Georgia on board our steamer. The guns on the parapet were mostly field-pieces, mounted on frameworks of wood instead of regular carriages. There is no mistake about the spirit of these people. They seize upon every spot of 'vantage ground and prepare it for defence. There were very few ships in the river; the yacht *Camilla*, better known as the *America*, the property of Captain Deasy, and several others of those few sailing under British colours, for most of the cotton ships are gone. After steaming down the river about twelve miles the sea opened out to the sight, and on a long, marshy, narrow island near the bar, which was marked by the yellowish surf, Fort Pulaski threw out the Confederate flag to the air of the Georgian 1st of May. The water was too shallow to permit the steamer to go up to the jetty, and the party landed at the wharf in boats.

A guard was on duty at the landing—tall, stout young fellows, in various uniforms, or in rude mufti, in which the Garibaldian red shirt and felt slouched hats predominated. They were armed with smooth-bore muskets (date 1851), quite new, and their bayonets, barrels and locks were bright and clean. The officer on duty was dressed in the blue frock-coat dear to the British linesman in days gone by, with brass buttons, emblazoned with the arms of the State, a red silk sash, and glazed *kepi*, and straw-coloured gauntlets. Several wooden huts, with flower-gardens in front, were occupied by the officers of the garrison; others were used as hospitals, and were full of men suffering from measles of a mild type.

A few minutes' walk led us to the fort, which is an irregular pentagon, with the base line or curtain face inlands, and the other faces casemated and bearing on the approaches. The curtain, which is simply crenellated, is covered by a redan surrounded by a deep ditch, inside the parapet of which are granite platforms ready for the reception of guns. The parapet is thick, and the scarp and counterscarp are faced with solid masonry.

A drawbridge affords access to the interior of the redan, whence the gate of the fort is approached across a deep and broad moat, which is crossed by another drawbridge. As the commodore entered the redan the guns of the fort broke out into a long salute, and the band at the gate struck up almost as noisy a welcome. Inside, the parade presented a scene of life and animation very unlike the silence of the city we had left. Men were busy clearing out the casemates, rolling away stores and casks of ammunition and provisions, others were at work at the gin and shears, others building sand-bag traverses to guard the magazine doors, as though expecting an immediate attack. Many officers were strolling under the shade of an open gallery at the side of the curtain which contained their quarters in the lofty bomb-proof casemates. Some of them had seen service in Mexico or border warfare; some had travelled over Italian and Crimean battle-fields; others were West Point graduates of the regular army; others young planters, clerks, or civilians, who rushed with ardour into the First Georgian Regiment.

The garrison of the fort is some six hundred and fifty men, and fully that number were in and about the work, their tents being pitched inside the redan or on the *terrep'ein* of the parapets. The walls are exceedingly solid and well built of gray brick, strong as iron, and upward of six feet in thickness, the casemates and bomb-proofs being lofty, airy, and capacious as any I have ever seen, though there is not quite depth enough between the walls at the salient and the gun-carriages. The work is intended for one hundred and twenty-eight guns, of which about one fourth are mounted on the casemates. They are long 32's, with a few 42's, and columbiads. The armaments will be exceeding heavy when all the guns are mounted, and they are fast getting the ten-inch columbiads into position *en barbette*.

Everything which could be required, except mortars, was in abundance—the platforms and gun carriages are solid and well made, the embrasures of the casemates are admirably constructed, and the ventilation of the bomb-proof carefully provided for. There are three furnaces for heating red-hot shot. Nor is discipline neglected, and the officers with whom I went round the works were as sharp in tone and manner to their men as volunteers well could be, though the latter often are enlisted for only three years by the State of Georgia. An excellent lunch was spread in the casemated bomb-proof, which served as the colonel's quarter, and before sunset the party were steaming towards Savannah through a tideway full of leaping sturgeon and porpoises, leaving the garrison intent on the approach of a large ship, which had her sails aback off the bar and hoisted the Stars and Stripes, but which turned out to be nothing more formidable than a Liverpool cotton ship.

It will take some hard blows before Georgia is driven to let go her grip of Fort Pulaski. The channel is very narrow, and passes close to the guns of the fort. The means of completing the armament have been furnished by the stores of Norfolk Navy Yard, where between seven hundred and eight hundred guns have fallen into the hands of the Confederates; and, if there are no columbiads among them, the *Merrimac* and other ships, which have been raised, as we hear, with guns uninjured, will yield up their Dahlgrens to turn their muzzles against their old masters.

May 2.—May-day was so well kept yesterday that the exhausted editors cannot "bring out" their papers, and consequently there is no news; but there is, nevertheless, much to be said concerning "Our President's" message, and there is a suddenness of admiration for pacific tendencies which can with difficulty be accounted for, unless the news from the North these last few days has something to do with it. Not a word now about an instant march on Washington! No more threats to seize on Faneuil Hall! The Georgians are by no means so keen as the Carolinians on their border—nay, they are not so belligerent today as they were a week ago.

Mr. Jefferson Davis's message is praised for its "moderation," and for other qualities which were by no means in such favour while the Sumter fever was at its height. Men look grave and talk about the interference of England and France, which "cannot allow this thing to go on." But the change which has come over them is unmistakable, and the best men begin to look grave. As for me, I must prepare to open my lines of retreat—my communications are in danger.

Letter 7

Montgomery, May 16, 1861.

Although I have written two letters since my arrival at Charleston, I have not been able to give an account of many things which have come under my notice, and which appeared to be noteworthy; and now that I am fairly on my travels once more, it seems only too probable that I shall be obliged to pass them over altogether. The roaring fire of the revolution is fast sweeping over the prairies, and one must fly before it or burn. I am obliged to see all that can be seen of the South at once, and then, armed with such safeguards as I can procure, to make an effort to recover my communications. Bridges broken, rails torn up, telegraphs pulled down—I am quite in the air, and air charged with powder and fire.

One of the most extraordinary books in the world could be made out of the cuttings and parings of the newspapers which have been published within the last few days. The judgments, statements, asseverations of the press, everywhere necessarily hasty, ill-sifted, and off-hand, do not aspire to even an ephemeral existence here. They are of use if they serve the purpose of the moment, and of the little boys who commence their childhood in deceit, and continue to adolescence in iniquity, by giving vocal utterance to the "sensation" headings in the journals they retail so sharply and curtly.

Talk of the superstition of the Middle Ages, or of the credulity of the more advanced periods of rural life; laugh at the Holy Coat of Treves, or groan over the Lady of Salette; deplore the faith in winking pictures, or in a *communiquè* of the *Moniteur*, moralize on the superstition which discovers more in the liquefaction of the ichor of St. Gennaro than a chemical trick; but if you desire to understand how far faith can see and trust among the people who consider themselves

57

the most civilized and intelligent in the world, you will study the American journals, and read the telegrams which appear in them. One day the 7th New York regiment is destroyed for the edification of the South, and is cut up into such small pieces that none of it is ever seen afterward. The next day it marches into Washington, or Annapolis, all the better for the process.

Another, in order to encourage the North, it is said that hecatombs of dead were carried out of Fort Moultrie, packed up, for easy travelling, in boxes. Again, to irritate both, it is credibly stated that Lord Lyons is going to interfere, or that an Anglo-French fleet is coming to watch the ports, and so on through a wild play of fancy, inexact in line as though the batteries were charged with the *aurora borealis* or summer lightning, instead of the respectable, steady, manageable offspring of acid and metal, to whose staid deportment we are accustomed at a moderate price for entrance. As is usual in such periods, the contending parties accuse each other of inveterate falsehood, perfidy, oppression, and local tyranny and persecution. "Madness rules the hour."

It was only a day or two ago I took up a local journal of considerable influence, in which were two paragraphs which struck me as being inexpressibly absurd. In the first it was stated that a gentleman who had expressed strong Southern sentiments in a New York hotel, had been mobbed and thrown into the street, and the writer indulged in some fitting reflections on the horrible persecution which prevailed in New York, and on the atrocity of such tyrannical mob-lawlessness in a civilized community. In another column there was a pleasant little narrative how citizens of Opelika, in Georgia, had waited on a certain person, who was "suspected" of entertaining Northern views, and had deported him on a rustic conveyance, known as a rail, which was considered by the journalist a very creditable exercise of public spirit.

Nay, more; in a *naive* paragraph relative to an attempt to burn the huge hotel of Willard, at Washington, in which some hundreds of people were residing, the paper, to account satisfactorily for the attempt, and to assign some intelligible and laudable motive for it, adds, that he supposes it was intended to burn out the "Border ruffians" who were lodged there—a reproduction of the excuse of our Anglo-Irish lord, who apologized for setting fire to a cathedral, on the ground that he imagined the bishop was inside. The exultation of the South when the flag of the United States was lowered at Sumter, has been answered by a shout of indignation and a battle-cry from the North, and the excitement at Charleston has produced a reflex action there, the energy of which cannot be described.

The apathy which struck me at New York, when I landed, has been succeeded by violent popular enthusiasm, before which all Laodicean policy has melted into fervent activity. The truth must be, that the New York population did not believe in the strength and unanimity of the South, and that they thought the Union safe, or did not care about it. I can put down the names of gentlemen who expressed the strongest opinions that the Government of the United States had no power to coerce the South, and who have since put down their names and their money to support the Government in the attempt to recover the forts which have been taken. As to the change of opinion in other quarters, which has been effected so rapidly and miraculously, that it has the ludicrous air of a vulgar juggler's trick at a fair, the public regard it so little, that it would be unbecoming to waste a word about it.

I expressed a belief in my first letter, written a few days after my arrival, that the South would never go back into the Union. The North thinks that it can coerce the South, and I am not prepared to say they are right or wrong; but I am convinced that the South can only be forced back by such a conquest as that which laid Poland prostrate at the feet of Russia. It may be that such a conquest can be made by the North, but success must destroy the Union as it has been constituted in times past. A strong government must be the logical consequence of victory, and the triumph of the South will be attended by a similar result, for which, indeed, many Southerners are very well disposed. To the people of the Confederate States there would be no terror in such an issue, for it appears to me they are pining for a strong government exceedingly.

The North must accept it, whether they like it or not. Neither party, if such a term can be applied to the rest of the United States and to those States which disdain the authority of the Federal Government, was prepared for the aggressive or resisting power of the other. Already the Confederate States perceive that they cannot carry all before them with a rush, while the North have learnt that they must put forth all their strength to make good a tithe of their lately uttered threats. But the Montgomery Government are now, they say, anxious to gain time, and to prepare a regular army. The North, distracted by apprehensions of vast disturbances in its complicated relations, is clamouring for instant action and speedy consummation. The counsels of the moderate men, as they were called, have been utterly overruled.

I am now, however, dealing with South Carolina, which has been the *fons et origo* of the secession doctrines, and their development into the full life of the Confederate States. The whole foundation on which South Carolina rests is cotton and a certain amount of rice, or rather she bases her whole fabric on the necessity which exists in Europe for those products of her soil, believing and asserting, as she does, that England and France cannot and will not do without them. Cotton, without a market, is so much flocculent matter encumbering the ground. Rice, without demand for it, is unsalable grain in store and on the field. Cotton at ten cents a pound is boundless prosperity, empire, and superiority, and rice or grain need no longer be regarded. In the matter of slave labour, South Carolina argues pretty much in this way: England and France require our products.

In order to meet their wants, we must cultivate our soil. There is only one way of doing so. The white man cannot live on our land at certain seasons of the year; he cannot work in the manner required by the crops. We must, therefore, employ a race suited to the labour, and that is a race which will only work when it is obliged to do so. That race was imported from Africa, under the sanction of the law, by our ancestors, when we were a British colony, and it has been fostered by us, so that its increase here has been as that of the most nourishing people in the world. In other places where its labour was not productive, or imperatively essential, that race has been made free, sometimes with disastrous consequences to itself and to industry.

But we will not make it free. We cannot do so. We hold that slavery is essential to our existence as producers of what Europe requires; nay, more, we maintain it is in the abstract right in principle; and some of us go so far as to maintain that the only proper form of society, according to the law of God and the exigencies of man, is that which has slavery as its basis. As to the slave, he is happier far in his state of servitude, more civilized and religious than he is or could be if free or in his native Africa.

I have already endeavoured to describe the portion of the State through which I travelled, and the aspect of Charleston, and I will now proceed, at the risk of making this letter longer than it should be, to make a few observations on matters which struck me during my visit to one or two of the planters of the many who were kind enough to give me invitations to their residences in the State.

Early one fine morning I started in a coasting steamer to visit a plantation in the Pedee and Maccamaw district, in the island coast of the State, north of Charleston. The only source of uneasiness in the mind of the party arose from the report that the United States squadron was coming to blockade the port, which would have cut off our line of retreat, and compelled us to make a long detour and a somewhat difficult journey by land, seeing that the roads are mere sand tracts, as the immense number of rivers and creeks offers excuse for not improving the means of land communication.

Passing Sumter, on which men are busily engaged, under the Confederate flag, in making good damages, and mounting guns, we put out a few miles to sea, and with the low sandy shore, dotted with soldiers, and guard-houses, and clumps of trees, on our left, in a few hours pass the Santee River, and enter an estuary into which the Pedee and Maccamaw Rivers run a few miles further to the northwest. The arid, barren, pine-covered sand-hills, which form the shores of this estuary, are guarded by rude batteries, mounted with heavy guns, and manned by the State troops, some of whom we can see strolling along the beach, or, with arms glancing in the sunlight, pacing up and down on their posts. On the left hand side there are said to be plantations, the sites of which are marked by belts of trees, and after we had proceeded a few miles from the sea, the steamer ran alongside a jetty and pier, which was crowded by men in uniform, waiting for the news, and for supplies of creature comforts.

Ladies were cantering along the fine hard beach, and some gigs and tax-carts, fully laden, rolled along very much as one sees them at Scarborough. The soldiers on the pier were all gentlemen of the county. Some, dressed in gray tunics and yellow facings, in high felt hats and plumes, and jack-boots, would have done no discredit in face, figure, and bearing, to the gayest cavaliers who ever thundered at the heels of Prince Rupert. Their horses, full of Carolinian fire and metal, stood picketed under the trees along the margin of the beach. Among these men, who had been doing the duty of common troopers in patrolling the sea-coast, were gentlemen possessed of large estates and princely fortunes; and one who stood among them was pointed out to me as captain of a company for whose uses his liberality provided unbounded daily libations of champagne, and the best luxuries which French ingenuity can safely imprison in those well-known caskets, with which Crimean warriors were not unacquainted at the close of the campaign.

They were eager for news, which was shouted out to them by their friends in the steamer, and one was struck by the intimate personal cordiality and familiar acquaintance which existed among them.

Three heavy guns, mounted in an earthwork, defended by palisades, covered the beach and landing-place, and the garrison was to have been re-enforced by a regiment from Charleston, which, however, had not got in readiness to go up on our steamer, owing to some little difficulties between the volunteers, their officers, and the quartermaster-general's department.

I mention these particulars to give an idea of the state of defence in which South Carolina holds itself, for, unless Georgetown, which lies at the head of this inlet, could be considered an object of attack, one seeks in vain for any reason to induce an enemy to make his appearance in this direction. A march on Charleston by land would be an operation of extreme difficulty, through a series of sand-hills, alternating with marshes, water-course, rivers, and flooded rice-fields. As to Georgetown, which we have now reached, nothing can be said by way of description more descriptive than the remark of its inhabitants, that it was a finished town a hundred years ago. It is a dozy, sleepy, sandy, lifeless, straggling village, with wooden houses drawn up in right lines on the margins of great, straight, grass-grown pathways, lined with trees, and known to the natives as streets.

As the Nina approaches the tumble-down wharf, two or three citizens advance from the shade of shaky sheds to welcome us, and a few country vehicles and light phaetons are drawn forth from the same shelter to receive the passengers, while the negro boys and girls, who have been playing upon the bales of cotton and barrels of rice, which represent the trade of the place on the wharf, take up commanding positions for the better observation of our proceedings. One or two small yachts and coasting schooners are moored by the banks of the broad, full stream, the waters of which we had previously crossed in our journey from the dismal swamp.

There is an air of quaint simplicity and old-fashioned quiet about Georgetown, refreshingly antagonistic to the bustle and tumult of most American cities, and one can, without much stretch of imagination, fancy the old loyal burghers in cocked hats, small-swords, and long, square-cut sober suits, stalking solemnly down its streets, rejoicing in the progress of the city which recalled the name of the king and the old country, or hastening down to the river's side to hear the tidings brought from home by the Bristol bark that has just anchored in the stream. Instead thereof, however, there are the tall, square forms of eager citizens bowed over their newspapers in the shade before the bar-room, or the shuffling negro delighting in the sunshine, and kicking up the dust in the centre of the road as he goes on his errand.

While waiting for our vehicle, we enjoyed the hospitality of one of our friends, who took us into an old-fashioned angular wooden mansion, more than a century old, still sound in every timber, and testifying, in its quaint wainscotings and the rigid framework of door and window, to the durability of its cypress timbers, and the preservative character of the atmosphere. In early days it was the crack house of the old settlement, and the residence of the founder of the female branch of the family of our host, who now only makes it his halting-place when passing to and fro between Charleston and his plantation, leaving it the year round in charge of an old servant and her grandchild. Rose trees and flowering shrubs clustered before the porch, and filled the garden in front, and the establishment gave one a good idea of a London merchant's retreat about Chelsea a hundred and fifty years ago.

At length we were ready for our journey, and, mounted in two light covered vehicles, proceeded along the sandy track which, after a while, led us to a cut, deep in the bosom of the woods, where silence was only broken by the cry of a woodpecker, the boom of a crane, or the sharp challenge of the jay. For miles we passed through the shades of this forest, meeting only two or three vehicles containing female planterdom on little excursions of pleasure or business, who smiled their welcome as we passed. Not more than twice in a drive of two hours did we come upon any settlement or get a view of any white man's plantation, and then it was only when we had emerged from the wood and got out upon the broad, brown plains, where bunds, and water-dykes, and machinery for regulating the flooding of the lake indicated the scenes of labour. These settlements consisted of rows of some ten or twelve quadrangular wooden sheds, supported upon bricks, so as to allow the air, the children, and the chickens to play beneath; sometimes with brickwork chimneys at the side, occasionally with ruder contrivances of mud and woodwork to serve the same purpose.

Arrived at a deep chocolate-coloured stream, called Black River, full of fish and alligators, we find a flat large enough to accommodate vehicles and passengers, and propelled by two negroes pulling upon a stretched rope, in the manner usual in the ferryboats of Switzerland, ready for our reception. Another drive through a more open country, and we reach a fine grove of pine and live oak, which melts away into a shrubbery, guarded by a rustic gateway, passing through which we are brought by a sudden turn into the planter's house, buried in trees, which dispute with the green sward, and with wild flower beds, every yard of the space which lies between the hall-door and the waters of the Pedee; and in a few minutes, as we gaze over the expanse of fields, just tinged with green by the first life of the early rice crops, marked by the deep water-cuts, and bounded by a fringe of unceasing forest, the chimneys of the steamer we had left at Georgetown gliding, as it were, through the fields, indicate the existence of another navigable river still beyond.

Leaving with regret the veranda which commanded so enchanting a foreground of flowers, rare shrubbery, and bearded live oaks, with each graceful sylvan outline distinctly penciled upon the waters of the river, we enter the house, and are reminded by its low-browed, old-fashioned rooms, of the country houses yet to be found in parts of Ireland or the Scottish border, with additions made by the luxury and love of foreign travel of more than one generation of educated Southern planters. Paintings from Italy illustrate the walls in juxtaposition with interesting portraits of early Colonial governors and their lovely womankind, limned with no uncertain hand, and full of the vigour of touch and naturalness of drapery, of which Copley has left us too few exemplars, and one portrait of Benjamin West claims for itself such honour as his own pencil can give.

An excellent library, filled with collections of French and English classics, and with those ponderous editions of Voltaire, Rousseau, the *Memoires pour Servir*, books of travel and history, such as delighted our forefathers in the last century, and many works of American and general history, afford ample occupation for a rainy day. But alas! these, and all good things which the house affords, can be enjoyed but for a brief season. Just as nature has expanded every charm, developed every grace, and clothed the scene with all the beauty of opened flower, of ripening grain, and of mature vegetation, on the wings of the wind the poisoned breath comes borne to the home of the white man, and he must fly before it or perish. The books lie unopened on their shelves, the flower blooms and dies unheeded, and, pity 'tis 'tis true, the old Madeira, garnered 'neath the roof, settles down for a fresh lease of life, and sets about its solitary task of acquiring a finer flavour for the infrequent lips of its banished master and his welcome visitors.

This is the story, at least, that we hear on all sides, and such is the tale repeated to us beneath the porch, when the full moon enhances, while softening, the loveliness of the scene, and the rich melody of hundreds of mocking-birds fills the grove.

Within these hospitable doors Horace might banquet better than he did with Nasidienus, and drink such wine as can be only found among the descendants of an ancestry who, improvident enough in all else, learned the wisdom of bottling up choice old Bual and Sercial ere the demon of odium had dried up their generous sources for ever. To these must be added excellent bread, ingenious varieties of the *gallette*, compounded now of rice and now of Indian meal, delicious butter and fruits, all good of their kind. What more is needed for one who agrees with Mr. Disraeli in thinking bread and wine man's two first luxuries and his best? And is there anything bitter rising up from the bottom of the social bowl? My black friends who attend on me are grave as Mussulman *khitmutgars*. They are attired in liveries, and wear white cravats and Berlin gloves. At night, when we retire, off they go to their outer darkness in the small settlement of negrohood, which is separated from our house by a wooden palisade. Their fidelity is undoubted. The house breathes an air of security. The doors and windows are unlocked. There is but one gun, a fowling-piece, on the premises. No planter hereabouts has any dread of his slaves.

But I have seen within the short time that I have been here in this part of the world several dreadful accounts of the murder and violence in which masters suffered at the hands of their slaves. There is something suspicious in the constant, never-ending statement, that "We are not afraid of our slaves." The curfew and the night patrol in the streets, the prisons and watch-houses, and the police regulations prove that strict supervision, at all events, is needed and necessary. My host is a kind man and a good master. If slaves are happy anywhere, they should be so with him.

These people are fed by their master. They have upward of half a pound *per diem* of fat pork, and corn in abundance. They rear poultry, and sell their chickens and eggs to the house. They are clothed by their master. He keeps them in sickness as in health. Now and then there are gifts of tobacco and molasses for the deserving. There was little labour going on in the fields, for the rice has been just exerting itself to get its head above water. These fields yield plentifully, for the waters of the river are fat, and they are let in, whenever the planters require it, by means of floodgates and small canals, through which the flats can carry their loads of grain to the river for loading the steamers.

Letter 8

FACTS AND OPINIONS AT THE CONFEDERATE CAPITAL

Montgomery, Capital of the Confederate States
of America, May 8, 1861.

In my last letter I gave an account of such matters as passed under my notice on my way to this city, which I reached, as you are aware, on the night of Saturday, May 4. I am on difficult ground, the land is on fire, the earth is shaking with the tramp of armed men, and the very air is hot with passion. My communications are cut off, or are at best accidental, and in order to re-open them I must get further away from them, paradoxical as the statement may appear to be. It is impossible to know what is going on in the North, and it is almost the same to learn what is doing in the South out of eyeshot; it is useless to inquire what news is sent to you to England. Events hurry on with tremendous rapidity, and even the lightning lags behind them. The people of the South at last are aware that the "Yankees" are preparing to support the Government of the United States, and that the secession can only be maintained by victory in the field.

There has been a change in their war policy. They now aver that "they only want to be let alone," and they declare that they do not intend to take Washington, and that it was merely as a feint they spoke about it. The fact is, there are even in the compact and united South men of moderate and men of extreme views, and the general tone of the whole is regulated by the preponderance of one or other at the moment. I have no doubt on my mind that the government here intended to attack and occupy Washington—not the least that they had it much at heart to reduce Fort Pickens as soon as possible. Now some of their friends say that it will be a mere matter of convenience whether they attack Washington or not, and that, as for Fort Pickens, they will certainly let it alone, at all events for the present, inasmuch as the menacing attitude of General Bragg obliges the enemy to keep a squadron of their best ships there, and to retain a force of regulars they can ill spare, in a position where they must lose enormously from diseases incidental to the climate.

They have discovered, too, that the position is of little value so long as the United States hold Tortugas and Key West. But the Confederates are preparing for the conflict, and when they have organized their forces, they will make, I am satisfied, a very resolute advance all along the line. They are at present strong enough, they suppose, in their domestic resources, and in the difficulties presented to a hostile force by the nature of the country, to bid defiance to invasion, or, at all events, to inflict a very severe chastisement on the invaders, and their excited manner of speech so acts upon the minds that they begin to think they can defy, not merely the United States, but the world. Thus it is that they declare they never can be conquered, that they will die to a man, woman, and child first, and that if fifty thousand, or any number of thousands of Black Republicans get one hundred miles into Virginia, not one man of them shall ever get out alive. Behind all this talk, however, there is immense energy, great resolution, and fixed principles of action.

Their strategy consists in keeping quiet till they have their troops well in hand, in such numbers and discipline as shall give them fair grounds for expecting success in any campaign with the United States troops. They are preparing with vigour to render the descent of the Mississippi impossible, by erecting batteries on the commanding levees or embankments which hem in its waters for upward of eight hundred miles of bank, and they are occupying, as far as they can, all the strategical points of attack or defence within their borders. When everything is ready, it is not improbable that Mr. Jefferson Davis will take command of the army, for he is reported to have a high ambition to acquire reputation as a general, and in virtue of his office he is Generalissimo of the Armies of the Confederate States.

It will be remarked that this plan rests on the assumption that the United States cannot or will not wage an offensive war, or obtain any success in their attempts to recover the forts and other property of the Federal Government. They firmly believe the war will not last a year, and that 1862 will behold a victorious, compact, slave-holding Confederate power of fifteen States under a strong government, prepared to hold its own against the world, or that portion of it which may attack it. I now but repeat the sentiments and expectations of those around me. They believe in the irresistible power of cotton, in the natural alliance between manufacturing England and France and the cotton producing Slave States, in the force of their simple tariff, and in the interest which arise out of a system of free-trade, which, however, by a rigorous legislation they will interdict to their neighbours in the Free States, and only open for the benefit of their foreign customers. Commercially, and politically, and militarily, they have made up their minds, and never was there such confidence exhibited by any people in the future as they have, or pretended to have, in their destiny. Listen to their programme.

It is intended to buy up all the cotton crop which can be brought into the market at an average price, and to give bonds of the Confederate States for the amount, these bonds being, as we know, secured by the export duty on cotton. The government, with this cotton crop in its own hands, will use it as a formidable machine of war, for cotton can do anything, from the establishment of an empire to the securing of a shirt button. It is at once king and subject, master and servant, captain and soldier, artilleryman and gun. Not one bale of cotton will be permitted to enter the Northern States. It will be made an offence punishable with tremendous penalties, among which confiscation of property, enormous fines, and even the penalty of death, are enumerated, to send cotton into the Free States. Thus Lowell and its kindred factories will be reduced to ruin, it is said, and the North to the direst distress. If Manchester can get cotton and Lowell cannot, there are good times coming for the mill-owners.

The planters have agreed among themselves to hold over one-half of their cotton crop for their own purposes and for the culture of their fields, and to sell the other to the government. For each bale of cotton, as I hear, a bond will be issued on the fair average price of cotton in the market, and this bond must be taken at par as a circulating medium within the limits of the Slave States. This forced circulation will be secured by the act of the Legislature. The bonds will bear interest at 10 *per cent.*, and they will be issued on the faith and security of the proceeds of the duty of one-eighth of a cent on every pound of cotton exported. All vessels loading with cotton will be obliged to enter into bonds, or give security that they will not carry their cargoes to Northern ports, or let it reach Northern markets to their knowledge. The government will sell the cotton for cash to foreign buyers, and will thus raise funds amply sufficient, they contend, for all purposes.

I make these bare statements, and I leave to political economists the discussion of the question which may and will arise out of the acts of the Confederate States. The Southerners argue that by breaking from their unnatural alliance with the North they will save upward of $47,000,000, or nearly £10,000,000 sterling annually. The estimated value of the annual cotton crop is $200,000,000. On this the North formerly made at least $10,000,000, by advance, interest and exchanges, which in all came to fully 5 *per cent.* on the whole of the crop. Again, the tariff to raise revenue sufficient for the maintenance of the government of the Southern Confederacy is far less than that which is required by the government of the United States. The Confederate States propose to have a tariff which will be about 12½ *per cent.* on imports, which will yield $25,000,000. The Northern tariff is 30 *per cent.*, and as the South took from the North $70,000,000 worth of manufactured goods and produce, they contribute, they assert, to the maintenance of the North to the extent of the difference between the tax sufficient for the support of their government, and that which is required for the support of the Federal Government.

Now they will save the difference between 30 *per cent*, and 12½ *per cent.* (17½ *per cent*), which amounts to $37,000,000, which, added to the saving on commissions, exchanges, advances, &c., makes up the good round sum which I have put down higher up. The Southerners are firmly convinced that they have "kept the North going" by the prices they have paid for the protected articles of their manufacture, and they hold out to Sheffield, to Manchester, to Leeds, to Wolverhampton, to Dudley, to Paris, to Lyons, to Bordeaux, to all the centres of English manufacturing life, as of French taste and luxury, the tempting baits of new and eager and hungry markets. If their facts and statistics are accurate, there can be no doubt of the justice of their deductions on many points; but they can scarcely be correct in assuming that they will bring the United States to destruction by cutting off from Lowell the 600,000 bales of cotton which she usually consumes.

One great fact, however, is unquestionable—the government has in its hands the souls, the wealth, and the hearts of the people. They will give anything—money, labour, life itself—to carry out their theories. "Sir," said an ex-governor of this State to me today, "sooner than submit to the North, we will all become subject to Great Britain again." The same gentleman is one of the many who have given to the government a large portion of their cotton crop every year as a freewill offering. In his instance his gift is one of 500 bales of cotton, or £5,000 *per annum*, and the papers teem with accounts of similar "patriotism" and devotion. The ladies are all making sand-bags, cartridges, and uniforms, and, if possible, they are more fierce than the men. The time for mediation is past, if it ever were at hand or present at all; and it is scarcely possible now to prevent the processes of phlebotomiszation which are supposed to secure peace and repose.

There was no intelligence of much interest on Sunday, but there is a general belief that Arkansas and Missouri will send in their adhesion to the Confederacy this week, and the Commissioners from Virginia are hourly expected. The attitude of that State, however, gives rise to apprehensions lest there may be a division of her strength; and any aggression on her territories by the Federal Government, such as that contemplated in taking possession of Alexandria, would be hailed by the Montgomery Government with sincere joy, as it would, they think, move the State to more rapid action and decision.

Montgomery is on an undulating plain, and covers ground large enough for a city of two hundred thousand inhabitants, but its population is only twelve thousand. Indeed, the politicians here appear to dislike large cities, but the city designers certainly prepare to take them if they come. There is a large negro population, and a considerable number of a colour which forces me to doubt the evidences of my senses rather than the statements made to me by some of my friends, that the planters affect the character of parent in their moral relations merely with the negro race. A waiter at the hotel—a tall, handsome young fellow, with the least tinge of colour in his cheek, not as dark as the majority of Spaniards or Italians—astonished me in my ignorance today when, in reply to a question asked by one of our party, in consequence of a discussion on the point, he informed me he "was a slave."

The man, as he said so, looked confused; his manner altered. He had been talking familiarly to us, but the moment he replied, "I am a slave, Sir," his loquacity disappeared, and he walked hurriedly and in silence out of the room. The River Alabama, on which the city rests, is a wide, deep stream, now a quarter of a mile in breadth, with a current of four miles an hour. It is navigable to Mobile, upward of four hundred miles, and steamers ascend its waters for many miles beyond this into the interior. The country around is well wooded, and is richly cultivated in broad fields of cotton and Indian corn, but the neighbourhood is not healthy, and deadly fevers are said to prevail at certain seasons of the year. There is not much animation in the streets, except when "there is a difficulty among the citizens," or in the eternal noise

70

cf the hotel steps and bars. I was told this morning by the hotel keeper that I was probably the only person in the house, or about it, who had not loaded revolvers in his pockets, and one is aware occasionally of an unnatural rigidity scarcely attributable to the osseous structure in the persons of those who pass one in the crowded passages.

Monday, May 6.—Today I visited the Capitol, where the Provisional Congress is sitting. On leaving the hotel, which is like a small Willard's, so far as the crowd in the hall is concerned, my attention was attracted to a group of people to whom a man was holding forth in energetic sentences. The day was hot, but I pushed near to the spot, for I like to hear a stump speech, or to pick up a stray morsel of divinity in the *via sacra* of strange cities, and it appeared as though the speaker was delivering an oration or a sermon. The crowd was small. Three or four idle men in rough, homespun, makeshift uniforms, leaned against the iron rails inclosing a small pond of foul, green-looking water, surrounded by brick-work which decorates the space in front of the Exchange Hotel. The speaker stood on an empty deal packing case.

A man in a cart was listening with a lack-lustre eye to the address. Some three or four others, in a sort of vehicle, which might either be a hearse or a piano-van, had also drawn up for the benefit of the address. Five or six other men, in long black coats and high hats, some whittling sticks, and chewing tobacco, and discharging streams of discoloured saliva, completed the group. "Nine h'hun'nerd and fifty dollars! Only nine h-hun'nerd and fifty dollars offered for him," exclaimed the man, in the tone of injured dignity, remonstrance, and surprise, which can be insinuated by all true auctioneers into the driest numerical statements. "Will *no one* make any advance on nine hundred and fifty dollars?"

A man near me opened his mouth, spat, and said, "Twenty-five."

"Only nine hundred and seventy-five dollars offered for him. Why, at's radaklous—only nine hundred and seventy-five dollars! Will no one," &c. Beside the orator auctioneer stood a stout young man of five-and-twenty years of age, with a bundle in his hand. He was a muscular fellow, broad-shouldered, narrow-flanked, but rather small in stature; he had on a broad, greasy, old wide-awake, a blue jacket, a coarse cotton shirt, loose and rather ragged trowsers, and broken shoes. The expression of his face was heavy and sad, but it was by no means disagreeable, in spite of his thick lips, broad nostrils, and high cheek-bones.

71

On his head was wool instead of hair. I am neither sentimentalist, nor Black Republican, nor negro-worshiper, but I confess the sight caused a strange thrill through my heart. I tried in vain to make myself familiar with the fact that I could, for the sum of nine hundred and seventy-five dollars, become as absolutely the owner of that mass of blood, bones, sinew, flesh, and brains, as of the horse which stood by my side. There was no sophistry which could persuade me the man was not a man—he was, indeed, by no means my brother, but assuredly he was a fellow creature. I have seen slave markets in the East, but somehow or other the Orientalism of the scene cast a colouring over the nature of the sales there which deprived them of the disagreeable harshness and matter-of-fact character of the transaction before me. For Turk, or Smyrniote, or Egyptian, to buy and sell slaves, seemed rather suited to the eternal fitness of things than otherwise.

The turbaned, shawled, loose-trowsered, pipe-smoking merchants, speaking an unknown tongue, looked as if they were engaged in a legitimate business. One knew that their slaves would not be condemned to any very hard labour, and that they would be in some sort the inmates of the family and members of it. Here it grated on my ear to listen to the familiar tones of the English tongue as the medium by which the transfer was effected, and it was painful to see decent-looking men in European garb engaged in the work before me. Perchance these impressions may wear off, for I meet many English people who are the most strenuous advocates of the slave system, although it is true that their perceptions may be quickened to recognize its beauties by their participation in the profits. The negro was sold to one of the bystanders, and walked off with his bundle, God knows where. "Niggers is cheap," was the only remark of the bystanders. I continued my walk up a long, wide, straight street, or, more properly, an unpaved sandy road, lined with wooden houses on each side, and with trees by the side of the footpath.

The lower of the two storeys is generally used as a shop, mostly of the miscellaneous store kind, in which all sorts of articles are to be had, if there is any money to pay for them; and, in the present case, if any faith is to be attached to the conspicuous notices in the windows, credit is of no credit, and the only thing that can be accepted in exchange for the goods is "cash." At the end of this long street, on a moderate eminence, stands a whitewashed or painted edifice, with a gaunt, lean portico, supported on lofty, lanky pillars, and surmounted by a subdued and dejected-looking little cupola.

Passing an unkempt lawn, through a very shabby little gateway in a brick frame, and we ascend a flight of steps into a hall, from which a double staircase conducts us to the vestibule of the Chamber. Anything much more offensive to the eye cannot well be imagined than the floor and stairs. They are stained deeply by tobacco juice, which have left its marks on the white stone steps, and on the base of the pillars outside. In the hall which we have entered there are two tables, covered with hams, oranges, bread and fruits, for the refreshment of members and visitors, over which two sable goddesses, in portentous crinoline, preside. The door of the chamber is open, and we are introduced into a lofty, well-lighted and commodious apartment, in which the Congress of the Confederate States hold its deliberations.

A gallery runs half round the room, and is half filled with visitors—country cousins, and farmers of cotton and maize, and, haply, seekers of places, great or small. A light and low semi-circular screen separates the body of the house, where the members sit, from the space under the gallery, which is appropriated to ladies and visitors. The clerk sits at a desk above this table, and on a platform behind him are the desk and chair of the presiding officer or Speaker of the Congress. Over his head hangs the unfailing portrait of Washington, and a small engraving, in a black frame, of a gentleman unknown to me. Seated in the midst of them, at a senator's desk, I was permitted to "assist," in the French sense, at the deliberations of the Congress. Mr. Howell Cobb took the chair, and a white-headed clergyman was called upon to say prayers, which he did, upstanding, with outstretched hands and closed eyes, by the side of the Speaker. The prayer was long and sulphurous. One more pregnant with gunpowder I never heard, nor could aught like it have been heard since

Pulpit, drum ecclesiastic,
Was beat with fist instead of a stick.

The Rev. gentleman prayed that the Almighty might be pleased to inflict on the arms of the United States such a defeat, that it might be the example of signal punishment forever; that this President might be blessed, and that the other President might be the other thing; that the gallant, devoted young soldiers, who were fighting for their country, might not suffer from exposure to the weather or from the bullets of their enemies; and that the base mercenaries who were fighting on the other side might come to sure and swift destruction; and so on.

Are right and wrong mere geographical expressions? The prayer was over at last, and the House proceeded to business. Although each State has several delegates in Congress, it is only entitled to one vote on a strict division. In this way some curious decisions may be arrived at, as the smallest State is equal to the largest, and a majority of the Florida representatives may neutralize a vote of all the Georgia representatives.

For example, Georgia has ten delegates; Florida has only three. The vote of Florida, however, is determined by the action of any two of its three representatives, and these two may, on a division, throw the one State vote into the scale against that of Georgia, for which ten members are agreed. The Congress transacts all its business in secret session, and finds it a very agreeable and commendable way of doing it. Thus, today, for example, after the presentation of a few unimportant motions and papers, the Speaker rapped his desk, and announced that the House would go into secret session, and that all who were not members should leave.

As I was returning to the hotel there was another small crowd at the fountain. Another auctioneer, a fat, flabby, perspiring, puffy man, was trying to sell a negro girl who stood on the deal-box beside him. She was dressed pretty much like a London servant girl of the lower order out of place, except that her shoes were mere shreds of leather patches, and her bonnet would have scarce passed muster in the New Cut. She, too, had a little bundle in her hand, and looked out at the buyers from a pair of large sad eyes. "Niggers were cheap;" still here was this young woman going for an upset price of $610, but no one would bid, and the auctioneer, after vain attempts to raise the price and excite competition, said, "Not sold today, Sally; you may get down."

Tuesday, May 7.—The newspapers contain the text of the declaration of the state of war on the part of President Davis, and of the issue of letters of marque and reprisal, &c. But it may be asked, who will take these letters of marque? Where is the government of Montgomery to find ships? The answer is to be found in the fact that already numerous applications have been received from the shipowners of New England, from the whalers of New Bedford, and from others in the Northern States, for these very letters of marque, accompanied by the highest securities and guaranties! This statement I make on the very highest authority. I leave it to you to deal with the facts.

Today I proceeded to the Montgomery Downing Street and Whitehall to present myself to the members of the Cabinet, and to be introduced to the President of the Confederate States of America. There is no sentry at the doors, and access is free to all, but there are notices on the doors warning visitors that they can only be received during certain hours. The President was engaged with some gentlemen when I was presented to him, but he received me with much kindliness of manner, and when they had left entered into conversation with me for some time on general matters.

Mr. Davis is a man of slight, sinewy figure, rather over the middle height, and of erect, soldier-like bearing. He is about fifty-five years of age; his features are regular and well-defined, but the face is thin and marked on cheek and brow with many wrinkles, and is rather careworn and haggard. One eye is apparently blind, the other is dark, piercing, and intelligent. He was dressed very plainly in a light gray summer suit. In the course of conversation he gave an order for the Secretary of War to furnish me with a letter as a kind of passport in case of my falling in with the soldiers of any military posts who might be indisposed to let me pass freely, merely observing that I had been enough within the lines of camps to know what was my duty on such occasions.

I subsequently was presented to Mr. Walker, the Secretary of War, who promised to furnish me with the needful documents before I left Montgomery. In his room were General Beauregard and several officers, engaged over plans and maps, apparently in a little council of war, which was, perhaps, not without reference to the intelligence that the United States troops were marching on Norfolk Navy Yard, and had actually occupied Alexandria. On leaving the Secretary I proceeded to the room of the Attorney General, Mr. Benjamin, a very intelligent and able man, whom I found busied in preparations connected with the issue of letters of marque. Everything in the offices looked like earnest work and business.

On my way back from the State Department I saw a very fine company of infantry and three field pieces, with about one hundred and twenty artillerymen, on their march to the railway station for Virginia. The men were all well equipped, but there were no ammunition wagons for the guns, and the transport consisted solely of a few country carts drawn by poor horses, out of condition. There is no lack of muscle and will among the men. The troops which I see here are quite fit to march and fight as far as their *personnel* is concerned, and there is no people in the world so crazy with military madness. The very children in the streets ape the air of soldiers, carry little flags, and wear cockades as they strut in the highways; and mothers and fathers feed the fever by dressing them up as *Zouaves* or *Chasseurs*.

Mrs. Davis had a small levee today in right of her position as wife of the President. Several ladies there probably looked forward to the time when their States might secede from the new Confederation, and afford them the pleasure of holding a reception. Why not Presidents of the State of Georgia, or Alabama? Why not King of South Carolina, or Emperor of Florida? Soldiers of fortune, make your game! Gentlemen politicians, the ball is rolling. There is, to be sure, a storm gathering at the North, but it cannot hurt you, and already there are *condottieri* from all parts of the world flocking to your aid, who will eat your Southern beeves the last of all.

One word more as to a fleet. The English owners of several large steamers are already in correspondence with the government here for the purchase of their vessels. The intelligence which had reached the government that their commissioners have gone on to Paris is regarded as unfavourable to their claims, and as a proof that as yet England is not disposed to recognize them. It is amusing to hear the tone used on both sides toward Great Britain. Both are most anxious for her countenance and support, although the North blusters rather more about its independence than the South, which professes a warm regard for the mother country. "But," says the North, "if Great Britain recognizes the South, we shall certainly look on it as a declaration of war."

"And," says the South, "if Great Britain does not recognize our privateers' flag, we shall regard it as proof of hostility and of alliance with the enemy." The government at Washington seeks to obtain promises from Lord Lyons that our government will not recognize the Southern Confederacy, but at the same time refuses any guaranties in reference to the rights of neutrals. The blockade of the Southern ports would not occasion us any great inconvenience at present, because the cotton-loading season is over; but if it be enforced in October, there is a prospect of very serious and embarrassing questions arising in reference to the rights of neutrals, treaty obligations with the United States Government, the trade and commerce of England, and the law of blockade in reference to the distinctions to be drawn between measures of war and means of annoyance.

As I write the guns in front of the State Department are firing a salute, and each report marks a State of the Confederacy. They are now ten, as Arkansas and Tennessee are now out of the Union.

Letter 9

From Montgomery to Mobile.

Mobile, Alabama, May 11.

The wayfarer who confides in the maps of a strange country, or who should rely upon even the guide-books of the United States, which still lack a Murray or a Bradshaw, may be at times embarrassed by insuperable hills and unnavigable rivers. When, however, I saw the three towering stories of the high-pressure steamer *Southern Republic*, on board of which we tumbled down the steep bank of the Alabama River at Montgomery, any such misgivings vanish from my mind. So colossal an ark could have ascended no mythical stream, and the existence and capabilities of the Alabama were demonstrated by its presence.

Punctuality is reputed a rare virtue in the river steamers of the West and South, which seldom leave their wharves until they have bagged a fair complement of passengers, although steaming up and ringing gongs and bells every afternoon for a week or more before their departure, as if travellers were to be swarmed like bees. Whether stimulated by the infectious activity of these "war times," or convinced that the "politeness of kings" is the best steamboat policy, the grandson of Erin who owns and commands the Southern Republic casts off his fastenings but half an hour after his promised start, and the short puff of the engine is enlivened by the wild strains of a steam-organ called a "calliope," which gladdens us with the assurance that we are in the incomparable "land of Dixie."

Reserving for a cooler hour the attractions of the lower floor—a Hades consecrated to machinery, freight, and negroes—we betake ourselves to the second landing, where we find a long dining-hall surrounded by two tiers of state rooms, the upper one accessible by a stairway leading to a gallery, which divides the "saloon" between floor and roof. We are shown to our quarters, which leave much to be desired and nothing to spare, and rush from their suffocating atmosphere to the outer balcony, where a faint breeze stirs the air. There is a roofed balcony above us that corresponds to the second tier of state rooms, from which a party of excited secessionists are discharging revolvers at the dippers on the surface and the cranes on the banks of the river.

After we have dropped down five or six miles from Montgomery, the steam whistle announces our approach to a landing, and, as there is no wharf in view, we watch curiously the process by which our top-heavy craft, under the sway of a four-knot current, is to swing round in her invisible moorings. As we draw nigh to a wagon-worn indenture in the bank, the "scream" softens into the dulcet pipes of the "calliope," and the steamer doubles upon her track, like an elephant turning at bay, her two engines being as independent of each other as Seceding States, and, slowly stemming the stream, lays her nose upon the bank, and holds it there, with the judicious aid of her paddles, until a long plank is run ashore from her bow, over which three passengers, with valises, make way for a planter and his family, who come on board. The gang-plank is hauled in, the steamer turns her head down stream with the expertness of a whale in a canal, and we resume our voyage. We renew these stoppages at various times before dark, landing here a barrel and there a box, and occasionally picking up a passenger.

After supper, which is served on a series of parallel tables running athwart the saloon, we return to enjoy from the balcony the cool obscurity of the evening in this climate, where light means heat. As we cleave the glass surface of the black water, the timber-clad banks seem to hem us in more closely and to shut up in the vista before us, and while we glide down with a rapidity which would need but the roar of rapids to prefigure a cataract beyond, we yield to the caprice of fancy, instituting comparisons between the dark perspective ahead and the mystery of the future.

Again a scream, and a ruddy light flashes from our prow and deepens the shades around us. This proceeds from the burning of "light wood"—a highly resinous pine—in a wire basket hung on gimbals and held like a landing-net below the bow of the steamer, so as to guide without blinding the pilot, who is ensconced like a Hansom cabman upon its roof. The torch-bearer raises his cresset as we steam up to the bank, and plants it in a socket, when a hawser is seized round a tree, and the crew turned ashore to "wood up."

There is a steep high bank above us, and while dusky forms are flitting to and fro with food for our furnaces, we survey a long stairway ascending the bank at a sharp angle in a cut, which is lost in the sheds that crown the eminence over head. This stair is flanked on either side by the bars of an iron tramway, up which freight is hauled when landed, and parallel to it is a wooden slide, down which bales of cotton and sacks of corn are shot upon the steamer. One or two passengers slowly ascend, and a voice in the air notifies us that a team is at hand with a load of ladies, who shortly after are seen picking their way down the flight of steps. The cresset is constantly replenished with fresh light wood, and the shadows cast by its flickering flame make us regret that we have not with us a Turner to preserve this scene, which would have been a study for Rembrandt or Salvator Rosa.

At midnight we halt for a couple of hours at Selma, a "rising town," which has taken a start of late, owing to the arrival of a branch railway, that connects it with Tennessee and the Mississippi River. Here a huge *embarcadere*, several stories high, seems fastened to the side of the bank, and affords us an opportunity of stepping out from either story of the Southern Republic upon a corresponding landing. Upon one of these floors there are hackmen and hotel runners, competing for those who land, and indicating the proximity of a town, if not a city. Our captain had resolved upon making but a short stay, in lieu of tying up until morning—his usual practice—when an acquaintance comes on board and begs him to wait an hour for a couple of ladies and some children, whom he will hunt up a mile or so out of town. Times are hard, and the captain very cheerfully consents, not insensible to the flattering insinuation: "You know our folks never go with anyone but you, if they can help it."

The next day and evening are a repetition of the foregoing scenes, with more plantations in view and a general air of tillage and prosperity. We are struck by the uniformity of the soil, which everywhere seems of inexhaustible fertility, and by the unvarying breadth of the stream, which, but for its constantly recurring sinuosities, might pass for a broad ship canal. We also remark that the bluffs rarely sink into bottoms susceptible of overflow, and admire the verdure of the primitive forest, a tangle of magnolias in full flower, of laurel, and of various oaks peculiar to this region, and which, though never rising to the dignity of that noble tree in higher latitudes, are many of them extremely graceful.

All this sylva of moderate stature is intertwined with creepers, and at intervals we see the Spanish moss, indicating the malarious exhalations of the soil beneath. The Indian corn, upon which the Southerners rely principally for food, has attained a height of two feet, and we were told that, in consequence of the war, it is sown in greater breadth than usual. The cotton plant has but just peeped above the earth, and, alluding to its tenderness, those around us express anxieties about that crop, which, it seems, are never allayed until it has been picked, bagged and pressed, shipped and sold.

As I am not engaged upon an itinerary, let these sketches suffice to convey an idea of the four hundred and seventeen miles of winding river which connect Montgomery with Mobile, to which place the Southern Republic conveyed us in thirty-four hours, stoppings included.

One of the Egyptian pyramids owes its origin to the strange caprice of a princess, and the Southern Republic is said to have been built with the proceeds of an accidental "haul" of Gold Coast natives, who fell into the net of her enterprising proprietor. This worthy, born of Irish parents in Milk street, is too striking a type of what the late Mr. Webster was wont to call a "Northern man with Southern principles," not to deserve something more than a passing notice.

For out-and-out Southern notions there is nothing in Dixie's Land like the successful emigrant from the North and East. Captain Meagher had at his fingers' ends all the politico-economical facts and figures of the Southern side of the question, and rested his reasoning solely upon the more sordid and material calculations of the secessionists. It was a question of tariffs. The North had, no doubt, provided the protection of a navy, the facilities of mails, the construction of forts, Custom Houses, and Post Offices, in the South, and placed countless well-paid offices at the disposal of gentlemen fond of elegant leisure; but for all these the South had been paying more than their value, and when abolitionists were allowed to elect a Sectional President, and the system of forced labour, which is the basis of Southern prosperity, was threatened, the South were too happy to take a "snap judgment," as in a *pie poudre* court, and declare the Federal compact forfeited and annulled forever.

During the long second day of our voyage, we examined the faces of the proletarians, whose colour and constitutions so well adapted them for the Cyclopean realms of the main deck. Among them we detect several physiognomies which strike us as resembling seedlings from the Gold Coast rather than the second or third fruits of ancient transplantation. A fellow traveller gratifies at the same time our curiosity and our penetration. There are several native Africans, or, as they are called in Cuba, *bozales*, on board. They are the property of the argumentative captain, and were acquired by a *coup de main*, at which I have already hinted in this letter. It seems that a club of planters in this State and one or two others resolved, little more than a year ago, to import a cargo of Africans. They were influenced partly by cupidity and partly by fancy to set the United States laws at defiance, and to evince their contempt for New England philanthropy. The job was accepted by an Eastern house, which engaged to deliver the cargo at a certain point on the coast within certain limits of time.

Whether the shipment arrived earlier than anticipated, or whether Captain Meagher was originally designed as the person to whom the bold and delicate manoeuvre of landing them should be intrusted, it is certain that on a certain Sunday in last July he took a little coasting trip in his steamer *Czar*, and appeared at Mobile on the following morning in season to make his regular voyage up river. It is no less certain that he ran the dusky strangers in at night by an unfrequented pass, and landed them among the cane-brakes of his own plantation with sufficient celerity to be back at the moorings of the *Czar* without his absence having been noticed. The vessel from which the *bozales* were delivered was scuttled and sunk, and her master and crew found their way North by rail.

But the parties in interest soon claimed to divide the spoils, when, to their infinite disgust, the enterprising captain very coolly professed to ignore the whole business, and defied them to seek to recover by suit at law property the importation of which was regarded and would be punished as felony, if not as piracy, by the judicial tribunals. A case was made and issue joined, when the captain proved a circumstantial *alibi*, and, having cast the claimants, doled them out a few *bonzes*, perhaps to escape assassination, as shells, while he kept the oyster in the shape of the pick of the importation, which he still holds, reconciling his conscience to the transaction by interpreting it as *salvage*.

All this is told us by our interlocutor, who was one of the losers by the affair, and who stigmatized the conduct of its hero as having been treacherous. The latter, after repeated jocular inquiries, suffers his vanity to subdue his reticence, and finishes by "acknowledging the corn."

In the forenoon of the second day we meet two steamers ascending the river, with heavy cargoes, and are told that they are the *Keyes* and the *Lewis*, recently warned off, and *not seized* by the blockading squadron off Pensacola. They are deep with provisions for the forces of the Confederate States Army before Pickens, which must now be dispatched from Montgomery by rail.

In Mobile, for the first time since leaving Washington, "we realize" the entire stagnation of business. There are but five vessels in port, chiefly English, which will suffice to carry away the *débris* of the cotton crop. Exchange on the North is unsalable, owing to the impossibility of importing coin through the unsettled country, and bills on London are of slow sale at par, which would leave a profit of seven *per cent.* upon the importation of gold from your side.

Mobile, Sunday, May 11.

The heat of the city rendered an excursion to which I was invited, for the purpose of visiting the forts at the entrance of the bay, exceedingly agreeable, and I was glad to get out from the smell of warm bricks to the breezy waters of the sea. The party comprised many of the leading merchants and politicians of this city, which is the third in importance as a port of exportation in the United States of America. There was not a man among them who did not express, with more or less determination, the resolve never to submit to the rule of the accursed North. Let there be no mistake whatever as to the unanimity which exists at present in the South to fight for what it calls its independence, and to carry on a war to the knife with the government of the United States.

I have frequently had occasion to remark the curious operation of the doctrine of State Rights on the minds of the people: but an examination of the institutions of the country as they actually exist leads to the inference that, where the tyranny of the majority is at once irresponsible and cruel, it is impossible for any man, where the doctrine prevails, to resist it with safety or success. It is the inevitable result of the action of this majority, as it operates in America, first to demoralize and finally to absorb the minority; and even those who have maintained what are called "Union doctrines," and who are opposed to secession or revolution, have bowed their heads before the majesty of the mass, and have hastened to signify their acquiescence in the decisions which they have hitherto opposed.

The minority, cowardly in consequence of the arbitrary and vindictive character of the overwhelming power against which it has struggled, and disheartened by defeat, of which the penalties are tremendous in such conflicts as these, hastens to lick the feet of the conqueror, and rushes with frantic cheers after the chariot in the triumph which celebrates its own humiliation. If there be a minority at all on this great question of secession in the Southern States, it hides in holes and corners, inaccessible to the light of day, and sits there in darkness and sorrow, silent and fearful, if not dumb and hopeless. There were officers who had served with distinction under the flag of the United States, now anxious to declare that it was not their flag, and that they had no affection for it, although they were ready to admit they would have continued to serve under it if the States had not gone out.

A man's State, in fact, under the operation of these majority doctrines to which I have adverted, holds hostages for his fidelity to the majority, not only in such land or fortune as he may possess within her bounds, but in his family, his relatives, and kin, and if the State revolts, the officer who remains faithful to the flag of the United States is considered by the authorities of the revolting State a traitor, and, what is worse, he is treated in the persons of those he leave behind him as the worst kind of political renegade. General Scott, but a few months ago the most honoured of men in a Republic which sets such store on military success, is now reviled and abused because, being a Virginian by birth, he did not immediately violate his oath, abandon his post, and turn to fight against the flag which he has illustrated by repeated successes, during a career of half a century, the moment his State passes an ordinance of Secession.

An intelligent and accomplished officer, who accompanied me today around the forts under his command, told me that he had all along resisted Secession, but that when his State went out he felt it was necessary to resign his commission in the United States Army, and to take service with the Confederates. Among the most determined opponents of the North, and the most vehement friends of what are called here "domestic institutions," are the British residents, English, Irish, and Scotch, who have settled here for trading purposes, and who are frequently slave-holders. These men have no State rights to uphold, but they are convinced of the excellence of things as they are, or find it their interest to be so.

The waters of two rivers fall into the head of the Bay of Mobile, which is, in fact, a narrow sea creek between low, sandy banks, covered with pine and forest trees, broken here and there into islands, and extending some thirty miles inland, with a breadth varying from three to seven miles. No attempt has been made apparently to improve the waters or to provide docks or wharfage for the numerous cotton ships which lie out at the mouth of the bay, more than twenty-five miles from Mobile. All the cotton has to be sent down to them in lighters, and the number of men thus employed in the cotton season in loading the barges, navigating and transferring the cargoes to the ships, is very considerable, and their rate of wages is high.

The horror entertained by a merchant captain of the shore is well known, and skippers are delighted at an anchorage so far from land, which at the same time detains the crews in the ships and prevents absenteeism and "running." At present there are but seven ships at the anchorage, nearly all British, and one of the latter appears in the distance hard and fast ashore, though whether she got there in consequence of the light not being burning or from neglect, it is impossible to say. Fort Gaines, on the right bank of the channel, near the entrance, is an unfinished shell of a fort, which was commenced by the United States engineers some time ago, and which it would not be easy to finish without a large outlay of money and labour. It is not well placed to resist either a land attack or an assault by boats.

A high sand-bank in front of one of the faces screens the fire, and a wood on another side, if occupied by riflemen, would render it difficult to work the barbette guns. It is not likely, however, that the fort will be attacked. The channel it commands is only fit for light vessels. From this fort to the other side of the channel, where Fort Morgan stands, the distance is over three miles, and the deep water channel is close to the latter fort. The position at Gaines is held by a strong body of Alabama troops—stout, sturdy men, who have volunteered from farm, field, or desk. They are armed with ordinary muskets of the old pattern, and their uniform is by no means uniform; but the men look fit for service. The fort would take a garrison of five hundred men if fully mounted, but the parapets are mere partition walls of brickwork crenelled; the bomb-proofs are unfinished, and but for a few guns mounted on the sand-hills, the place is a defenceless shell-trap.

There are no guns in the casemates, and there is no position ready to bear the weight of a gun in barbette. The guns which are on the beach are protected by sand-bags traversed, and are more formidable than the whole fortress. The steamer proceeded across the channel to Fort Morgan, which is a work of considerable importance, and is assuming a formidable character under the superintendence of Colonel Hardee, formerly of the United States army. It has a regular trace, bastion, and curtain, with a dry ditch and drawbridge, well-made casemates and bomb-proofs, and a tolerable armament of columbiads, 42 and 32-pounders, a few 10-inch mortars, and light guns in the external works at the salients. The store cf ammunition seems ample. Some of the fuses are antiquated, and the gun-carriages are old-fashioned. The open parade and the unprotected gorges of the casemates would render the work extremely unpleasant under a shell fire, and the buildings and barracks inside are at present open to the influence of heat. The magazines are badly traversed and inadequately protected.

A very simple and apparently effective contrivance for dispensing with the use of the sabot in shells was shown to me by Colonel Maury, the inventor. It consists of two circular grummets of rope, one at the base and the other at the upper circumference of the shell, made by a simple machinery to fit tightly to the sphere, and bound together by thin copper wire. The grummets fit the bore of the gun exactly, and act as wads, allowing the base of the shell to rest in close contact with the charge, and breaking into oakum on leaving the muzzle. Those who know what mischief can be done by the fragments of the sabot when fired over the heads of troops will appreciate this simple invention, which is said to give increased range to the horizontal shell. There must be about sixty guns in this work; it is over-garrisoned, and, indeed, it seems to be the difficulty here to know what to do with the home volunteers. Rope mantlets are used on the breeches of some of the *barbette* guns. At night the harbour is in perfect darkness. Notwithstanding the defences I have indicated, it would be quite possible to take Fort Morgan with a moderate force well supplied with the means of vertical fire.

"Are there any mosquitoes here?" inquired I of the waiter, on the day of my arrival.

"Well, there's a few, I guess; but I wish there were ten times as many."

"In the name of goodness why do you say so?" asked I, with some surprise and indignation.

"Because we'd get rid of the —— Black Republicans out of Fort Pickens all the sooner," replied he.

There is a strange unilateral tendency in the minds of men in judging of the operation of causes and results in such a contest as that which now prevails between the North and the South. The waiter reasoned and spoke like many of his betters. The mosquitoes, for whose aid he was so anxious, were regarded by him as true Southerners, who would only torture his enemies. The idea of these persecuting little fiends being so unpatriotic as to vex the Confederates in their sandy camp never entered into his mind for a moment. In the same way a gentleman of intelligence, who was speaking to me of the terrible sufferings which would be inflicted on the troops at Tortugas and at Pickens by fever, dysentery, and summer heats, looked quite surprised when I asked him "whether these agencies would not prove equally terrible to the troops of the Confederates?"

Letter 10

Mobile, May 16, 1861.

Our little schooner lay quietly at the wharf all night, but no one was allowed to come on board without a pass, for these wild-looking sentries are excellent men of business, and look after the practical part of soldiering with all the keenness which their direct personal interest imparts to their notions of duty. The enemy is to them the incarnation of all evil, and they hunt his spies and servants very much as a terrier chases a rat—with intense traditional and race animosity. The silence of the night is not broken by many challenges, or the "All's well" of patrols; but there is warlike significance enough in the sound of the shot which the working parties are rolling over the wooden jetty, with a dull, ponderous thumping on board the flats that are to carry them off for the food and *nourriture* of the batteries.

With the early morning, however, came the moral signs of martial existence. I started up from among my cockroaches, knocked my head against the fine pine beams over my hammock, and then, considerably obfuscated by the result, proceeded to investigate all the grounds that presented themselves to me as worthy of consideration in reference to the theory which had suddenly forced itself upon my mind that I was in the Crimea. For close at hand, through the sleepy organs of the only sense which was fully awake, came the well-known *réveillée* of the Zouaves, and then French clangours, rolls, ruffles, and calls ran along the line, and the volunteers got up, or did not, as seemed best to them.

An ebony and aged Ganymede, however, appeared with coffee, and told me, "the cap'n wants ask weder you take some bitters, Sir;" and, indeed, "the captain" did compound some amazing preparation for the judges and colonels present on deck and below, that met the approval of them all, and was recommending it for its fortifying qualities in making a redan and Malakhoff of the stomach. Breakfast came in due time; not much Persic apparatus to excite the hate of the simple-minded, but a great deal of substantial matter, in the shape of fried onions, ham, eggs, biscuit, with accompaniments of iced water, Bordeaux, and coffee. Our guests were two—a broad, farmer-like gentleman, weighing some sixteen stone, dressed in a green frieze tunic, with gold lace and red and scarlet worsted facings, and a felt wide awake, who, as he wiped his manly brow, informed me he was a "rifleman."

We have some volunteers quite as corpulent, and not more patriotic, for our farmer was a man of many bales, and, in becoming an officer in his company of braves, had given an unmistakable proof of devotion to his distant home and property. The other, a quiet, modest, intelligent-looking young man, was an officer in a different battalion, and talked with sense about a matter with which sense has seldom anything to do—I mean uniform. He remarked that in a serious action and close fighting, or in night work, it would be very difficult to prevent serious mistakes, and even disasters, owing to the officers of the Confederate States' troops wearing the same distinguishing marks of rank and similar uniforms, whenever they can get them, to those used in the regular service of the United States, and that much inconvenience will inevitably result from the great variety and wonderful diversity of the dresses of the immense number of companies forming the different regiments of volunteers.

The only troops near us which were attired with a regard to military exactness, were the regiment of *Zouaves* from New Orleans. Most of these are Frenchmen or Creoles, some have belonged to the battalions which the Crimea first made famous, and were present before Sevastopol and in Italy, and the rest are Germans and Irish. Our friends went off to see them drill, but, as a believer in the enchanting power of distance, I preferred to look on at such of the manoeuvres as could be seen from the deck. These *Zouaves* look exceedingly like the real article. They are, perhaps, a trifle leaner and taller, and are not so well developed at the back of the head, the heels, and the ankles, as their prototypes. They are dressed in the same way, except that I saw no turban on the *fez* cap. The jacket, the cummerbund, the baggy red breeches, and the gaiters, are all copies of the original. They are all armed with rifle-musket and sword-bayonet, and their pay is at the usual rate of $11, or something like £2 6s. a month, with rations and allowances.

The officers do their best to be the true "*chacal*." I was more interested, I confess, in watching the motions of vast shoals of mullet and other fish, which flew here and there, like flocks of plover, before the red fish and other enemies, and darted under our boat, than in examining *Zouave* drill. Once, as a large fish came gambolling along the surface close at hand, a great gleam of white shot up in the waves beneath, and a boiling whirl marked with a crimson pool, which gradually melted off in the tide, showed where a monster shark had taken down a part of his breakfast. "That's a ground-shark," quoth the skipper. "There's quite a many of them about here." Porpoises passed by in a great hurry for Pensacola, and now and then a turtle showed his dear little head above the enviable fluid which he honoured with his presence. Far away in the long stretch of water toward Pensacola are six British merchantmen in a state of blockade; that is, they have only fifteen days to clear out, according to the reading of the law adopted by the United States officers.

The Navy Yard looks clean and neat in the early morning, and away on the other side of the channel Fort Pickens—*teterrima causa*—raises its dark front from the white sand and green sward of the glacis, on which a number of black objects invite inspection through a telescope, and obligingly resolve themselves into horses turned out to graze on the slope. Fort M'Rae, at the other side of the channel, as if to irritate its neighbour, flings out a flag to the breeze, which is the counterpart of the "Stars and Stripes" that wave from the rival flagstaff, and is at this distance identical to the eye until the glass detects the solitary star in its folds instead of the whole galaxy.

On the dazzling snowy margin of sand that separates the trees and brushwood from the sea, close at hand, the outline of the batteries which stud the shore for miles is visible. Let us go and make a close inspection. Mr. Ellis, a lieutenant in the Louisiana regiment, who is *aide-de-camp* to Brigadier-General Bragg, has just arrived with a message from his chief to escort me round all the works, and wherever else I like to go, without any reservation whatever. He is a handsome, well-built, slight young fellow, very composed and staid in manner, but full of sentiment for the South. Returned from a tour in Europe, he is all admiration for English scenery, life, and habits. "After all, nature has been more bountiful to you than to us."

He is dressed in a tight undress cavalry jacket and trowsers of blue flannel, with plain gold lace pipings and buttons, but on his heels are heavy brass spurs, worthy of the heaviest of field officers. Our horses are standing in the shade of a large tree near the wharf, and mine is equipped with a saddle of ponderous brass-work, on raised pummel and cantle, and housings, and emblazoned cloth, and mighty stirrups of brass fit for the stoutest marshal that ever led an army of France to victory; General Braxton Bragg is longer in the leg than Marshal Pelissier or Canrobert, or the writer, and as we jogged along over the deep, hot sand, my kind companion, in spite of my assurances that the leathers were quite comfortable, made himself and me somewhat uneasy on the score of their adjustment, and, as there was no implement at hand to make a hole, we turned into the general's courtyard to effect the necessary alterations.

The cry of "Orderly" brought a smart, soldierly young man to the front, who speedily took me three holes up, and as I was going away he touched his cap and said, "I beg your pardon, Sir, but I often saw you in the Crimea." His story as he told it was brief. He had been in the 11th Hussars, and on the day of the 25th of October he was following, as he said, close after Lord Cardigan and Captain Nolan, when his horse was killed under him. As he tried to make his escape, the Cossacks took him prisoner, and for eleven months he was in captivity, but was exchanged at Odessa.

"Why did you leave the service?"

"Well, Sir, I was one of the two sergeants that was permitted to leave in each regiment on the close of the war, and I came away."

"But here you are soldiering again?"

"Yes, Sir; I came over here to better myself, as I thought, and I had to enter one of their cavalry regiments, but now I am an orderly."

He told me further, that his name was Montague, and that he "thought his father lived near Windsor, twenty-one miles from London;" and I was pleased to find his superior officers spoke of him in very high terms, although I could have wished those who spoke so were in our own service.

I do not think that any number of words can give a good idea of a long line of detached batteries. I went through them all, and I certainly found stronger reasons than ever for distrusting the extraordinary statements which appear in the American journals in reference to military matters, particularly on their own side of the question. Instead of hundreds of guns, there are only ten. They are mostly of small calibre, and the gun-carriages are old and unsound, or new and rudely made. There are only five "heavy" guns in all the works, but the mortar batteries, three in number, of which one is unfinished, will prove very damaging, although they will only contain nine or ten mortars.

The batteries are all sand-bag and earthworks, with the exception of Fort Barrancas. They are made after all sorts of ways, and are of very different degrees of efficiency. In some the magazines will come to speedy destruction; in others they are well made. Some are of the finest white sand, and will blind the gunners, or be blown away with shells; others are cramped, and hardly traversed; others, again, are very spacious, and well constructed. The embrasures are usually made of sand-bags, covered with raw hide, to save the cotton bags from the effect of the fire of their own guns. I was amused to observe that most of these works had galleries in the rear, generally in connection with the magazine passages, which the constructors called "rat-holes," and which are intended as shelter to the men at the guns, in case of shells falling inside the battery. They may prove to have a very different re-sult, and are certainly not so desirable in a military point of view as good traverses.

A rush for the "rat-holes" will not be very dignified or improving to the *morale* every time a bomb hurtles over them; and assuredly the damage to the magazines will be enormous if the fire from Pickens is accurate and well sustained. Several of the batteries were not finished, and the men who ought to have been working were lying under the shade of trees, sleeping or smoking—long-limbed, long-bearded fel-lows in flannel shirts and slouched hats, uniformless in all save bright, well-kept arms, and resolute purpose. We went along slowly from one battery to the other. I visited nine altogether, not including Fort Bar-rancas, and there are three others, among which is Fort M'Rae. Per-haps there may be fifty guns of all sorts in position for about three miles, along a line exceeding 136 deg. around Fort Pickens, the aver-age distance being about $1^{1}/_{3}$ mile.

The mortar batteries are well placed among brushwood, quite out of view to the fort, at distances varying from 2,500 to 2,800 yards, and the mortars are generally of calibres nearly corresponding with our 10-inch pieces. Several of the gun batteries are put on the level of the beach; others have more command, and one is particularly well placed, close to the White Lighthouse, on a raised plateau, which dominates the sandy strip that runs out to Fort M'Rae. Of the latter I have al-ready spoken. Fort Barrancas is an old fort—I believe of Spanish con-struction, with a very meagre trace—a plain curtain-face toward the sea, protected by a dry ditch and an outwork, in which, however, there are no guns. There is a drawbridge in the rear of the work, which is a simple parallelogram, showing twelve guns mounted *en barbette* on the sea-face. The walls are of brick, and the guns are protected by thick merlons of sand-bags.

The sole advantage of the fort is in its position; it almost looks down into the casemates of Pickens opposite, at its weakest point, and it has a fair command of the sea entrance, but the guns are weak, and there are only three pieces mounted which can do much mischief. While I was looking round there was an entertaining dispute going on between two men, whom I believe to have been officers, as to the work to be done, and I heard the inferior intimate pretty broadly his conviction that his chief did not know his own business in reference to some orders he was conveying.

The amount of ammunition which I saw did not appear to me to be at all sufficient for one day's moderate firing, and many of the shot were roughly cast and had deep flanges from the moulds in their sides, very destructive to the guns as well as to accuracy. In the rear of these batteries, among the pine woods and in deep brush, are three irregular camps, which, to the best of my belief, could not contain more than 2,700 men. There are probably 3,000 in and about the batteries, the Navy Yard, and the suburbs, and there are also, I am informed, 1,500 at Pensacola, but I doubt exceedingly that there are as many as 8,000 men, all told, of effective strength under the command of Gen. Bragg. It would be a mistake to despise these Irregulars.

One of the Mississippi regiments out in camp was evidently composed of men who liked campaigning, and who looked as though they would like fighting. They had no particular uniforms—the remark will often be made—but they had pugnacious physiognomies, and the physical means of carrying their inclinations into effect, and every man of them was, I am informed, familiar with the use of arms. Their tents are mostly small and bad, on the ridge-pole pattern, with side flys to keep off the sun. In some battalions they observe regularity of line, in others they follow individual or company caprice. The men use green boughs and bowers, as our poor fellows did in the old hot days in Bulgaria, and many of them had benches and seats before their doors, and the luxury of boarded floors to sleep upon.

There is an embarrassing custom in America, scarcely justifiable in any code of good manners, which in the South at least is too common, and which may be still more general in the North; at all events, to a stranger it is productive of the annoyance which is experienced by one who is obliged to inquire whether the behaviour of those among whom he is at the time is intentional rudeness or conventional want of breeding. For instance, my friend and myself, as we are riding along, see a gentleman standing near his battery or his tent—"Good-morrow, Colonel," or "General" (as the case may be), says my friend.

"Good-morrow (imagining military rank according to the notion possessed by speaker of the importance of the position of a general's A. D. C.), Ellis."

"Colonel, &c., allow me to introduce to you Mr. Jones of London."

The colonel advances with effusion, holds out his hand, grasps Jones's hand rigidly, and says warmly, as if he had just gained a particular object of his existence, "Mr Jones, I am very glad to make your acquaintance, Sir. Have you been pretty well since you have been in this country, Sir?" &c.

But it is most likely that the colonel will just walk away when he pleases, without saying a word to or taking the least notice of the aforesaid Jones, as to whose acquaintance he had just before expressed such friendly feelings, and in whose personal health he had taken so deep an interest; and Jones, till he is accustomed to it, feels affronted. The fact is, that the introduction means nothing; you are merely told each other's names, and if you like you may improve your acquaintance. The hand shaking is a remnant of barbarous times, when men with the same coloured skin were glad to see each other.

The country through which we rode was most uninteresting, thick brushwood and pine trees springing out of deep sand, here and there a *nullah* and some dirty stream—all flat as ditchwater. On our return we halted at the general's quarters. I had left a note for him, in which I inquired whether he would have any objection to my proceeding to Fort Pickens from his command, in case I obtained permission to do so, and when I entered General Bragg's room he was engaged in writing not merely a very courteous and complimentary expression of his acquiescence in my visit, but letters of introduction to personal friends in Louisiana, in the hope of rendering my sojourn more agreeable.

He expressed a doubt whether my comrades would be permitted to enter the fort, and talked very freely with me in reference to what I had seen at the batteries but I thought I perceived an indication of some change of purpose with respect to the immediate urgency of the attack on Fort Pickens, compared with his expressions last night. At length I departed with many thanks to General Bragg for his kindness and confidence, and returned to a room full of generals and colonels, who made a levee of their visits.

On my return to the schooner I observed that the small houses on the side of the long sandy beach were filled with men, many of whom were in groups round the happy possessors of a newspaper, and listened with the utmost interest to the excited delivery of the oracular sentences. How much of the agony and bitterness of this conflict—nay, how much of its existence—may be due to these same newspapers, no man can say, but I have very decided opinions, or rather a very strong belief, on the subject. There were still more people around the various bar-rooms than were attracted even by the journalists. Two of our companions were on board when I got back to the quay. The Mobile gentlemen had gone off to Pensacola, and had not returned to time, and under any circumstances it was not probable that they would be permitted to land, as undoubtedly they were no friends to the garrison or to the cause of the United States.

Our skipper opened his eyes and shook his rough head when he was ordered to get under way for Fort Pickens, and to anchor off the jetty. Up went the flag of truce to the fore once more, but the ever-watchful sentry, diverted for the time from his superintendence of the men who were fishing at our pier, forbade our departure till the corporal of the guard had given leave, and the corporal of the guard would not let the fair *Diana* cast off her warp till he had consulted the sergeant of the guard, and so there was some delay occasioned by the necessity for holding an interview with that functionary, who finally permitted the captain to proceed on his way, and with a fair light breeze the schooner fell round into the tideway and glided off towards the fort. We drew up with it rapidly, and soon attracted the notice of the lookout men and some officers who came down to the jetty.

We anchored a cable's length from the jetty. In reply to the sentry's hail, the skipper asked for a boat to put off for us. "Come off in your own boat." Skiff of Sharon! But there was no choice. With all the pathos of that remarkable structure, it could not go down in such a short row. And if it did? Well, "there is not a more terrible place for sharks along this coast," the captain had told us incidentally *en route*. Our boat was inclined to impartiality in its relation with the water, and took quite as much inside as it could hold, but we soused into it, and the men pulled like Doggett's Badgers, and soon we were out of shark depth and alongside the jetty, where were standing to receive us Mr. Brown, our friend of yesterday, Captain Vogdes, and Captain Berry, commanding a United States battery in the fort.

94

The soldiers of the guard were United States regular troops of the artillery, wore blue uniforms with brass buttons and remarkably ugly slouched hats, with an ornament in the shape of two crossed cannons. Captain Vogdes informed me that Col. Moore had sent off a reply to my letter to the fleet, stating that he would gladly permit me to go over the fort, but that he would not allow anyone else, under any circumstances, whatever, to visit it. My friends were, therefore, constrained to stay outside; but one of them picked up a friend on the beach, and got up an impromptu ride along the island.

The way from the jetty to the entrance of the fort is in the universal deep sand of this part of the world; the distance from the landing place to the gateway is not much more than two hundred yards, and the approach to the portal is quite unprotected. There is a high ramp and glacis on the land side, but the face and part of the curtain in which the gate is situate are open, as it was not considered likely that it would ever be attacked by Americans. The sharp angle of the bastion on this face is so weak that men are now engaged in throwing up an extempore glacis to cover the base of the wall and the casemates from fire.

The ditch is very broad, and the scarp and counterscarp are riveted with brick-work. The curvette has been cleared out, and in doing so, as a proof of the agreeable character of the locality, I may observe, upwards of sixty rattlesnakes were killed by the workmen. An abattis has been made along the edge of this part of the ditch—a rough inclined fence of stakes and boughs of trees. "Yes, Sir; at one time when those terrible fire-eating gentlemen at the other side were full of threats, and coming to take the place every day, there were only seventy men in this fort, and Lieut. Slemmer threw up this abattis to delay his assailants, if it were only for a few minutes, and to give his men breathing time to use their small arms."

The casemates here are all blinded, and the hospital is situated in the bomb-proofs inside. The gate was closed. At a talismanic knock it was opened, and from the external silence we passed into a scene full of activity and life, through the dark gallery which served at first as a framework to the picture. The parade of the fort was full of men, and at a *coup d'œil* it was obvious that great efforts had been made to prepare Fort Pickens for a desperate defence. In the parade were several tents of what is called Sibley's pattern, like our bell tents, but without the lower side wall, and provided with a ventilating top, which can be elevated or depressed at pleasure.

The parade ground has been judiciously filled with deep holes, like inverted cones, in which shells will be comparatively innocuous; and, warned by Sumter, everything has been removed which could prove in the least degree combustible. The officer on duty led me straight across to the opposite angle of the fort. As the rear of the casemates and bomb-proofs along this side will be exposed to a plunging fire from the opposite side, a very ingenious screen has been constructed by placing useless gun platforms and parts of carriages at an angle against the wall, and piling them up with sand and earth for several feet in thickness. A passage is thus left between the base of the wall and that of the screen through which a man can walk with ease.

Turning into this passage we entered a lofty bomb-proof, which was the bedroom of the commanding officer, and passed through into the casemate which serves as his headquarters. Colonel Harvey Brown received me with every expression of politeness and courtesy. He is a tall, spare, soldierly-looking man, with a face indicative of great resolution and energy, as well as of sagacity and kindness, and his attachment to the Union was probably one of the reasons of his removal from the command of Fort Hamilton, New York, to the charge of this very important fort. He has been long in the service, and he belonged to the first class of graduates who passed at West Point after its establishment in 1818. After a short and very interesting conversation, he proceeded to show me the works, and we mounted upon the parapet, accompanied by Captain Berry, and went over all the defences.

Fort Pickens has a regular bastioned trace, in outline an oblique and rather narrow parallelogram, with the obtuse angles facing the sea at one side and the land at the other. The acute angle, at which the bastion toward the enemy's batteries is situated, is the weakest part of the work; but it was built for sea defence, as I have already observed, and the trace was prolonged to obtain the greatest amount of fire on the sea approaches. The crest of the parapet is covered with very solid and well-made merlons of heavy sand-bags, but one face and the gorge of the bastion are exposed to an enfilading fire from Fort M'Rae, which the colonel said he intended to guard against if he got time.

All the guns seemed in good order, the carriages being well constructed, but they are mostly of what are considered small calibres now-a-days, being 32-pounders, with some 42-pounders and 24-pounders. There are, however, four heavy columbiads, which command the enemy's works on several points very completely. It struck me that the bastion guns were rather crowded. But, even in its present state, the defensive preparations are most creditable to the officers, who have had only three weeks to do the immense amount of work before us. The brick copings have been removed from the parapets, and strong sand-bag traverses have been constructed to cover the gunners, in addition to the "rat-holes" at the bastions.

More heavy guns are expected, which, with the aid of a few more mortars, will enable the garrison to hold their own against everything but a regular siege on the land side, and so long as the fleet covers the narrow neck of the island with its guns, it is not possible for the Confederates to effect a lodgement. If Fort M'Rae were strong and heavily armed, it could inflict great damage on Pickens; but it is neither one nor the other, and the United States officers are confident that they will speedily render it quite untenable.

The *bouches à feu* of the fort may be put down at forty, including the available pieces in the casemates, which sweep the ditch and the faces of the curtains. The walls are of the hardest brick, of nine feet thickness in many places, and the crest of the parapets on which the merlons and traverses rest are of turf. From the walls there is a splendid view of the whole position, and I found my companions were perfectly well acquainted with the strength and *locus* of the greater part of the enemy's works. Of course I held my peace, but I was amused at their accuracy. "There are the quarters of our friend, General Bragg." "There is one of their best batteries just beside the lighthouse." The tall chimney of the Warrington Navy Yard was smoking away lustily.

The colonel called my attention to it. "Do you see that, Sir? They are casting shot there. The sole reason for their 'forbearance' is that navy yard. They know full well that if they open a gun upon us we will lay that yard and all the work in ruins."

Captain Vogdes subsequently expressed some uneasiness on a point as to which I could have relieved his mind very effectually. He had seen something which led him to apprehend that the Confederates had a strong intrenched camp in the rear of their works. Thereupon I was enabled to perceive that in Captain Vogdes' mind there was a strong intention to land and carry the enemy's position. Why, otherwise, did you care about an intrenched camp, most excellent engineer? But now I may tell you that there is no intrenched camp at all, and that your vigilant eye, Sir, merely detected certain very absurd little furrows which the Confederates have in some places thrown up in the soft sand in front of their camps, which would cover a man up to the knee or stomach, and are quite useless as a breastwork.

If they thought a landing probable, it is unpardonable in them to neglect such a protection. These furrows are quite straight, and even if they are deepened the assailants have merely to march round them, as they extend only for some forty or fifty yards, and have no flanks. The officers of the garrison are aware the enemy have mortar batteries, but they think the inside of the fort will not be easily hit, and they said nothing to show that they were acquainted with the position of the mortars.

From the parapet we descended by a staircase into the casemates. The Confederates are greatly deceived in their expectation that the United States troops will be much exposed to the sun or heat in Pickens. More airy, well-ventilated quarters cannot be imagined, and there is quite light enough to enable the men to read in most of them. The plague of flies will infest both armies, and is the curse of every camp in summer. As to mosquitoes, the Confederates will probably suffer, if not more, at least as much as the States' troops. The effect of other tormentors, such as yellow fever and dysentery, will be in all probability felt on both sides; but, unless the position of the fort is peculiarly unhealthy, the men, who are under no control in respect to their libations, will probably suffer more than those who are restrained by discipline and restricted to a regular allowance. Water can always be had by digging, and is fit to use if drunk immediately. Vegetables and fresh provisions are not of course so easily had as on shore, but there is a scarcity of them in both camps, and the supplies from the store-ships are very good and certain. The bread baked by the garrison is excellent, as I had an opportunity of ascertaining, for I carried off two loaves from the bakehouse on board our schooner.

Our walk through the casemates was very interesting. They were crowded with men, most of whom were reading. They were quiet, orderly-looking soldiers—a mixture of old and young—scarcely equal in stature to their opponents, but more to be depended upon, I should think, in a long struggle. Everything seemed well arranged. Those men who were in bed had mosquito curtains drawn, and were reading or sleeping at their ease. In the casemates used as a hospital there were only some twelve men sick out of the whole garrison, and I was much struck by the absence of any foul smell, and by the cleanliness and neatness of all the arrangements. The colonel spoke to each of the men kindly, and they appeared glad to see him. The dispensary was as neat as care and elbow-grease could make it, and next door to it, in strange juxtaposition, was the laboratory for the manufactory of fusees and deadly implements, in equally good order.

Everything is ready for immediate service. I am inclined to think it will be some time before it is wanted. Assuredly, if the enemy attack Fort Pickens, they will meet with a resistance which will probably end in the entire destruction of the navy yard and of the greater part of their works. A week's delay will enable Colonel Brown to make good some grave defects; but delay is of more advantage to his enemy than it is to him, and if Fort Pickens were made at once *point d'appui* for a vigorous offensive movement by the fleet and by a land force, I have very little doubt in my mind that Pensacola must fall, and that General Bragg would be obliged to retire. In a few weeks the attitude of affairs may be very different. The railroad is open to General Bragg, and he can place himself in a very much stronger attitude than he now occupies.

At last the time came for me to leave. The colonel and Captain Berry came down to the beach with me. Outside we found Captain Vogdes kindly keeping my friends in conversation and in liquid supplies in the shade of the bakehouse shed, and, after a little more pleasant conversation, we were afloat once more. Probably no living man was ever permitted to visit the camps of two enemies within sight of each other before this under similar circumstances, for I was neither spy nor herald, and I owe my best thanks to those who trusted me on both sides so freely and honourably.

A gentleman who preceded me did not fare quite so well. He landed on the island and went up to the fort, where he represented himself to be the correspondent of an American journal. But his account of himself was not deemed satisfactory. He was sent off to the fleet. Presently there came over a flag of truce from General Bragg, with a warrant signed by a justice of the peace, for the correspondent, on a charge of felony; but the writ did not run in Fort Pickens. The officers regarded the message as a clever ruse to get back a spy, and the correspondent is still in durance vile, or in safety, as the case may be, on board the squadron.

All sails filled, the *Diana* stood up toward the Navy Yard once more in the glare of the setting sun. The sentinels along the battery and beach glared at us with surprise as the schooner, with her flag of truce still flying, ran past them. The pier was swept with the glass for the Mobile gentlemen; they were not visible. "Hollo! Mr. Captain, what's that you're at?" His mate was waving the Confederate flag from the deck.

"It's only a signal, Sir, to the gentlemen on shore."

"Wave some other flag, then, while there's a flag of truce flying, and while we are in these waters."

After backing and filling for some time, the party were descried in the distance. Again, the watery skiff was sent off, and in a few minutes they were permitted, thanks to their passes, to come off. Some confidential person had informed them the attack was certainly coming off in a very short time. They were anxious to stay. They had seen friends at Pensacola, and were full of praises of "the quaint old Spanish settlement," but mine is, unfortunately, not an excursion of pleasure, and it was imperative that I should not waste time. Everything had been seen that was necessary for my purpose. It was beyond my power to state the reasons which led me to think no fight would take place, for doing so would have been to betray confidence. And so we parted company: they to feast their eyes on a bombardment—and if they only are near enough to see it, they will heartily regret their curiosity, or I am mistaken—and we to return to Mobile.

It was dark before the *Diana* was well down off Fort Pickens again, and, as she passed out to sea, between it and Fort M'Rae, it was certainly to have been expected that one side or other would bring her to. Certainly our friend Mr. Brown, in his clipper *Oriental*, would overhaul us outside; and there lay a friendly bottle in a nest of ice waiting for the gallant sailor, who was to take farewell of us according to promise. Out we glided into night, and into the cold sea breeze, which blew fresh and strong from the north. In the distance the black form of the Powhatan could be just distinguished; the rest of the squadron could not be made out by either eye or glass, nor was the schooner in sight. A lantern was hoisted by my orders, and was kept aft some time after the schooner was clear of the forts. Still no schooner. The wind was not very favourable for running toward the *Powhatan*, and it was too late to approach her with perfect confidence from the enemy's side. Besides, it was late; time pressed.

The *Oriental* was surely lying off somewhere to the west-ward, and the word was given to make all sail, and soon the *Diana* was bowling along shore, where the sea melted away in a fiery line of foam so close to us that a man could, in nautical phrase, "shy a biscuit" on the sand. The wind was abeam, and the *Diana* seemed to breathe it through her sails, and flew along at an astonishing rate through the phosphorescent waters with a prow of flame and a bubbling wake of dancing meteor-like streams flowing from her helm, as though it were a furnace whence boiled a stream of liquid metal.

"No sign of the *Oriental* on our lee bow?"

"Nothin' at all in sight, Sir."

The sharks and huge rays flew off from the shore as we passed and darted out seawards, making their runs in brilliant trails of light. On sped the *Diana*, but no *Oriental* came in sight.

I was tired. The sun had been very hot; the ride through the batteries, the visits to quarters, the excursion to Pickens had found out my weak places, and my head was aching and legs fatigued, and so I thought I would turn in for a short time, and I dived into the shades below, where my comrades were already sleeping, and kicking off my boots, lapsed into a state which rendered me indifferent to the attentions no doubt lavished upon me by the numerous little familiars who recreate in the well-peopled timbers. It never entered into my head, even in my dreams, that the captain would break the blockade if he could—particularly as his papers had not been indorsed, and the penalties would be sharp and sure if he were caught. But the confidence of coasting captains in the extraordinary capabilities of their craft is a madness—a hallucination so strong that no danger or risk will prevent their acting upon it whenever they can.

I was assured once by the "captain" of a *Billyboy*, that he could run to windward of any frigate in her majesty's service, and there is not a skipper from Hartlepool to Whitstable who does not believe his own *Mary Ann*, or *Three Grandmothers*, is, on certain "pints," able to bump her fat bows and scuttle-shaped stern faster through the seas than any clipper which ever flew a pendant. I had been some two hours and a half asleep when I was awakened by a whispering in the little cabin. Charley, the negro cook, ague-stricken with terror, was leaning over the bed, and in broken French was chattering through his teeth—"*Monsieu, Monsieu, nous sommes perdus! The bateman de guerre nous poursuit. Il n'a pas encore tiré. Il va tirer bientôt! Oh mon Dieu! mon Dieu!*"

Through the hatchway I could see the skipper was at the helm, glancing anxiously from the compass to the quivering reef points of his mainsail. "What's all this we hear, captain?"

"Well, Sir, there's been somethin' a runnin' after us these two hours" (very slowly). "But I don't think he'll keech us up no how this time."

"But, good heavens. you know, it may be the *Oriental*, with Mr. Brown on board."

"Ah wall—may bee. But he kep quite close upon me in the dark—it gev me quite a stark when I seen him. May bee, says I, he's a pri-

101

vateerin' chap, and so I draws in on shore close as I cud,—gets mee centerboard in, and, says I, I'll see what yer med of, mee boy. He an't a gaining much on us."

I looked, and sure enough, about half or three-quarters of a mile astern, and somewhat to leeward of us, a vessel, with sails and hull all blended into a black lump, was standing on in pursuit. I strained my eyes and furbished up the glasses, but I could make out nothing definite. The skipper held grimly on. The shore was so close we could have almost leaped into the surf, for the *Diana*, when her centre-board is up, does not draw much over four feet. "Captain, I think you had better shake your wind, and see who he is. It may be Mr. Brown."

"Meester Brown or no I can't help carrine on now. I'd be on the bank outside in a minit if I didn't hold my course."

The captain had his own way; he argued that if it was the *Oriental* she would have fired a blank gun long ago to bring us to; and as to not calling us when the sail was discovered, he took up the general line of the cruelty of disturbing people when they're asleep. Ah! captain, you know well it was Mr. Brown, as you let out when we were safe off Fort Morgan. By keeping so close in shore in shoal water the *Diana* was enabled to creep along to windward of the stranger, who evidently was deeper than ourselves. See there! Her sails shiver! so one of the crew says; she's struck! But she's off again, and is after us. We are just within range, and one's eyes become quite blinky, watching for the flash from the bow, but, whether privateer or United States schooner, she was too magnanimous to fire. A stern chase is a long chase. It must now be somewhere about two in the morning. Nearer and nearer to shore creeps the *Diana*.

"I'll lead him into a pretty mess, whoever he is, if he tries to follow me through the Swash," grins the skipper. The Swash is a very shallow, narrow, and dangerous passage into Mobile Bay, between the sand-banks on the east of the main channel and the shore. Our pursuer holds on, but gains nothing. The *Diana* is now only some nine or ten miles from Fort Morgan, guarding the entrance to Mobile. Soon an uneasy, dancing motion, welcomes her approach to the Swash. "Take a cast of the lead, John!" "Nine feet." "Good! Again!" "Seven feet." "Good—Charley, bring the lantern." (Oh, Charley, why did that lantern go out just as it was wanted, and not only expose us to the most remarkable amount of "cussin," imprecation, and strange oaths our ears ever heard, but expose our lives and your head to more imminent danger?) But so it was, just at the critical juncture when a turn of the helm port or starboard made the difference perhaps between life and death, light after light went out, and the captain went dancing mad, after intervals of deadly calmness, as the mate sang out, "Five feet and a half! seven feet—six feet—eight feet—five feet—four and a half feet (oh Lord!)—six feet," and so on, through a measurement of death by inches, not at all agreeable.

And where was Mr. Brown all this time? Really we were so much interested in the state of the lead-line, and in the very peculiar behaviour of the lanterns, which would not burn, that we scarcely cared much when we heard from the odd hand and Charley that she had put about, after running aground once or twice, they thought, as soon as we entered the Swash, and had vanished rapidly in the darkness. It was little short of a miracle that we got past the elbow, for just at the critical moment, in a channel not more than one hundred yards broad, with only six feet water, the binnacle light, which had burned speedily for a minute, sank with a splutter into black night.

When the passage was accomplished the captain relieved his mind by chasing Charley into a corner, and with a shark which he held by the tail, as the first weapon that came to hand, inflicting on him condign punishment, and then returning to the helm. Charley, however, knew his master, for he slyly seized the shark and flung his defunct corpse overboard before another fit of passion came on, and by the morning the skipper was good friends with him, after he had relieved himself by a series of castigations of the negligent lamplighter with every variety of Rhadamanthine implement.

The *Diana* had thus distinguished her dirty little person by breaking a blockade, and giving an excellent friend of ours a great deal of trouble (if it was indeed Mr. Brown), as well as giving us a very unenviable character for want of hospitality and courtesy; and for both I beg to apologize with this account of the transaction. But she had a still greater triumph. As she approached Fort Morgan all was silence. The morning was just showing a grey streak in the east. "Why, they're all asleep at the fort," observed the indomitable captain, and, regardless of gun or sentries, down went his helm, and away the *Diana* thumped into Mobile Bay, and stole off in the darkness toward the opposite shore.

There was, however, a miserable day before us. When the light fairly broke we had got only a few miles inside, a stiff northerly wind blew right in our teeth, and the whole of the blessed day we spent tacking backward and forward between one low shore and another low shore, in water the colour of pea-soup, so that temper and patience were exhausted, and we were reduced to such a state that we took intense pleasure in meeting with a drowning alligator. He was a nice-looking young fellow, about ten feet long, and had evidently lost his way, and was going out to sea bodily, but it would have been the height of cruelty to take him on board our ship, miserable as he was, though he passed within two yards of us. There was, to be sure, the pleasure of seeing Mobile in every possible view, far and near, and east and west, and in a lump and run out, but it was not relished any more than our dinner, which consisted of a very gamy Bologna sausage pig, who had not decided whether he would be pork or bacon, and onions fried in a terrible preparation of Charley, the cook.

At five in the evening, however, having been nearly fourteen hours beating about twenty-seven miles, we were landed at an outlying wharf, and I started off for the Battle House and rest. The streets are filled with the usual rub-a-dubbing bands, and parades of companies of the citizens in grotesque garments and armament, all looking full of fight and secession. I write my name in the hotel book at the bar as usual. Instantly young Vigilance Committee, who has been resting his heels high in the air, with one eye on the staircase and the other on the end of his cigar, stalks forth and reads my style and title, and I have the satisfaction of slapping the door in his face as he saunters after me to my room, and looks curiously in to see how a man takes off his boots. They are all very anxious in the evening to know what I think about Pickens and Pensacola, and I am pleased to tell the citizens I think it will be a very tough affair on both sides whenever it comes. I proceed to New Orleans on Monday.

Letter 11

Mobile, May 18, 1861.

I avail myself of the departure of a gentleman who is going to New York by the shortest route he can find, to send you the accompanying letters. The mails are stopped; so are the telegraphs; and it is doubtful whether I can get to New Orleans by water. Of what I saw at Fort Pickens and Pensacola here is an account, written in a very hurried manner, and under very peculiar circumstances.

Tuesday, May 14, 1861.

Two New Orleans gentlemen, who came overland from Pensacola yesterday, give such an account of their miseries from heat, dust, sand, and want of accommodation, in the dreary waste through which they passed for more than seventeen hours, that I sought out some other way of going there, and at last heard of a small schooner, called the *Diana,* which would gladly undertake to run round by sea, if permitted to enter by the blockading squadron.

She was neither clean nor neat-looking; her captain, a tall, wild-haired young man, had more the air of a mechanic than of a sailor, but he knew his business well, as the result of the voyage showed. His crew consisted of three men and a negro cook. Three gentlemen of Mobile, who were anxious to visit General Bragg's camp, agreed to join me, but before I sailed I obtained a promise that they would not violate the character of neutrals as long as they were with me, and an assurance that they were not in any way engaged in or employed by the Confederate States' forces. " Surely you will not have Mr. R——hanged, Sir?" said the mayor of Mobile to me when I told him I could not consent to pass off the gentleman in question as a private friend.

"No, I shall do nothing to get Mr. R—— hanged. It will be his own act which causes it, but I will not allow Mr. R—— to accompany me under false pretences." Having concluded our bargain with the skipper at a tolerably fair rate, and laid in a stock of stores and provisions, the party sailed from Mobile at five in the evening of Tuesday, May 14, with the flag of the Confederate States flying; but, as a precautionary measure, I borrowed from our acting Consul, Mr. Magee, a British ensign, which, with a flag of truce, would win the favourable consideration of the United States squadron. Our craft, the somewhat Dutch build of which gave no great promise of speed, came, to our surprise and pleasure, up with the lights of Fort Morgan at nine o'clock, and we were allowed to pass unchallenged through a "swash," as a narrow channel over the bar is called, which, despite the absence of beacons and buoys, our skipper shot through under the guidance of a sounding-pole, which gave, at various plunges, but few inches to spare.

The shore is as flat as a pancake—a belt of white sand, covered with drift logs and timber, and with a pine forest; not a house or human habitation of any sort to be seen for forty miles, from Fort Morgan to the entrance of the harbour of Pensacola; cheerless, miserable, full of swamps, the haunts of alligators, cranes, snakes, and pelicans; with lagoons, such as the Perdida, swelling into inland seas; deep buried in pine woods, and known only to wild creatures and to the old filibusters,—swarming with mosquitoes. As the *Diana* rushed along within a quarter of a mile of this grim shore, great fish flew off from the shallows, and once a shining gleam flashed along the waters and winged its way alongside the little craft—a monster shark, which ploughed through the sea *pari passu* for some hundred yards leeward of the craft, and distinctly visible in the wonderful phosphorescence around it, and then dashed away with a trail of light seaward, on some errand of voracity, with tremendous force and vigour.

The wretched Spaniards who came to this ill-named Florida must often have cursed their stars. How rejoiced were they when the Government of the United States relieved them from their dominion! Once during the night some lights were seen on shore, as if from a camp fire. The skipper proposed to load an old iron carronade and blaze away at them, and one of the party actually got out his revolver to fire, but I objected very strongly to these valorous proceedings, and, suggesting that they might be friends who were there, and that, friends or foes, they were sure to return our fire, succeeded in calming the martial ardour on board the *Diana*.

The fires were very probably made by some of the horsemen lately sent out by General Bragg to patrol the coast, but the skipper said that in all his life-long experience he had never seen a human creature or a light on that shore before. The wind was so favourable and the *Diana* so fast, that she would have run into the midst of the United States squadron off Fort Pickens had she pursued her course. Therefore, when she was within about ten miles of the station she hove to, and lay off and on for about two hours. Before dawn the sails were filled, and off she went once more, bowling along merrily, till with the first flush of day there came in sight Fort M'Rae, Fort Pickens, and the masts of the squadron, just rising above the blended horizon of low shore and sea.

The former, which is on the western shore of the mainland, is in the hands of the Confederate troops. The latter is just opposite to it, on the extremity of the sand-bank called Santa Rosa Island, which for forty-five miles runs in a belt parallel to the shore of Florida, at a distance varying from one and a quarter to four miles. To make smooth water of it, the schooner made several tacks shoreward. In the second of these tacks the subtle entrance of Perdida Creek is pointed out, which, after several serpentine and re-entering undulations of channel, one of which is only separated from the sea for a mile or more by a thin wall of sand-bank, widens to meet the discharge of a tolerably spacious inland lake. The Perdida is the dividing line between the States of Alabama and Florida.

The flagstaff of Fort M'Rae soon became visible, and in fainter outline beyond it that of Fort Pickens and the hulls of the fleet, in which one can make out three war steamers, a frigate, and a sloop-of-war, and then the sharp-set canvas of a schooner, the police craft of this beat, bearing down upon us. The skipper, with some uneasiness, announces the small schooner that is sailing in the wind's eye as the *Oriental*, and confesses to have already been challenged and warned off by her sentinel master. We promised him immunity for the past and safety for the future, and, easing off the main sheet, he lays the *Diana* on her course for the fleet.

Fort M'Rae, one of the obsolete school of fortresses, rounds up our left. Beyond it, on the shore, is Barrancas, a square-faced work, half a mile further up the channel, and more immediately facing Fort Pickens. A thick wood crowns the low shore which treads away to the eastward, but amid the sand the glass can trace the outlines of the batteries. Pretty-looking detached houses line the beach; some loftier edifices gather close up to the shelter of a tall chimney which is vomiting out clouds of smoke, and a few masts and spars checker the white fronts of the large buildings and sheds, which, with a big shears, indicate the position of the navy yard of Warrington, commonly called that of Pensacola, although the place of that name lies several miles higher up the creek. Fort M'Rae seems to have sunk at the foundations; the crowns of many of the casemates are cracked, and the water-face is poor-looking. Fort Pickens, on the contrary, is a solid, substantial-looking work, and reminds one something of Fort Paul at Sevastopol, as seen from the sea, except that it has only one tier of casemates, and is not so high.

As the *Oriental* approaches, the *Diana* throws her foresail aback, and the pretty little craft, with a full-sized United States ensign flying, and the muzzle of a brass howitzer peeping over her forecastle, ranges up luff, and taking an easy sweep lies alongside us. A boat is lowered from her and is soon alongside, steered by an officer; her crew are armed to the teeth with pistols and cutlasses.

"Ah, I think I have seen you before. What schooner is this?"

"The *Diana*, from Mobile."

The officer steps on deck, and announces himself as Mr. Brown, Master in the United States Navy, in charge of the boarding vessel *Oriental*. The crew secure their boat and step up after him. The skipper, looking very sulky, hands his papers to the officer. "Now, sir, make sail, and lie to under the quarter of that steamer, the guardship *Powhatan*."

Mr. Brown was exceedingly courteous when he heard who the party were. The Mobilians, however, looked as black as thunder; nor where they at all better pleased when they heard the skipper ask if he did not know there was a strict blockade of the port. The *Powhatan* is a paddle steamer of 2,200 tuns and 10 guns, and is known to our service as the flag-ship of Commodore Tatnall, in Chinese waters, when that gallant veteran gave us timely and kindly proof of the truth of his well-known expression, "*Blood is thicker than water.*" Upon her spar-deck there is a stout, healthy-looking crew, which seems quite able to attend to her armament of ten heavy 10-inch Dahlgren columbiads, and the formidable 11-inches of the same family on the forecastle.

Her commander, Captain Porter, though only a lieutenant, commanding, has seen an age of active service, both in the navy and in the merchant steam marine service, to which he was detailed for six or seven years after the discovery of California. The party were ushered into the cabin, and Captain Porter received them with perfect courtesy, heard our names and object, and then entered into general conversation, in which the Mobilians, thawed by his sailorly frankness, gradually joined, as well as they could. Over and over again I must acknowledge the exceeding politeness and civility with which your correspondent has been received by the authorities on both sides in this unhappy war.

Though but little beyond the age of forty, Captain Porter has been long enough in the navy to have imbibed some of those prejudices which by the profane are stigmatized as fogyisms. Until the day previous he had, he told me, felt disposed to condemn rifled cannon of a small calibre as "gimcracks," but had been rapidly converted to the "Armstrong faith" by the following experiment: He was making target-practice with his heavy gun at a distance of some 2,600 yards. At anything like a moderate elevation the experiment was unsatisfactory; and, while his gunners were essaying to harmonize cause and effect, the charge and the elevation, he bethought him of a little rifled brass plaything which Captain Dahlgren had sent on board a day or two before his departure. To his astonishment the ball, after careering until he thought "it would never stop going," struck the water 1,000 yards beyond the target, and established a reputation he had never believed possible for a howitzer of 6lb. calibre carrying a 12lb. bolt. He observed that the ancient walls of Fort M'Rae would not resist this new missile for half an hour.

If it comes to fighting, you will hear more of the *Powhatan* and Captain Porter. He has been repeatedly in the harbour and along the enemy's works at night in his boat, and knows their position thoroughly; and he showed me on his chart the various spots marked off whence he can sweep their works and do them immense mischief. "The *Powhatan* is old, and if she sinks I can't help it." She is all ready for action; boarding-nettings triced up, fieldpieces and howitzers prepared against night boarding, and the whole of her bows padded internally, with dead wood and sails, so as to prevent her main deck being raked as she stands stern on toward the forts. Her crew are as fine a set of men as I have seen of late days on board a man-of-war. They are healthy, well fed, regularly paid, and can be relied on to do their duty to a man.

As far as I could judge, the impression of the officers was that General Bragg would not to expose himself to the heavy chastisement which, in their belief, awaits him, if he is rash enough to open fire upon Fort Pickens. As Captain Porter is not the senior officer of the fleet, he signalled to the flag-ship, and was desired to send us on board.

One more prize has been made this morning—a little schooner with a crew of Italians and laden with vegetables. This master, a Roman of Civita Vecchia, pretends to be in great trouble, in order to squeeze a good price out of the captain for his *"tutti fruti e cosi diversi."* The officers assured me that all the statements made by the coasting skippers, when they return to port from the squadron, are lies from beginning to end.

A ten-oared barge carried the party to the United States frigate *Sabine*, on board of which Flag-Captain Adams hoists his pennant. On our way we had a fair view of the *Brooklyn*, whose armament of twenty two heavy guns is said to be the most formidable battery in the American navy. Her anti-type, the *Sabine*, an old-fashioned fifty-gun frigate, as rare an object upon modern seas as an old post-coach is upon modern roads, is reached at last. As one treads her decks, the eyes, accustomed for so many weeks to the outlandish uniforms of brave but undisciplined Southern Volunteers, feel *en pays de connaissance*, when they rest upon the solid mass of three hundred or four hundred quid-rolling, sunburnt, and resolute-looking blue-shirted tars, to whom a three years' cruise has imparted a family aspect, which makes them almost as hard to distinguish apart as so many Chinamen.

A believer in the serpent-symbol might feel almost tempted to regard the log of the *Sabine* as comprising the *Alpha* and the *Omega* of, at least, the last half century of the American Republic. Her keel was laid shortly after our last war with Brother Jonathan, and so long as the Temple of Janus remained closed—her size having rendered her unfit to participate in what is called the Mexican war—she remained in the shiphouse of the Navy Yard which had witnessed her baptism. In the year 1858 she was summoned from her retirement to officiate as flagship of the "Paraguay expedition," and after having conveyed the American commissioner to Montevideo, whence he proceeded with a flotilla of steamers and sloops-of-war up to Corrientes, and thence in the temporary flagship, the steamer *Fulton*, to Assumpcion, she brought him back to New York in May, 1859, and was then dispatched to complete her cruise as part of the Home Squadron in the Caribbean Sea and Gulf of Mexico.

During the concluding months of her cruise the political complications of North and South burst into the present rupture, and the day before our visit one of her lieutenants, a North Carolinian, had

110

left her to espouse, as nearly all the Southern officers of both army and navy have done, the cause of his native State. Captain Adams is in a still more painful predicament. During his eventful voyage, which commenced a six days' experience in the terrible Bermuda cyclone of November, 1858, he had been a stranger to the bitter sectional animosities engendered by the last election; and had recently joined the blockade of this port, where he finds a son enlisted in the ranks of the C. S. A., and learns that two others from part of the Virginia divisions of Mr. Jefferson Davis's forces. Born in Pennsylvania, he married in Louisiana, where he has a plantation and the remainder of his family, and he smiles grimly as one of our companions brings him the playful message from his daughter, who has been elected *vivandière* of a New Orleans regiment, "that she trusts he may be starved while blockading the South, and that she intends to push on to Washington and get a lock of Old Abe's hair"—a Sioux lady would have said his scalp.

The veteran sailor's sad story demands deep sympathy. I, however, cannot help enjoying at least the variety of hearing a little of the *altera pars*. It is now nearly six weeks since I entered "Dixie's Land," during which period I must confess I have had a sufficiency of the music and drums, the cavaliering and the roistering of the Southern gallants. As an impartial observer. I may say I find less bitterness and denunciation, but quite as dogged a resolution upon the Roundhead side. Some experience, or at least observation of the gunpowder argument, has taught us that attack is always a more grateful office than defence, and, if we are to judge of the sturdy resolution of the inmates of Fort Pickens by the looks of the officers and crews of the fleet, Fort Pickens will fall no easy prize, if at all.

After some conversation with Captain Adams, and the ready hospitality of his cabin, he said finally he would take on himself to permit me and the party to land at the navy yard and to visit the enemy's quarters, relying on my character as a neutral and a subject of Great Britain that no improper advantage would be taken of the permission. In giving that leave he was, he said, well aware that he was laying himself open to attack, but he acted on his own judgment and responsibility. We must, however, hoist a flag of truce, as he had been informed by General Bragg that he considered the intimation he had received from the fleet of the blockade of the port was a declaration of war, and that he would fire on any vessel from the fleet which approached his command. I bade goodbye to Captain Adams with sincere regret, and if—but I may not utter the wish here.

Our barge was waiting to take us to the *Oriental*, in which we sailed pleasantly away down to the *Powhatan* to inform Captain Porter I had received permission to go on shore. Another officer was in his cabin when I entered—Captain Poore, of the *Brooklyn*—and he seemed a little surprised when he heard that Captain Adams had given leave to all to go on shore. "What, all these editors of Southern newspapers who are with you, Sir?" I assured him they were nothing of the kind, and after a few kind words I made my *adieu*, and went on board the *Diana* with my companions.

Hoisting one of our two table-cloths to the masthead as a flag of truce, we dropped slowly with the tide through the channel that runs parallel to one face of Fort Pickens. The wind favoured us but little, and the falling breeze enabled all on board to inspect deliberately the seemingly artistic preparations for the threatened attack which frowns and bristles from three miles of forts and batteries arrayed around the slight indenture opposite. Heavy sand-bag traverses protect the corners of the parapet, and seem solid enough to defy the heavy batteries ensconced in earthworks around the lighthouse, which to an outside glance seems the most formidable point of an attack, directed as it is against the weaker flank of the fort at its most vulnerable angle.

A few soldiers and officers upon the rampart appeared to be inhaling the freshening breeze which arose to waft the schooner across the channel, and enable her to coast the mainshore, so that all could take note of the necklace of bastions, earthworks, and columbiads with which General Bragg hopes to throttle his adversary. We passed by Barrancas, the nearest point of attack (a mile and a quarter), the commander-in-chief's headquarters, the barracks, and the hospital successively, and as the vessel approached the landing-pier of the Navy Yard one could hear the bustle of the military and the hammers of the artificers, and descry the crimson and blue trappings of *Zouaves*, recalling Crimean reminiscences. A train of heavy tumbrils, drawn by three or four pairs of mules, was the first indication of a transport system in the army of the Confederate States, and the high-bred chargers mounted by the escorts of these ammunition wagons corroborated the accounts of the wealth and breeding of its volunteer cavalry.

The *Diana* now skirted the navy yard, the neat dwellings of which, and the profusion of orange and fig groves in which they are embosomed, have an aspect of tropical shade and repose, much at variance with the stern preparations before us. Our skipper let go his anchor at a respectful distance from the quay, evincing a regard for martial law that contrasted strangely with the impatience of control elsewhere manifested throughout this land, and almost inspiring the belief that no other rule can ever restore the lost bump of veneration to American craniology.

While the master of the *Diana* was skulling his leaky punt ashore to convey my letters of introduction to the commander-in-chief, I had leisure to survey the long, narrow, low sand belt of the island opposite, which loses itself in the distance, and disappears in the ocean forty-seven miles from Fort Pickens. It is so nearly level with the sea that I could make out the main-yards of the *Sabine* and the *Brooklyn*, anchored outside the island within range of the Navy Yard, which is destined to receive immediate attention whenever the attack shall begin. Pursuing my reflections upon the *morale* of the upper and nether millstones between which the *Diana* is moored, I am sadly puzzled by the anomalous ethics or metaphysics of this singular war, the preparations for which vary so essentially—it were sin to say ludicrously—from all ancient and modern belligerent usages. Here we have an important fortress, threatened with siege for the last sixty days, suffering the assailants of the flag it defends to amass battery upon battery, and string the whole coast of low hills opposite with every variety of apparatus for its own devastation, without throwing a timely shell to prevent their establishment.

War has been virtually declared, since letters of marque and a corresponding blockade admit of no other interpretation, and yet but last week two Mobile steamers, laden with £50,000 worth of provisions for the beleaguering camp, were stopped by the blockading fleet, and, though not permitted to enter this harbour, were allowed to return to Mobile untouched, the commander thinking it quite punishment enough for the Rebels to thus compel them to return to Mobile, and carry up the Alabama River to Montgomery this mass of eatables, which would have to be dispatched thence by rail to this place! Such practical jokes lend a tinge of innocence to the premonitories of this strife which will hardly survive the first bloodshed.

The skipper returned from shore with an orderly, who brought the needful permission to haul the *Diana* alongside the wharf, where I landed, and was conducted by an *aide* of the quartermaster-general through the shady streets of this graceful little village, which covers an inclosure of three hundred acres. and, with the adjoining forts, cost the United States over £6,000,000 sterling, which may have something to do with the President's determination to hold a property under so heavy an hypothecation. Irish landlords, with encumbered estates, have no such simple mode of obtaining an acquittal.

The Navy Yard is, properly speaking, a settlement of exceedingly neat detached houses, with gardens in front, porticoes, pillars, verandahs, and Venetian blinds to aid the dense trees in keeping off the scorching rays of the sun, which is intensely powerful in the summer, and is now blazing so fiercely as to force one to admit the assertion that the average temperature is as high as that of Calcutta to be very probable. The grass-plots under these tree are covered with neat piles of cannon balls, mostly of small size; two obsolete mortars—one dated 1776—are placed in the main Avenue.

Tents are pitched under the trees, and the houses are all occupied by officers, who are chatting, smoking, and drinking at the open windows. A number of men in semi-military dresses of various sorts and side arms are lounging about the quays and the lawns before the houses. Into one of these I am escorted, and find myself at a very pleasant mess, of whom the greater number are officers of the *Zouave* Corps, from New Orleans—one, a Dane, has served at Idstedt, Kiel, Frederichstadt; another foreigner has seen service in South America; another has fought in half the insurrectionary wars in Europe. The wine is abundant, the fare good, the laughter and talk loud. Mr. Davis has been down all day from Montgomery, accompanied by Mrs. Davis, Mr. Maloney, and Mr. Wigfall, and they all think his presence means immediate action.

The only ship here is the shell of the old *Fulton*, which is on the stocks, but the works of the Navy Yard are useful in casting shot, shell, and preparing munitions of war. An *aide-de-camp* from General Bragg entered as we were sitting at table, and invited me to attend him to the general's quarters. The road, as I found, was very long and very disagreeable, owing to the depth of the sand, into which the foot sank at every step up to the ankle. Passing the front of an extended row of the clean, airy, pretty villas inside the Navy Yard, we passed the gate on exhibiting our passes, and proceeded by the sea beach, one side of which is lined with houses, a few yards from the surf. These houses are all occupied by troops, or are used as bar-rooms or magazines. At intervals a few guns have been placed along the beach, covered by sand-bags, parapets, and traverses.

As we toiled along in the sand, the *aide* hailed a cart, pressed it into the service, and we continued our journey less painfully. Suddenly a tall, straight-backed man in a blue frock-coat, with a star on the epaulette strap, a smart *kepi*, and trowsers with gold stripe, and large brass spurs, rode past on a high-stepping, powerful charger, followed by an orderly. "There is General Bragg," said his *aide*. The general turned round, reined up, and I was presented as I sat in my state chariot.

The commander of the Confederated States Army at Pensacola is about forty-two years of age, of a spare and powerful frame; his face is dark, and marked with deep lines, his mouth large, and squarely set in determined jaws, and his eyes, sagacious, penetrating, and not by any means unkindly, look out at you from beetle brows which run straight across and spring into a thick tuft of black hair, which is thickest over the nose, where naturally it usually leaves an intervening space. His hair is dark, and he wears such regulation whiskers as were the delight of our generals a few years ago. His manner is quick and frank, and his smile is very pleasing and agreeable. The general would not hear of my continuing my journey to his quarters in a cart, and his orderly brought up an ambulance, drawn by a smart pair of mules, in which I completed it satisfactorily.

The end of the journey through the sandy plain was at hand, for in an inclosure of a high wall there stood a well-shaded mansion, amid trees of live oak and sycamore, with sentries at the gate and horses held by orderlies under the portico. General Bragg received me at the top of the steps which lead to the verandah, and, after a few earnest and complimentary words, conducted me to his office, where he spoke of the contest in which he was to play so important a part in terms of unaffected earnestness. Why else had he left his estates? After the Mexican war he had retired from the United States Artillery; but when his State was menaced he was obliged to defend her. He was satisfied the North meant nothing but subjugation. All he wanted was peace. Slavery was an institution for which he was not responsible; but his property was guaranteed to him by law, and it consisted of slaves. Why did the enemy take off slaves from Tortugas to work for them at Pickens? Because whites could not do their work.

It was quite impossible to deny his earnestness, sincerity, and zeal as he spoke, and one could only wonder at the difference made by the "stand point" from which the question is reviewed. General Bragg finally, before we supped, took down his plans and showed me the position of every gun in his works and all his batteries. He showed the greatest clearness of unreserved openness in his communications, and was anxious to point out that he had much greater difficulties to contend with than General Beauregard had at Charleston. The inside of

Pickens is well known to him, as he was stationed there the very first tour of duty which he had after he left West Point. It was late at night when I returned on one of the general's horses toward the navy yard.

The orderly who accompanied me was, he said, a Mississippi planter, but he had left his wife and family to the care of the negroes, had turned up all his cotton land and replanted it with corn, and had come off to the wars. Once only were we challenged, and I was only required to show my pass as I was getting on board the schooner. Before I left General Bragg he was good enough to say he would send down one of his *aides-de-cam*p and horses early in the morning, to give me a look at the works.

Letter 12

New Orleans, May 25, 1861.

There are doubts arising in my mind respecting the number of armed men actually in the field in the South, and the amount of arms in the possession of the Federal forces. The constant advertisements and appeals for "a few more men to complete" such and such companies furnish some sort of evidence that men are still wanting. But a painful and startling insight into the manner in which "Volunteers" have been sometimes obtained has been afforded to me at New Orleans. In no country in the world have outrages on British subjects been so frequent and so wanton as in the States of America. They have been frequent, perhaps, because they have generally been attended with impunity. Englishmen, however, will be still a little surprised to hear that within a few days British subjects living in New Orleans have been seized, knocked down, carried off from their labour at the wharf and the workshop, and forced by violence to serve in the "Volunteer" ranks!

These cases are not isolated. They are not in twos and threes, but in tens and twenties; they have not occurred stealthily or in by-ways, they have taken place in open day, and in the streets of New Orleans. These men have been dragged along like felons, protesting in vain that they were British subjects. Fortunately, their friends bethought them that there was still a British Consul in the city, who would protect his countrymen—English, Irish, or Scotch. Mr. Mure, when he heard of the reports and of the evidence, made energetic representations to the authorities, who, after some evasion, gave orders that the impressed "Volunteers" should be discharged, and the "Tiger Rifles" and other companies were deprived of the services of thirty-five British subjects whom they had taken from their usual avocations. The mayor promises it shall not occur again.

It is high time that such acts should be put a stop to, and that the mob of New Orleans should be taught to pay some regard to the usages of civilized nations. There are some strange laws here and elsewhere in reference to compulsory service on the part of foreigners which it would be well to inquire into, and Lord John Russell may be able to deal with them at a favourable opportunity. As to any liberty of opinion or real freedom here, the boldest Southerner would not dare to say a shadow of either exists. It may be as bad in the North, for all I know; but it must be remembered that in all my communications I speak of things as they appear to me to be in the place where I am at the time.

The most cruel and atrocious acts are perpetrated by the rabble who style themselves citizens. The national failing of curiosity and prying into other people's affairs is now rampant, and assumes the name and airs of patriotic vigilance. Every stranger is watched, every word is noted, espionage commands every keyhole and every letter-box; love of country takes to eavesdropping, and freedom shaves men's heads, and packs men up in boxes for the utterance of "Abolition sentiments." In this city there is a terrible substratum of crime and vice, violence, misery, and murder, over which the wheels of Cotton King's chariot rumble gratingly, and on which rest in dangerous security the feet of his throne. There are numbers of negroes who are sent out on the streets every day with orders not to return with less than seventy-five cents—anything more they can keep.

But if they do not gain that—about three shillings and six pence a day—they are liable to punishment; they may be put into jail on charges of laziness, and may be flogged *ad libitum*, and are sure to be half starved. Can anything, then, be more suggestive than this paragraph, which appeared in last night's papers. "*Only* three coroners inquests were held yesterday on persons found drowned in the river, names unknown!" The italics are mine. Over and over again has the boast been repeated to me that on the plantations lock and key are unknown or unused in the planters' houses. But in the cities they are much used, though scarcely trusted. It appears, indeed, that unless a slave has made up his or her mind to incur the dreadful penalties of flight, there would be no inducement to commit theft, for money or jewels would be useless; search would be easy, detection nearly certain. That all the slaves are not indifferent to the issues before them, is certain.

At one house of a planter, the other day, one of them asked my friend, "Will we be made to work, massa, when ole English come?"

An old domestic in the house of a gentleman in this city said, "There are few whites in this place who ought not to be killed for their cruelty to us."

Another said, "Oh, just wait till they attack Pickens!"

These little hints are significant enough coupled with the notices of runaways, and the lodgements in the police jails, to show that all is not quiet below the surface. The holders, however, are firm, and there have been many paragraphs stating that slaves have contributed to the various funds for State defence, and that they generally show the very best spirit.

By the proclamation of Governor Magoffin, a copy of which I inclose, you will see that the Governor of the Commonwealth of Kentucky and commander-in-chief of all her military forces on land or water, warns all States, separated or united, especially the United States and the Confederate States, that he will fight their troops if they attempt to enter his Commonwealth. Thus Kentucky sets up for herself, while Virginia is on the eve of destruction, and an actual invasion has taken place of her soil. It is exceedingly difficult of comprehension that, with the numerous troops, artillery, and batteries, which the Confederate journals asserted to be in readiness to repel attack, an invasion which took place in face of the enemy, and was effected over a broad river, with shores readily defensible, should have been unresisted.

Here it is said there is a mighty plan, in pursuance of which the United States troops are to be allowed to make their way into Virginia, that they may at some convenient place be eaten up by their enemies; and if we hear that the Confederates at Harper's Ferry retain their position one may believe some such plan really exists, although it is rather doubtful strategy to permit the United States forces to gain possession of the right bank of the Potomac. Should the position at Harper's Ferry be really occupied with a design of using it as a *point d'appui* for movements against the North, and any large number of troops be withdrawn from Annapolis, Washington, and Baltimore, so as to leave those places comparatively undefended, an irruption in force of the Confederates on the right flank and in rear of General Scott's army, might cause most serious inconvenience and endanger his communications, if not the possession of the places indicated.

Looking at the map, it is easy to comprehend that a march southwards from Alexandria could be combined with an offensive movement by the forces said to be concentrated in and around Fortress Monroe, so as to place Richmond itself in danger, and, if any such measure is contemplated, a battle must be fought in that vicinity, or the *prestige* of the South will receive very great damage. It is impossible for anyone to understand the movements of the troops on both sides. These companies are scattered broadcast over the enormous expanse of the States, and, where concentrated in any considerable numbers, seem to have had their position determined rather by local circumstances than by considerations connected with the general plan of a large campaign.

In a few days the object of the present movement will be better understood, and it is probable that your correspondent at New York will send, by the same mail which carries this, exceedingly important information, to which I, in my present position, can have no access. The influence of the blockade will be severely felt, combined with the strict interruption of all intercourse by the Mississippi. Although the South boasts of its resources and of its amazing richness and abundance of produce, the constant advices in the journals to increase the breadth of land under corn, and to neglect the cotton crop in consideration of the paramount importance of the cause, indicate an apprehension of a scarcity of food if the struggle be prolonged.

Under any circumstances, the patriotic ladies and gentlemen who are so anxious for the war must make up their minds to suffer a little in the flesh. All they can depend on is a supply of home luxuries; Indian corn and wheat, the flesh of pigs, eked out with a small supply of beef and mutton, will constitute the staple of their food. Butter there will be none, and wine will speedily rise to an enormous price. Nor will coffee and tea be had, except at a rate which will place them out of the reach of the mass of the community. These are the smallest sacrifices of war. The blockade is not yet enforced here, and the privateers of the port are extremely active, and have captured vessels with more energy than wisdom.

The day before yesterday, ships belonging to the United States in the river were seized by the Confederation authorities, on the ground that war had broken out, and that the time of grace accorded to the enemy's traders had expired. Great was the rush to the Consul's office to transfer the menaced property from ownership under the Stars and Stripes to British hands; but Mr. Mure refused to recognize any transactions of the kind, unless sales *bona fide* had been effected before the action of the Confederate marshals.

At Charleston the blockade has been raised, owing, apparently, to some want of information or of means on the part of the United States Government, and considerable inconvenience may be experienced by them in consequence. On the 11th, the United States steam frigate *Niagara* appeared outside and warned off several British ships, and on the 13th she was visited by Mr. Bunch, our consul, who was positively assured by the officers on board that eight or ten vessels would be down to join in enforcing the blockade.

On the 15th, however, the *Niagara* departed, leaving the port open, and several vessels have since run in and obtained fabulous freights, suggesting to the minds of the owners of the vessels which were warned off the propriety of making enormous demands for compensation. The Southerners generally believe not only that their Confederacy will be acknowledged, but that the blockade will be disregarded by England. Their affection for her is proportionably prodigious, and reminds one of the intensity of the gratitude which consists in lively expectations of favours to come.

New Orleans, May 21, 1861.

Yesterday morning early I left Mobile in the steamer *Florida*, which arrived in the Lake of Pontchartrain late at night, or early this morning. The voyage, if it can be called so, would have offered, in less exciting times, much that was interesting—certainly, to a stranger, a good deal that was novel—for our course lay inside a chain, almost uninterrupted, of reefs, covered with sand and pine trees, exceedingly narrow, so that the surf and waves of the ocean beyond could be seen rolling in foam through the foliage of the forest, or on the white beach, while the sea lake on which our steamer was speeding lay in a broad, smooth sheet, just crisped by the breeze, between the outward barrier and the wooded shores of the mainland. Innumerable creeks, or "bayous," as they are called, pierce the gloom of these endless pines. Now and then a sail could be made out, stealing through the mazes of the marshy waters.

If the mariner knows his course, he may find deep water in most of the channels from the outer sea into these inner waters, on which the people of the South will greatly depend for any coasting trade, and supplies coastwise, they may require, as well as for the safe retreat of their privateers. A few miles from Mobile, the steamer turning out of the bay, entered upon the series of these lakes through a narrow channel called Grant's Pass, which some enterprising person, not improbably of Scottish extraction, constructed for his own behoof by an ingenious watercut, and for the use of which, and of a little iron light-house that he has built close at hand, on the model of a pepper-castor, he charges toll on passing vessels. This island is scarcely three feet above the water; it is not over twenty yards broad and one hundred and fifty yards long. A number of men were, however, busily engaged in throwing up the sand, and arms gleamed amid some tents pitched around the solitary wooden shed in the centre.

A schooner lay at the wharf, laden with two guns and sand-bags, and as we passed through the narrow channel several men in military uniform, who were on board, took their places in a boat which pushed off for them, and were conveyed to their tiny station, of which one shell would make a dust-heap. The Mobilians are fortifying themselves as best they can, and seem, not unadvisedly, jealous of gunboats and small war steamers. On more than one outlying sand-bank toward New Orleans are they to be seen at work on other batteries, and they are busied in repairing, as well as they can, old Spanish and new United States works which had been abandoned, or which were never completed.

The news has just been reported, indeed, that the batteries they were preparing on Ship Island have been destroyed and burnt by a vessel of war of the United States. For the whole day we saw only a few coasting craft and the return steamers from New Orleans; but in the evening a large schooner, which sailed like a witch and was crammed with men, challenged my attention, and on looking at her through the glass I could make out reasons enough for desiring to avoid her if one was a quiet, short-handed, well-filled old merchant-man. There could be no mistake about certain black objects on the deck. She lay as low as a yacht, and there were some fifty or sixty men in the waist and forecastle.

On approaching New Orleans, there are some settlements rather than cities, although they are called by the latter title, visible on the right hand, embowered in woods and stretching along the beach. Such are the "Mississippi City," Pass Cagoula, and Pass Christian, &c.—all resorts of the inhabitants of New Orleans during the summer heats and the epidemics which play such havoc with life from time to time. Seen from sea, these huge hamlets look very picturesque. The detached villas, of every variety of architecture, are painted brightly and stand in gardens in the midst of magnolias and rhododendrons. Very long and slender piers lead far into the sea before the very door, and at the extremity of each there is a bathing box for the inmates.

The general effect of one of these settlements, with its light domes and spires, long lines of whitewashed railings, and houses of every hue set in the dark green of the pines, is very pretty. The steamer touched at two of them. There was a motley group of coloured people on the jetty, a few whites, of whom the males were nearly all in uniform; a few bales of goods were landed or put on board, and that was all one could see of the life of that place. Our passengers never ceased talking politics all day, except when they were eating or drinking, for I regret to say they can continue to chew and to spit while they are engaged in political discussion. Some were rude provincials in uniform. One was an acquaintance from the far East, who had been a lieutenant on board of the *Minnesota*, and had resigned his commission in order to take service under the Confederate flag.

The fiercest among them all was a thin little lady, who uttered certain energetic aspirations for the possession of portions of Mr. Lincoln's person, and who was kind enough to express intense satisfaction at the intelligence that there was smallpox among the garrison at Monroe. In the evening a little difficulty occurred among some of the military gentlemen, during which one of the logicians drew a revolver, and presented it at the head of the gentleman who was opposed to his peculiar views, but I am happy to say that an arrangement, to which I was an unwilling "party," for the row took place within a yard of me, was entered into for a fight to come off on shore in two days after they landed, which led to the postponement of immediate murder.

The entrance to Pontchartrain Lake is infamous for the abundance of its mosquitoes, and it was with no small satisfaction that we experienced a small tornado, a thunderstorm, and a breeze of wind which saved us from their fury. It is a dismal canal through a swamp. At daylight the vessel lay alongside a wharf surrounded by small boats and bathing stations. A railway-shed receives us on shore, and a train is soon ready to start for the city which is six miles distant. For a few hundred yards the line passes between wooden houses, used as restaurants, or "*restaurats*," as they are called hereaway, kept by people with French names and using the French tongue; then the rail plunges through a swamp, dense as an Indian jungle, and with the overflowings of the Mississippi creeping in feeble, shallow currents over the black mud.

Presently the spires of churches are seen rising above the underwood and rushes. Then we come out on a wide marshy plain, in which flocks of cattle up to the belly in mud are floundering to get at the rich herbage on the unbroken surface. Next comes a wide-spread suburb of exceedingly broad lanes, lined with small one-storied houses. The inhabitants are pale, lean, and sickly, and there is about the men a certain look, almost peculiar to the fishy-fleshy populations of Levantine towns, which I cannot describe, but which exists all along the Mediterranean seaboard, and crops out here again. The drive through badly-paved streets enables us to see that there is an air of French civilization about New Orleans.

The streets are wisely adapted to the situation; they are not so wide as to permit the sun to have it all his own way from rising to setting. The shops are "*magasins*;" *cafés* abound. The coloured population looks well dressed, and is going to mass or market in the early morning. The pavements are crowded with men in uniform, in which the taste of France is generally followed. The carriage stops at last, and rest comes gratefully after the stormy night, the mosquitoes, "the noise of the captains" (at the bar), and the shouting.

May 22.—The prevalence of the war spirit here is in everything somewhat exaggerated by the fervour of Gallic origin, and the violence of popular opinion and the tyranny of the mass are as potent as in any place in the South. The great house of Brown Brothers, of Liverpool and New York, has closed its business here in consequence of the intimidation of the mob, or, as the phrase is, of the "citizens," who were "excited" by seeing that the firm had subscribed to the New York fund, on its sudden resurrection after Fort Sumter had fallen. Some other houses are about to pursue the same course; all large business transactions are over for the season, and the migratory population which comes here to trade has taken wing much earlier than usual. But the streets are full of "*Turcos*" and "*Zouaves*" and "*Chasseurs*;" the tailors are busy night and day on uniforms; the walls are covered with placards for recruits, the seamstresses are sewing flags, the ladies are carding lint and stitching cartridge bags. The newspapers are crowded with advertisements relating to the formation of new companies of volunteers and the election of officers.

There are Pickwick Rifles, Lafayette, Beauregard, Irish, German, Scotch, Italian, Spanish, Crescent, McMahon—innumerable—Rifle Volunteers of all names and nationalities, and the Meagher Rifles, indignant with "that valiant son of Mars" because he has drawn his sword for the North, have re-baptized themselves, and are going to seek glory under a more auspicious nomenclature. About New Orleans I shall have more to say when I see more of it.

At present it looks very like an outlying suburb of Chalons when the Grand Camp is at its highest military development, although the thermometer is rising gradually, and obliges one to know occasionally that it can be 95° in the shade already. In the course of my journeying southward I have failed to find much evidence that there is any apprehension on the part of the planters of a servile insurrection, or that the slaves are taking much interest in the coming contest, or know what it is about. But I have my suspicions that all is not right; paragraphs meet the eye, and odd sentences strike the ear, and little facts here and there come to the knowledge which arouse curiosity and doubt. There is one stereotyped sentence which I am tired of: "Our negroes, Sir, are the happiest, the most contented, and the best off of any people in the world."

The violence and reiterancy of this formula cause one to inquire whether anything which demands such insistance is really in the condition predicated, and, for myself, I always say, "It may be so, but as yet I do not see the proof of it. The negroes do not look to be what you say they are." For the present that is enough as to one's own opinions. Externally the paragraphs which attract attention, and the acts of the authorities, are inconsistent with the notion that the negroes are all very good, very happy, or at all contented, not to speak of their being in the superlative condition of enjoyment; and, as I only see them, as yet, in the most superficial way, and under the most favourable circumstances, it may be that when the cotton-picking season is at its height, and it lasts for several months, when the labour is continuous from sunrise to sunset, there is less reason to accept the assertions as so largely and generally true of the vast majority of the slaves.

"There is an excellent gentleman over there," said a friend to me, "who gives his overseers a premium of $10 on the birth of every child on his plantation."

"Why so?"

"Oh, in order that the overseers may not work the women in the family-way overmuch."

There is little use in this part of the world in making use of inferences. But where overseers do not get the premium, it may be supposed they do work the pregnant women too much. Here are two paragraphs which do not look very well as they stand:

Those negroes who were taken with a sudden leaving on Sunday night last will save the country the expenses of their burial if they keep dark from these parts. They and other of the 'breden' will not be permitted to express themselves quite so freely in regard to their *braggadocio* designs upon virtue in the absence of volunteers.—Wilmington (Clintock County, Ohio,) *Watchman* (Republican).

Served him right.—One day last week some coloured individual, living near South Plymouth, made a threat that, in case a civil war should occur, 'he would be one to ravish the wife of every Democrat, and to help murder their offspring and wash his hands in their blood.' For this diabolical assertion he was hauled up before a committee of white citizens, who adjudged him forty stripes on his naked back. He was accordingly stripped, and the lashes were laid on with such good will, that the blood flowed at the end of the castigation.—Washington (Fayette County, Ohio,) *Register* Neutral).

It is reported that the patrols are strengthened, and I could not help hearing a charming young lady say to another, the other evening, that "she would not be afraid to go back to the plantation, though Mrs. Brown Jones said she was afraid her negroes were after mischief."

There is a great scarcity of powder, which is one of the reasons, perhaps, why it has not yet been expended as largely as might be expected from the tone and temper on both sides. There is no sulphur in the States—nitre and charcoal abound. The sea is open to the North. There is no great overplus of money on either side. In Missouri, the interest on the State debt due in July will be used to procure arms for the State volunteers to carry on the war. The South is preparing for the struggle by sowing a most unusual quantity of grain, and in many fields corn and maize have been planted instead of cotton. "Stay laws," by which all inconveniences arising from the usual, dull, old-fashioned relations between debtor and creditor are avoided (at least by the debtor), have been adopted in most of the Seceding States. How is it that the State Legislatures seem to be in the hands of the debtors, and not of the creditors?

There are some who cling to the idea that there will be no war, after all; but no one believes that the South will ever go back of its own free will, and the only reason that can be given for those who hope rather than think in that way, is to be found in the faith that the North will accept some mediation, and will let the South go in peace.

But could there, can there be peace? The frontier question, the adjustment of various claims, the demands for indemnity, or for privileges or exemptions, in the present state of feeling, can have but one result. The task of mediation is sure to be as thankless as abortive.

Assuredly the proffered service of England would, on one side at least, be received with something like insult. Nothing but adversity can teach these people its own most useful lessons. Material prosperity has puffed up the citizens to an unwholesome state. The toils and sacrifices of the Old World have been taken by them as their birthright, and they have accepted the fruits of all that the science, genius, suffering, and trials of mankind in time past have wrought out, perfected, and won as their own peculiar inheritance, while they have ignorantly rejected the advice and scorned the lessons with which these were accompanied.

May 23.—The Congress at Montgomery, having sat with closed doors almost since it met, has now adjourned till July the 20th, when it will reassemble at Richmond, in Virginia, which is thus designated, for the time, capital of the Confederate States of America. Richmond, the principal city of the old Dominion, is about one hundred miles in a straight line south by west of Washington. The rival capitals will thus be in very close proximity by rail and by steam, by land and by water. The movement is significant. It will tend to hasten a collision between the forces which are collected on the opposite sides of the Potomac. Hitherto, Mr. Jefferson Davis has not evinced all the sagacity and energy, in a military sense, which he is said to possess. It was bad strategy to menace Washington before he could act. His Secretary of War, Mr. Walker, many weeks ago, in a public speech, announced the intention of marching upon the capital.

If it was meant to do so, the blow should have been struck silently. If it was not intended to seize upon Washington, the threat had a very disastrous effect on the South, as it excited the North to immediate action, and caused General Scott to concentrate his troops on points which present many advantages in the face of any operations which may be considered necessary along the lines either of defence or attack. The movement against the Norfolk Navy Yard strengthened Fortress Monroe, and the Potomac and Chesapeake were secured to the United States. The fortified ports held by the Virginians and the Confederate States troops, are not of much value as long as the streams are commanded by the enemy's steamers; and General Scott has shown that he has not outlived either his reputation or his vigour by the steps, at once wise and rapid, he has taken to curb the malcontents in Maryland, and to open his communications through the city of Baltimore. Although immense levies of men may be got together on both sides for purposes of local defence or for State operations, it seems to me that it will be very difficult to move these masses in regular armies. The men are not disposed for regular, lengthened service, and there is an utter want of field trains, equipment, and commissariat, which cannot be made good in a day, a week, or a month.

The bill passed by the Montgomery Congress, entitled "An act to raise an additional military force to serve during the war," is, in fact, a measure to put into the hands of the government the control of irregular bodies of men, and to bind them to regular military service. With all their zeal, the people of the South will not enlist. They detest the recruiting sergeant, and Mr. Davis knows enough of war to feel hesitation in trusting himself in the field to volunteers. The bill authorizes Mr. Davis to accept volunteers, who may offer their services, without regard to the place of enlistment, "to serve during the war, unless sooner discharged." They may be accepted in companies, but Mr. Davis is to organize them into squadrons, battalions, or regiments, and the appointment of field and staff officers is reserved especially to him. The company officers are to be elected by the men of the company, but here again Mr. Davis reserves to himself the right of veto, and will only commission those officers whose election he approves.

The absence of cavalry and the deficiency of artillery may prevent either side obtaining any decisive results in one engagement, but no doubt there will be great loss whenever these large masses of men are fairly opposed to each other in the field. Of the character of the Northern regiments I can say nothing more from actual observation, nor have I yet seen in any place such a considerable number of the troops of the Confederate States moving together, as would justify me in expressing any opinion with regard to their capacity for organized movements such as regular troops in Europe are expected to perform.

An intelligent and trustworthy observer, taking one of the New York State Militia regiments as a fair specimen of the battalions which will fight for the United States, gives an account of them which leads me to the conclusion that such regiments are much superior when furnished by the country districts to those raised in the towns and cities. It appears in this case, at least, that the members of the regular militia companies in general send substitutes to the ranks. Ten of these companies form the regiment, and in nearly every instance they have been doubled in strength by volunteers. Their drill is exceedingly incomplete, and in forming the companies there is a tendency for the different nationalities to keep themselves together. In the regiment in question, the rank and file often consists of quarrymen, mechanics, and canal boatmen, mountaineers from the Catskill, bark peelers and timber cutters—ungainly, square-built, powerful fellows, with a Dutch tenacity of purpose crossed with an English indifference to danger.

There is no drunkenness and no desertion among them. The officers are almost as ignorant of military training as their men. The colonel, for instance, is the son of a rich man in his district, well educated, and a man of travel. Another officer is a shipmaster. A third is an artist; others are merchants and lawyers, and they are all busy studying *Hardee's Tactics*, the best book for infantry drill in the United States. The men have come out to fight for what they consider the cause of "theo cuntry," and are said to have no particular hatred of the South or of its inhabitants, though they think they are "a darned deal too high and mighty, and require to be wiped down considerably." They have no notion as to the length of time for which their services will be required, and I am assured that not one of them has asked what his pay is to be.

Reverting to Montgomery, one may say without offence, that its claims to be the capital of a Republic which asserts that it is the richest, and believes that it will be the strongest in the world, are not by any means evident to a stranger. Its central position, which has reference rather to a map than to the hard face of matter, procured for it a distinction to which it had no other claim. The accommodations which suited the modest wants of a State Legislature vanished or were transmuted into barbarous inconveniences by the pressure of a central government, with its offices, its departments, and the vast crowd of applicants which flocked thither to pick up such crumbs of comfort as could be spared from the executive table.

Never shall I forget the dismay of myself, and of the friends who were travelling with me, on our arrival at the Exchange Hotel, under circumstances with some of which you are already acquainted. With us were men of high position, members of Congress, senators, ex-governors, and General Beauregard himself. But to no one was greater accommodation extended than could be furnished by a room held, under a sort of ryot-warree tenure, in common with a community of strangers. My room was shown to me. It contained four large fourpost beds, a rickety table, and some chairs of infirm purpose and fundamental unsoundness. The floor was carpetless, covered with litter of paper and ends of cigars, and stained with tobacco juice. The broken glass of the window afforded no ungrateful means of ventilation.

One gentleman sat in his shirt sleeves at the table reading the account of the marshalling of the Highlanders at Edinburgh in the Abbotsford edition of Sir Walter Scott; another, who had been wearied, apparently, by writing numerous applications to the government for some military post, of which rough copies lay scattered around, came in, after refreshing himself at the bar, and occupied one of the beds, which, by-the-bye, were ominously provided with two pillows apiece. Supper there was none for us in the house, but a search in an outlying street, enabled us to discover a restaurant, where roasted squirrels and baked opossums figured as luxuries in the bill of fare. On our return we found that due preparation had been made in the apartment by the addition of three mattresses on the floor. The beds were occupied by unknown statesmen and warriors, and we all slumbered and snored in friendly concert till morning.

Gentlemen in the South complain that strangers judge of them by their hotels, but it is a very natural standard for strangers to adopt, and in respect to Montgomery it is almost the only one that a gentleman can conveniently use; for, if the inhabitants of this city and its vicinity are not maligned, there is an absence of the hospitable spirit which the South lays claim to as one of its animating principles, and a little bird whispered to me that from Mr. Jefferson Davis down to the least distinguished member of his government, there was reason to observe that the usual attentions and civilities offered by residents to illustrious stragglers had been "conspicuous for their absence." The fact is, that the small planters, who constitute the majority of the land-owners, are not in a position to act the *Amphitrion*, and that the inhabitants of the district can scarcely aspire to be considered what we would call gentry in England, but are a frugal, simple, hog and hominy-living people, fond of hard work and, occasionally, of hard drinking.

New Orleans, May 24, 1861.

It is impossible to resist the conviction that the Southern Confederacy can only be conquered by means as irresistible as those by which Poland was subjugated. The South will fall, if at all, as a nation prostrate at the feet of a victorious enemy. There is no doubt of the unanimity of the people. If words mean anything, they are animated by only one sentiment, and they will resist the North as long as they can command a man or a dollar. There is nothing of a sectional character in this disposition of the South. In every State there is only one voice audible. Hereafter, indeed, State jealousies may work their own way. Whatever may be the result, unless the men are the merest braggarts—and they do not look like :-—they will fight to the last before they give in, and their confidence in their resources is only equalled by their determination to test them to the utmost.

There is a noisy vociferation about their declarations of implicit trust and, reliance on their slaves, which makes one think they do "protest too much," and it remains to be seen whether the slaves really will remain faithful to their masters should the Abolition army ever come among them as an armed propaganda. One thing is obvious here. A large number of men who might be usefully employed in the ranks are idling about the streets. The military enthusiasm is in proportion to the property interest of the various classes of the people; and the very boast that so many rich men are serving in the ranks is a significant proof either of the want of substratum, or of the absence of great devotion to the cause of any such layer of white people as may underlie the great slaveholding, mercantile, and planting oligarchy.

The whole State of Louisiana contains about 50,000 men liable to serve when called on. Of that number only 15,000 are enrolled and under arms in any shape whatever; and if one is to judge of the state of affairs by the advertisements which appear from the adjutant-general's office, there was some difficulty in procuring the 3,000 men—merely 3,000 volunteers—"to serve during the war," who are required by the Confederate Government. There is plenty of "prave lords," and if fierce writing and talking could do work, the armies on both sides would have been killed and eaten long ago. It is found out that "the lives of the citizens" at Pensacola are too valuable to be destroyed in attacking Pickens. A storm that shall drive away the ships, a plague, yellow fever, mosquitoes, rattlesnakes, smallpox—any of these agencies is looked to with confidence to do the work of shot, shell, and bayonet.

Our American "brethren in arms" have yet to learn that great law in American cookery, that "if they want to make omelets they must break eggs." The "moral suasion" of the lasso, of head-shaving, ducking, kicking, and such processes, are, I suspect, used not unfrequently to stimulate volunteers; and the extent to which the acts of the recruiting officer are somewhat aided by the arm of the law, and the force of the policeman and the magistrate, may be seen from paragraphs in the morning papers now and then, to the effect that certain gentlemen of Milesian extraction, who might have been engaged in pugilistic pursuits, were discharged from custody, unpunished, on condition that they enlisted for the war. With the peculiar views entertained of freedom of opinion and action by large classes of people on this continent, such a mode of obtaining volunteers is very natural, but resort to it evinces a want of zeal on the part of some of the 50,000 who are on the rolls; and, from all I can hear—and I have asked numerous persons likely to be acquainted with the subject—there are not more than those 15,000 men of whom I have spoken in all the State under arms, or in training, of whom a considerable proportion will be needed for garrison and coast defence duties.

It may be that the Northern States and Northern sentiments are as violent as the South, but I see some evidences to the contrary. For instance, in New York ladies and gentlemen from the South are permitted to live at their favourite hotels without molestation; and one hotel-keeper at Saratoga Springs advertises openly for the custom of his Southern patrons. In no city of the South which I have visited would a party of Northern people be permitted to remain for an hour if the "citizens" were aware of their presence. It is laughable to hear men speaking of the "unanimity" of the South. Just look at the peculiar means by which unanimity is enforced and secured. This is an extract from a New Orleans paper:

Charges of Abolitionism.—Mayor Monroe has disposed of some of the cases brought before him on charges of this kind by sending the accused to the workhouse.

A Mexican, named Bernard Cruz, born in Tampico, and living here with an Irish wife, was brought before the mayor this morning, charged with uttering abolition sentiments. After a full investigation, it was found that from the utterance of his incendiary language, that Cruz's education was not yet perfect in Southern classics, and his Honour therefore directed that he be sent for six months to the Humane Institution for the Amelioration of the Condition of Northern Barbarians and Abolition Fanatics, presided over by Professor Henry Mitchell, keeper of the workhouse, and who will put him through a course of study on Southern ethics and institutions.

The testimony before him on Saturday, however, in the case

of a man named David O'Keefe, was such as to induce him to commit the accused for trial before the Criminal Court. One of the witnesses testified positively that she heard him make his children shout for Lincoln; another, that the accused said, 'I am an Abolitionist,' &c. The witnesses, neighbours of the accused, gave their evidence reluctantly, saying they had warned him of the folly and danger of his conduct. O'Keefe says he has been a United States soldier, and came here from St. Louis and Kansas.

John White was arraigned before Recorder Emerson on Saturday for uttering incendiary language while travelling in the baggage car of a train of the New Orleans, Ohio and Great Western Railroad, intimating that the decapitator of Jefferson Davis would get $10,000 for his trouble, and the last man of us would be whipped like dogs by the Lincolnites. He was held under bonds of $500 to answer the charge on the 8th of June. "Nicholas Gento, charged with declaring himself an Abolitionist, and acting very much like he was one by harbouring a runaway slave, was sent to prison, in default of bail, to await an examination before the recorder.

Such is "freedom of speech" in Louisiana! But in Texas the machinery for the production of "unanimity" is less complicated, and there are no insulting legal formalities connected with the working of the simple appliances which a primitive agricultural people have devised for their own purposes. Hear the Texan correspondent of one of the journals of this city on the subject. "It is to us astonishing," he says:

That such unmitigated lies as those Northern papers disseminate as anarchy and disorder here in Texas, dissension among ourselves, and especially from our German, &c., population, with dangers and anxieties from the fear of insurrection among the negroes, &c., should be deemed anywhere South worthy of a moment's thought. It is surely notorious enough that in no part of the South are Abolitionists or other disturbers of the public peace so very unsafe as in Texas. The *lasso* is so *very* convenient!

Here is an excellent method of preventing dissension described by a stroke of the pen; and, as such, an ingenious people are not likely to lose sight of the uses of a revolution in developing peculiar principles to their own advantage, repudiation of debts to the North has been proclaimed and acted on. One gentleman has found it convenient to inform Major Anderson that he does not intend to meet certain bills which he had given the major for some slaves. Another declares he won't pay anybody at all, as he has discovered it is immoral and contrary to the laws of nations to do so. A third feels himself bound to obey the commands of the governor of his State, who has ordered that debts due to the North shall not be liquidated. As a *naive* specimen of the way in which the whole case is treated, take this article and the correspondence of "one of the most prominent mercantile houses of New Orleans:"

SOUTHERN DEBTS TO THE NORTH.

The Cincinnati Gazette copies the following paragraph from *The New York Evening Post*:

'Bad Faith.—The bad faith of the Southern merchants in their transactions with their Northern correspondents is becoming more evident daily. We have heard of several recent cases where parties in this city, retired from active business, have, nevertheless, stepped forward to protect the credit of their Southern friends. They are now coolly informed that they cannot be reimbursed for these advances until the war is over. We know of a retired merchant who in this way has lost $100,000.'—and adds:

'The same here. Men who have done most for the South are the chief sufferers. Debts are coolly repudiated by the Southern merchants, who have heretofore enjoyed a first-class reputation. Men who have grown rich upon the trade furnished by the West are among the first to pocket the money of their correspondents, asking, with all the impudence and assurance of a highwayman, "What are you going to do about it?" There is honour among thieves, it is said, but there is not a spark of honour among these repudiating merchants. People who have aided and trusted them to the last moment are the greatest losers. There is a future, however. This war will be over, and the Southern merchants will desire a resumption of their connections with the West. As the repudiators—such as Goodrich & Co. of New Orleans—will be spurned, there will be a grand opening for honest men.

'There are many honourable exceptions in the South, but dishonesty is the rule. The latter is but the development of latent rascality. The rebellion has afforded a pretext merely for the swindling operations. The parties previously acted honestly, only because that was the best policy. The sifting process that may now be conducted will be of advantage to Northern merchants in the future. The present losses will be fully made up by subsequent gains.'

We have been requested to copy the following reply to this tirade from one of our most prominent mercantile houses, Messrs. Goodrich & Co.:

'New Orleans, May 24, 1861.
'*Cincinnati Gazette.*—We were handed, through a friend of ours, your issue of the 18th inst., and attention directed to an article contained therein, in which you are pleased to particularize us out of a large number of highly respectable merchants of this and other Southern cities as repudiators, swindlers, and other epithets, better suited to the mouths of the Wilson Regiment of New York than from a once respectable sheet, but now has sunk so low in the depths of niggerdom, that it would take all the soap in Porkopolis and the Ohio River to cleanse it from its foul pollution.

'We are greatly indebted to you for using our name in the above article, as we deem it the best card you could publish for us, and may add greatly to our business relations in the Confederate States, which will enable us in the end to pay our indebtedness to those who propose cutting our throats, destroying our property, stealing our negroes, and starving our wives and children, to pay such men in times of war. You may term it rascality, but we beg leave to call it patriotism.

'Giving the sinews of war to your enemies have ever been considered as treason.—Kent.

'Now for 'repudiating.' We have never, nor do we ever expect to repudiate any debt owing by our firm. But this much we will say, never will we pay a debt due by us to a man, or any company of men, who is a known Black Republican, and marching in battle array to invade our homes and firesides, until every such person shall be driven back, and their polluted footsteps shall, now on our once happy soil, be entirely obliterated.

'We have been in business in this city for twenty years, have passed through every crisis with our names untarnished or credit impaired, and would at present sacrifice all we have made, were it necessary, to sustain our credit in the Confederacy, but care nothing for the opinions of such as are open and avowed enemies. We are sufficiently known in this city not to require the indorsement of *The Cincinnati Gazette*, or any such sheet, for a character.

'The day is coming, and not far distant, when there will be an awful reckoning, and we are willing and determined to stand by our Confederate flag, sink or swim, and would like to meet some of *The Gazette's* editors *vis-à-vis* on the field of blood, and see who would be the first to flinch.

'Our senior partner has already contributed one darkey this year to your population, and she is anxious to return, but we have a few more left which you can have, provided you will come and take them yourselves.

'We have said more than we intended, and hope you will give this a place in your paper.

Goodrich & Co.'

There is some little soreness felt here about the use of the word "repudiation," and it will do the hearts of some people good, and will carry comfort to the ghost of the Rev. Sydney Smith, if it can hear the tidings, to know I have been assured, over and over again, by eminent mercantile people and statesmen, that there is "a general desire" on the part of the repudiating States to pay their bonds, and that no doubt, at some future period, not very clearly ascertainable or plainly indicated, that general desire will cause some active steps to be taken to satisfy its intensity, of a character very unexpected, and very gratifying to those interested. The tariff of the Southern Confederation has just been promulgated, and I send herewith a copy of the rates. Simultaneously, however, with this document, the United States steam frigates *Brooklyn* and *Niagara* have made their appearance off the Pas-à-l'Outre, and the Mississippi is closed, and with it the port of New Orleans. The steam-tugs refuse to tow out vessels for fear of capture, and British ships are in jeopardy.

May 25.—A visit to the camp at Tangipao, about fifty miles from New Orleans, gave an occasion for obtaining a clearer view of the internal military condition of those forces of which one reads much, and sees so little, than any other way. Major-General Lewis of the

State Militia, and staff, and General Labuzan, a Creole officer, attended by Major Ranney, President of the New-Orleans, Jackson, and Great Northern Railway, and by many officers in uniform, started with that purpose at 4:30 this evening in a rail-carriage, carefully and comfortably fitted for their reception. The militia of Louisiana has not been called out for many years, and its officers have no military experience, and the men have no drill or discipline.

Emerging from the swampy suburbs, we soon pass between white clover pastures, which we are told invariably salivate the herds of small but plump cattle browsing upon them. Soon cornfields "in tassel," alternate with long narrow rows of growing sugar-cane, which, though scarcely a fourth of the height of the maize, will soon over-shadow it; and the cane-stalks grow up so densely together that nothing larger than a rattle-snake can pass between them.

From Kennersville, an ancient sugar plantation cut up into "town lots," our first halt, ten miles out, we shoot through a cypress swamp, the primitive forest of this region, and note a greater affluence of Spanish moss than in the woods of Georgia or Carolina. There it hung, like a hermit's beard, from the pensile branch. Here, to one who should venture to thread the snake and alligator haunted mazes of the jungle, its matted profusion must resemble clusters of stalactites pendent from the roof of some vast cavern; for the gloom of an endless night appears to pervade the deeper recesses, at the entrance of which stand, like outlying skeleton pickets, the unfelled and leafless patriarchs of the clearing, that for a breadth of perhaps fifty yards on either side seems to have furnished the road with its sleepers.

The gray swamp yields to an open savannah, beyond which, upon the left, a straggling line of sparse trees skirts the left bank of the Mississippi, and soon after the broad expanse of Lake Pontchartrain appears within gunshot of our right, only separated from the road by one hundred yards or more of rush-covered prairie, which seems but a feeble barrier against the caprices of so extensive a sheet of water subject to the influences of wind and tide. In fact, ruined shanties and outhouses, fields laid waste, and prostrate fences remain evidences of the ravages of the "Wash" which a year ago inundated and rendered the railroad impassable save for boats.

The down trains first notice of the disaster was the presence of a two-storey frame building, which the waves had transported to the road, and its passengers, detained a couple of days in what now strikes us as a most grateful combination of timber-skirted meadow and lake scenery, were rendered insensible to its beauties by the torments of hungry mosquitoes. Had its engineers given the road but eighteen inches more elevation its patrons would have been spared this suffering, and its stock-holders might have rejoiced in a dividend. Many of the settlers have abandoned their improvements. Others, chiefly what are here called Dutchmen, have resumed their tillage with unabated zeal, and large fields of cabbages, one of them embracing not less than sixty acres, testify to their energy.

Again through miles of cypress swamps the train passes on to what is called the "trembling prairie," where the sleepers are laid upon a trestle-work of heavier logs, so that the rails are raised by "cribs" of timber nearly a yard above the morass. Three species of rail, one of them as large as a curlew, and the summer duck, seem the chief occupants of the marsh, but white cranes and brown bitterns take the alarm, and falcons and long-tailed "blackbirds" sail in the distance.

Toward sunset a halt took place upon the long bridge that divides Lake Maurepas, a picturesque sheet of water which blends with the horizon on our left, from Pass Maunshae, an arm of Lake Pontchartrain, which disappears in the forest on our right. Half a dozen wherries and a small fishing-smack are moored in front of a rickety cabin, crowded by the jungle to the margin of the cove. It is the first token of a settlement that has occurred for miles, and when we have sufficiently admired the scene, rendered picturesque in the sunset by the dense copse, the water and the bright colours of the boats at rest upon it, a commotion at the head of the train arises from the unexpected arrival upon the "switch" of a long string of cars filled with half a regiment of volunteers, who had been enlisted for twelve months' service, and now refused to be mustered in for the war, as required by the recent enactment of the Montgomery Congress. The new comers are at length safely lodged on the "turn off," and our train continues its journey. As we pass the row of cars, most of them freight wagons, we are hailed with shouts and yells in every key by the disbanded volunteers, who seem a youngish, poorly-clad, and undersized lot, though noisy as a street mob.

After Maunshae, the road begins to creep up toward *terra firma*, and before nightfall there was a change from cypresses and swamp laurels to pines and beeches, and we inhale the purer atmosphere of dry land, with an occasional whiff of resinous fragrance, that dispels the fever-tainted suggestions of the swamp below. There we only breathed to live. Here we seem to live to breathe. The rise of the road is a grade of but a foot to the mile, and yet at the camp an elevation of not more than eighty feet in as many miles suffices to establish all the climatic difference between the malarious marshes and a much higher mountain region.

But during our journey the hampers have not been neglected. The younger members of the party astonish the night-owls with patriotic songs, chiefly French, and the French chiefly with the "*Marseillaise*," which, however inappropriate as the slogan of the Confederate States, they persist in quavering, forgetful, perhaps, that not three-quarters of a century ago Toussaint l'Ouverture caught the words and air from his masters, and awoke the lugubrious notes of the insurrection.

Towards nine p. m., the special car rests in the woods, and is flanked on one side by the tents and watch-fires of a small encampment, chiefly of navvy and cotton-handling Milesian volunteers, called "the Tigers," from their prehensile powers and predatory habits. A guard is stationed around the car; a couple of Ethiopians who have attended us from town are left to answer the query, *quis custodiet ipsos custodes?* and we make our way to the hotel, which looms up in the moonlight in a two-storied dignity. Here, alas! there have been no preparations made to sleep or feed us. The scapegoat " nobody" announced our coming. Some of the guests are club men, used to the small hours, who engage a room, a table, half a dozen chairs. and a brace of bottles to serve as candlesticks.

They have brought stearine and pasteboards with them, and are soon deep in the finesses of "*Euchre*." We quietly stroll back to the car, our only hope of shelter. At the entrance we are challenged by a sentry, apparently ignorant that he has a percussion cap on his brown rifle, which he levels at us cocked. From this unpleasant vision of an armed and reckless tiger rampant we are relieved by one of the dusky squires, who assures the sentinel that we are "all right," and proceeds to turn over a seat and arrange what might be called a sedan-chair bed, in which we prepare to make a night of it. Our party is soon joined by others in quest of repose, and in half an hour breathings, some of them so deep as to seem subterranean, indicate that all have attained their object—like Manfred's—forgetfulness.

An early breakfast of rashers and eggs was prepared at the *table d'hôte*, which we were told would be replenished half-hourly until noon, when a respite of an hour was allowed to the "help" in which to make ready a dinner, to be served in the same progression.

Through a shady dingle a winding path led to the camp, and, after trudging a pleasant half mile, a bridge of boards, resting on a couple of trees laid across a pool, was passed, and, above a slight embankment, tents and soldiers are revealed upon a "clearing" of some thirty acres in the midst of a pine forest. Turning to the left, we reach a double row of tents, only distinguished from the rest by their "fly roofs" and boarded floors, and, in the centre, halt opposite to one which a poster of capitals on a planed deal marks as "Headquarters." Major-General Tracy commands the camp.

The white tents crouching close to the shade of the pines, the parade alive with groups and colours as various as those of Joseph's coat, arms stacked here and there, and occasionally the march of a double file in green, or in mazarine blue, up an alley from the interior of the wood, to be dismissed in the open camp, resembles a militia muster, or a holiday experiment at soldiering, rather than the dark shadow of forthcoming battle. The cordon of sentinels suffer no volunteer to leave the precincts of the camp, even to bathe, without a pass or the word. There are neither wagons nor ambulances, and the men are rolling in barrels of bacon and bread and shouldering bags of pulse—good picnic practice and campaigning gymnastics in fair weather.

The arms of these volunteers are the old United States smoothbore musket, altered from flint to percussion, with bayonet—a heavy and obsolete copy of Brown Bess in bright barrels. All are in creditable order. Most of them have never been used, even to fire a parade volley, for powder is scarce in the Confederated States, and must not be wasted. Except in their material, the shoes of the troops are as varied as their clothing. None have as yet been served out, and each still wears the boots, the brogans, the patent leathers, or the Oxford ties in which he enlisted. The tents have mostly no other floor than the earth, and that rarely swept; while blankets, boxes, and utensils are stowed in corners with a disregard of symmetry that would drive a martinet mad. Camp stools are rare and tables invisible, save here and there in an officer's tent.

Still the men look well, and, we are told, would doubtless present a more cheerful appearance, but for some little demoralization occasioned by discontent at the repeated changes in the organic structure of the regiments, arising from misapprehensions between the State and Federal authorities, as well as from some favouritism toward certain officers, effected by political wire-pulling in the governing councils. The system of electing officers by ballot has made the camp as thoroughly a political arena as the poll districts in New Orleans before an election, and thus many heroes, seemingly ambitious of epaulettes, are in reality only "laying pipes" for the attainment of civil power or distinction after the war.

The volunteers we met at Maunshae the previous evening had been enlisted by the State to serve for twelve months, and had refused to extend their engagement for the war—a condition now made precedent at Montgomery to their being mustered into the army of the Confederate States. Another company, a majority of whom persist in the same refusal, were disbanded while we were patrolling the camp, and an officer told one of the party he had suffered a loss of six hundred volunteers by this disintegrating process within the last twenty-four hours. Some of these country companies were skilled in the use of the rifle, and most of them had made pecuniary sacrifices in the way of time, journeys, and equipments. Our informant deplored this reduction of volunteers, as tending to engender disaffection in the parishes to which they will return, and comfort when known to the Abolitionists of the North. He added that the war will not perhaps last a twelvemonth, and if unhappily prolonged beyond that period, the probabilities are in favour of the short-term recruits willingly consenting to a re-enlistment.

The encampment of the "Perrit Guards" was worthy of a visit. Here was a company of *professional gamblers*, one hundred and twelve strong, recruited for the war in a moment of banter by one of the patriarchs of the fraternity, who, upon hearing at the St. Charles Hotel one evening, that the vanity or the patriotism of a citizen, not famed for liberality, had endowed with $1,000 a company which was to bear his name, exclaimed that "he would give $1,500 to anyone who should be fool enough to form a company and call it after him." In less than an hour after the utterance of this caprice, Mr. Perrit was waited upon by fifty-six "professionals," who had enrolled their names as the "Perrit Guards," and unhesitatingly produced from his wallet the sum so sportively pledged.

The Guards are uniformed in Mazarin blue flannel with red facings, and the captain, a youngish-looking fellow, with a hawk's eye, who has seen service with Scott in Mexico and Walker in Nicaragua, informed us that there is not a pair of shoes in the company that cost less than six dollars, and that no money has been spared to perfect their other appointments. A sack of ice and half a dozen silver goblets enforced his invitation "to take a drink at his quarters," and we were served by an African in uniform, who afterward offered us cigars received by the last Havana steamer. Looking at the sable attendant, one of the party observes that if these "experts of fortune win the present fight, it will be a case of *couleur gagne*."

It would be difficult to find in the same number of men taken at hazard greater diversities of age, stature, and physiognomy; but in keenness of eye and imperturbility of demeanour they exhibit a family likeness, and there is not an unintelligent face in the company. The gamblers, or, as they are termed, the "sports," of the United States have an air of higher breeding and education than the dice-throwers and card-turners of Ascot or Newmarket—nay, they may be considered the Anglo-Saxon equals, minus the title, of those *âmes damnées* of the continental nobility who are styled Greeks by their Parisian victims. They are the Pariahs of American civilization, who are, nevertheless, in daily and familiar intercourse with their patrons, and not restricted, as in England, to a betting-ring toleration by the higher orders.

The Guards are the model company of Camp Moore, and I should have felt disposed to admire the spirit of gallantry with which they have volunteered in this war as a purification by fire of their maculated lives, were it not hinted that the "Oglethorpe Guards," and more than one other company of volunteers, are youths of large private fortunes, and that in the Secession, as in the Mexican War, these patriots will doubtless pursue their old calling with as much profit as they may their new one with valour.

From the Lower Camp we wind through tents, which diminish in neatness and cleanliness as we advance deeper, to the Upper Division, which is styled "Camp Tracy," a newer formation, whose brooms have been employed with corresponding success. The adjutant's report for the day sums up one thousand and seventy-three rank and file, and but two on the sick list. On a platform, a desk beneath the shade of the grove holds a Bible and prayer-book, that await the arrival at ten o'clock of the Methodist preacher, who is to perform Divine service. The green uniforms of the "Hibernian Guards," and the gray and light blue dress of other companies, appertain to a better appointed sort of men than the Lower Division.

There may be two thousand men in Camp Moore—not more, and yet every authority gives us a different figure. The lowest estimate acknowledged for the two camps is three thousand five hundred men, and *The Picayune* and other New Orleans papers still speak in glowing terms of the five thousand heroes assembled in Tangipao. Although the muster there presents a tolerable show of ball-stoppers, it would require months of discipline to enable them to pass for soldiers even at the North; and besides that General Tracy has never had other experience than in militia duty, there is not, I think, a single West Point officer in his whole command. The only hope of shaping such raw material to the purposes of war, would naturally be by the admixture of a proper allowance of military experience, and until those possessing it shall be awarded to Camp Moore, we must sigh over the delusion which pictures its denizens to the good people of New Orleans as "fellows ready for the fray."

While the hampers are being ransacked an express locomotive arrives from town with despatches for General Tracy, who exclaims when reading them, "Always too late!" from which expression it is inferred that orders have been received to accept the just-disbanded volunteers. The locomotive was hitched to the car and drew it back to the city. Our car was built in Massachusetts, the engine in Philadelphia, and the magnifier of its lamp in Cincinnati. What will the South do for such articles in future?

May 26.—In the evening, as I was sitting in the house of a gentleman in the city, it was related as a topic of conversation that a very respectable citizen named Bibb had had a difficulty with three gentlemen, who insisted on his reading out the news for them from his paper as he went to market in the early morning. Mr. Bibb had a revolver "casually" in his pocket, and he shot one citizen dead on the spot, and wounded the other two severely, if not mortally. "Great sympathy," I am told, "is felt for Mr. Bibb." There has been a skirmish somewhere on the Potomac, but Bibb has done more business "on his own hook" than any of the belligerents up to this date; and, though I can scarcely say I sympathize with him, far be it from me to say that I do not respect him.

One curious result of the civil war in its effects on the South will, probably, extend itself as the conflict continues—I mean the refusal of the employers to pay their workmen, on the ground of inability. The natural consequence is much distress and misery. The English Consul is harassed by applications for assistance from mechanics and skilled labourers who are in a state bordering on destitution and starvation. They desire nothing better than to leave the country and return to their homes. All business, except tailoring for soldiering and cognate labours, are suspended. Money is not to be had. Bills on New York are worth little more than the paper, and the exchange against London is enormous—18 *per cent.* discount from the par value of the gold in bank, good draughts on England having been negotiated yesterday at 92 *per cent.*

One house has been compelled to accept 4 *per cent.* on a draught on the North, where the rate was usually from ¼ *per cent.* to ½ *per cent.* There is some fear that the police force will be completely broken up, and the imagination refuses to guess at the result. The city schools will probably be closed—altogether, things do not look well at New Orleans. When all their present difficulties are over, a struggle between the mob and the oligarchy, or those who have no property and those who have, is inevitable; for one of the first acts of the legislature will probably be directed to establish some sort of qualification for the right of suffrage, relying on the force which will be at their disposal on the close of the war. As at New York, so at New Orleans. Universal suffrage is denounced as a curse, as corruption legalized, confiscation organized.

As I sat in a well-furnished club-room last night, listening to a most respectable, well-educated, intelligent gentleman descanting on the practices of "the Thugs"—an organized band who coolly and deliberately committed murder for the purpose of intimidating Irish and German voters, and were only put down by a Vigilance Committee, of which he was a member—I had almost to pinch myself to see that I was not the victim of a horrid nightmare.

Monday, May 27.—The Washington Artillery went off today to the wars—*quo fas et gloria ducunt*; but I saw a good many of them in the streets after the body had departed—spirits who were disembodied. Their uniform is very becoming, not unlike that of our own foot artillery, and they have one battery of guns in good order. I looked in vain for any account of Mr. Bibb's little affair yesterday in the papers. Perhaps, as he is so very respectable, there will not be any reference to it at all. Indeed, in some conversation on the subject last night it was admitted that when men were very rich they might find judges and jury-men as tender as Danae, and policeman as permeable as the walls of her dungeon. The whole question now is, "What will be done with the blockade?"

The Confederate authorities are acting with a high hand. An American vessel, the *Ariel*, which had cleared out of port with British subjects on board, has been overtaken, captured, and her crew have been put in prison. The ground is that she is owned in main by Black Republicans. The British subjects have received protection from the consul. Prizes have been made within a league of shore, and in one instance, when the captain protested, his ship was taken out to sea, and was then re-captured formally. I went round to several merchants to-day; they were all gloomy and fierce. In fact, the blockade of Mobile is announced, and that of New Orleans has commenced, and men-of-war have been reported off the Pas-à-l'Outre.

The South is beginning to feel that it is being bottled up all fermenting and frothing, and is somewhat surprised and angry at the natural results of its own acts, or, at least, of the proceedings which have brought about a state of war. Mr. Slidell did not seem at all contented with the telegrams from the North, and confessed that "if they had been received by way of Montgomery he should be alarmed." The names of persons liable for military service have been taken down in several districts, and British subjects have been included. Several applications have been made to Mr. Mure, the consul, to interfere in behalf of men who, having enlisted, are now under orders to march, and who must leave their families destitute if they go away; but he has, of course, no power to exercise any influence in such cases. The English journals to the 4th of May have arrived here today. It is curious to see how quaint in their absurdity the telegrams become when they have reached the age of three weeks.

I am in the hapless position of knowing, without being able to remedy, the evils from this source, for there is no means of sending through to New York political information of any sort by telegraph. The electric fluid may be the means of blasting and blighting many reputations, as there can be no doubt the revelations which the government at Washington will be able to obtain through the files of the despatches it has seized at the various offices, will compromise some whose views have recently undergone remarkable changes. It is a hint which may not be lost on governments in Europe when it is desirable to know friends and foes hereafter, and despotic rulers will not be slow to take a hint from "the land of liberty."

Orders have been issued by the governor to the tow-boats to take out the English vessels by the southwest passage, and it is probable they will all get through without any interruption on the part of the blockading force. It may be imagined that the owners and consignees of cargoes from England, China, and India, which are on their way here, are not at all easy in their minds. Two of the Washington Artillery died in the train on their way to that undefinable region called "the seat of war."

May 28.—The Southern States have already received the assistance of several thousands of savages, or red men, and "the warriors" are actually engaged in pursuing the United States troops in Texas in conjunction with the State Volunteers. A few days ago a deputation of the chiefs of the Five Nations, Creeks, Choctaws, Seminoles, Camanches, and others passed through New Orleans on their way to Montgomery, where they hoped to enter into terms with the government for the transfer of their pension list and other responsibilities from Washington, and to make such arrangements for their property and their rights as would justify them in committing their fortunes to the issue of war. These tribes can turn out twenty thousand warriors, scalping-knives, tomahawks, and all. The chiefs and principal men are all slaveholders.

May 29.—A new "affair" occurred this afternoon. The servants of the house in which I am staying were alarmed by violent screams in a house in the adjoining street, and by the discharge of firearms—an occurrence which, like the cry of "murder" in the streets of Havana, clears the streets of all wayfarers if they be wise, and do not wish to stop stray bullets. The cause is thus stated in the journals:

Sad family affray.—Last evening, at the residence of Mr. A. P. Withers, in Nayades street, near Thalia, Mr. Withers shot and dangerously wounded his stepson, Mr. A. F. W. Mather. As the police tell it, the nature of the affair was this: The two men were in the parlour, and talking about the Washington Artillery, which left on Monday for Virginia. Mather denounced the artillerists in strong language, and his step-father denied what he said. Violent language followed, and, as Withers says, Mather drew a pistol and shot at him once, not hitting him. He snatched up a Sharp's revolver that was lying near and fired four times at his stepson. The latter fell at the third fire, and as he was falling Withers fired a fourth time, the bullet wounding the hand of Mrs. Withers, wife of one and mother of the other, she having rushed in to interfere, and she being the only witness of the affair. Withers immediately went out into the street and voluntarily surrendered himself to officer Casson, the first officer he met. He was locked up. Three of his shots hit Mather, two of them in the breast. Last night Mather was not expected to live.

Another difficulty is connected with the free coloured people who may be found in prize ships. Read and judge of the conclusion:

> What shall be done with them?—On the 28th inst., Capt. O.W. Gregor, of the privateer *Calhoun*, brought to the station of this district about ten negro sailors, claiming to be free, found on board of the brigs *Panama, John Adams*, and *Mermaid*.
>
> The recorder sent word to the marshal of the Confederate States that said negroes were at his disposition. The marshal refused to receive them or have anything to do with them, whereupon the Recorder gave the following decision:
>
> "'Though I have no authority to act in this case, I think it is my duty as a magistrate and good citizen to take upon myself, in this critical moment, the responsibility of keeping the prisoners in custody, firmly believing it would not only be bad policy, but a dangerous one, to let them loose upon the community.'
>
> The following despatch was sent by the recorder to the Hon. J. P. Benjamin:

> New Orleans, May 23.
>
> To J. P. Benjamin, Richmond—*Sir:* Ten free negroes, taken by a privateer from on board three vessels returning to Boston, from a whaling voyage, have been delivered to me. The marshal refuses to take charge of them. What shall I do with them?
>
> Respectfully, A. Blache,
>
> Recorder, Second District.

The monthly statement I enclose of the condition of the New Orleans banks on the 25th inst., must be regarded as a more satisfactory exhibit to their depositors and shareholders, though of no greater benefit to the commercial community in this its hour of need than the tempting show of a pastry-cook's window to the famished street poor. These institutions show assets estimated at $54,000,000, of which $20,000,000 are in specie and sterling exchange, to meet $25,000,000 of liabilities, or more than two for one. But, with this apparent amplitude of resources, the New Orleans banks are at a deadlock, affording no discounts and buying no exchange—the latter usually their greatest source of profit in a mart which ships so largely of cotton, sugar, and flour, and the commercial movement of which for not over nine months of the year is the second in magnitude among the cities of the old Union.

As an instance of the caution of their proceedings, I have only to state that a gentleman of wealth and the highest respectability, who needed a day or two since some money for the expenses of an unexpected journey, was compelled, in order to borrow of these banks the sum of $1,500, to hypothecate, as security for his bill at 60 days, $10,000 of bonds of the Confederate States, and for which a month ago he paid par in coin—a circumstance which reflects more credit upon the prudence of the banks than upon the security pledged for this loan.

CASH RESPONSIBILITIES.

Circulation — Chartered Banks,	$5,323,376	
Circulation — Free Banks,	1,798,835	
		$7,122,211
Deposits — Chartered Banks,	$12,979,307	
Deposits — Free Banks,	4,929,544	
		$17,908,851
Total,		$25,031,062

CASH ASSETS.

Coin — Chartered Banks,	$10,808,812	
Coin — Free Banks,	4,183,722	
		$14,992,534
Exchange, chiefly sterling matured and maturing :		
Chartered Banks,	$4,481,140	
Free Banks,	1,083,928	
		$5,565,068
Total,		$20,557,602
Short commercial paper, 1 to 90 days, intended to meet cash responsibilities, and not renewable :		
Chartered Banks,	$7,235,077	
Free Banks,	4,670,979	
		$11,906,056
Total,		$32,463,658
Circulation of the Free Banks, secured by a deposit in the public Treasury, of State and New Orleans City Bonds, to the amount of,	$3,793,873	
The Chartered Banks hold of the same securities,	1,747,467	
		$5,541,340

DEAD WEIGHT.

Chartered Banks — bills and mortgaged bonds and other assets, not realizable in 90 days,	$14,140,925	
Free Banks — bills and mortgaged bonds and other assets, not realizable in 90 days,	2,606,249	
		$16,747,174
Total,		$54,752,172
Remarks :		
Amount of coin, as above,		$14,993,531
Amount of coin required by the Fundamental Bank Rules of Louisiana — one-third of the cash responsibilities, say, on $25,031,062, as above,		$8,343,137
Surplus,		$6,648,847
Amount of short notes maturing within a circle of 90 days, and exchange, as above,		$17,471,124
Amount required to be held by the Fundamental Bank Rules — at least two-thirds,		$16,687,378
Surplus,		$783,771

149

Letter 13

Natchez, Miss., June 14.

On the morning of the 3rd of June, I left New Orleans in one of the steamers proceeding up the Mississippi, along that fertile but uninteresting region of reclaimed swamp lands called "the Coast," which extends along both banks for one hundred and twenty miles above the city. It is so called from the name given to it, "La Cote," by the early French settlers. Here is the favoured land—alas! it is a fever-land too—of sugar-cane and Indian corn. To those who have very magnificent conceptions of the Mississippi, founded on mere arithmetical computations of leagues, or vague geographical data, it may be astonishing, but it is nevertheless true, the Mississippi is artificial for many hundreds of miles. Nature has, of course, poured out the waters, but man has made the banks. By a vast system of raised embankments, called levees, the river is constrained to abstain from overflowing the swamps, now drained and green with wealth-producing crops.

At the present moment the surface of the river is several feet higher than the land at each side, and the steamer moves on a level with the upper stories, or even the roofs of the houses, reminding one of such scenery as could be witnessed in the old days of *treckshuyt* in Holland. The river is not broader than the Thames at Gravesend, and is quite as richly coloured. But then it is one hundred and eighty feet deep, and for hundreds of miles it has not less than one hundred feet of water. Thus deeply has it scooped out the rich clay and marl in its course, but as it flows out to join the sea it throws down the vast precipitates which render the bars so shifting and difficult, and bring the mighty river to such a poor exit.

A few miles above the wharves and large levees of the city the country really appears to be a sea of light green, with shores of forest in the distance, about two miles away from the bank. This forest is the uncleared land, extending for a considerable way back, which each planter hopes to take into culture one day or other, and which he now uses to provide timber for his farm. Near the banks are houses of wood, with porticoes, pillars, verandahs, and sunshades, generally painted white and green.

There is a great uniformity of style, but the idea aimed at seems to be that of the old French *château*, with the addition of a colonnade round the ground storey. These dwellings are generally in the midst of small gardens, rich in semi-tropical vegetation, with glorious magnolias, now in full bloom rising in their midst, and groves of live-oak interspersed. The levee is as hard and dry as the bank of a canal. Here and there it is propped up by wooden revelments. Between it and the uniform line of palings which guards the river face of the plantations there is a carriage-road. In the enclosure near each residence there is a row of small wooden huts, white-washed, in which live the negroes attached to the service of the family. Outside the negroes who labour in the fields are quartered in similar constructions, which are like the small single huts, called "Maltese," which were plentiful in the Crimea. They are rarely furnished with windows; a wooden slide or a grated space admits such light and air as they want.

One of the most striking features of the landscape is its utter want of life. There were a few horsemen exercising in a field, some gigs and buggies along the levee roads, and little groups at the numerous landing-places, generally containing a few children in tom-fool costumes, as *zouaves, chasseurs,* or some sort of infantry, but the slaves who were there had come down to look after luggage or their masters. There were no merry, laughing, chattering gatherings of black faces and white teeth, such as we hear about. Indeed, the negroes are not allowed hereabouts to stir out of their respective plantations, or to go along the road without passes from their owners. The steamer *J. L. Cotten,* which was not the less popular, perhaps, because she had the words "Low pressure" conspicuous on her paddle-boxes, carried a fair load of passengers, most of whom were members of Creole families living on the coast.

The proper meaning of the word "Creole" is very different from that which we attach to it. It signifies a person of Spanish or French descent born in Louisiana or in the Southern and tropical countries. The great majority of the planters here are French Creoles, and it is said they are kinder and better masters than Americans or Scotch, the latter being considered the most severe. Intelligent on most subjects, they are resolute in the belief that England must take their cotton or perish. Even the keenest of their financiers, Mr. Forstall, an Irish Creole, who is representative of the house of Baring, seems inclined to this faith, though he is prepared with many ingenious propositions, which would rejoice Mr. Gladstone's inmost heart, to raise money for the Southern Confederacy, and make them rich exceedingly.

One thing has rather puzzled him. M. Baroche, who is in New Orleans, either as a looker-on or as an accredited *employé* of his father or of the French Government, suggested to him that it would not be possible for all the disposable mercantile marine of England and France together to carry the cotton crop, which hitherto gave employment to a great number of American vessels, now tabooed by the South, and the calculations seem to bear out the truth of the remark. Be that as it may, Mr. Forstall is quite prepared to show that the South can raise a prodigious revenue by a small direct taxation, for which the machinery already exists in every parish of the State, and that the North must be prodigiously damaged in the struggle, if not ruined outright.

One great source of strength in the South is its readiness—at least, its professed alacrity—to yield anything that it is asked. There is unbounded confidence in Mr. Jefferson Davis. Wherever I go, the same question is asked: "Well, Sir, what do you think of our President? Does he not strike you as being a very able man?" In finance he is trusted as much as in war. When he sent orders to the New Orleans banks, some time ago, to suspend specie payment, he exercised a power which could not be justified by any reading of the Southern Constitution. All men applauded. The President of the United States is far from receiving any such support or confidence, and it need not be said any act of his of the same nature as that of Mr. Davis would have created an immense outcry against him. But the South has all the unanimity of a conspiracy, and its unanimity is not greater than its confidence. One is rather tired of endless questions, "Who can conquer such men?" But the question should be, "Can the North conquer us?"

Of the fustian about dying in their tracks and fighting till every man, woman and child is exterminated, there is a great deal too much, but they really believe that the fate which Poland could not avert, to which France as well as the nations she overran bowed the head, can never reach them. With their faithful negroes to raise their corn, sugar and cotton while they are at the wars, and England and France to take the latter and pay them for it, they believe they can meet the

American world in arms. A glorious future opens before them. Illimitable fields tilled by multitudinous negroes open on their vision, and prostrate at the base of the mountain of cotton from which they rule the kings of the earth, the empires of Europe shall lie, with all their gold, their manufactures, and their industry, crying out, "Pray give us more cotton! All we ask is more!"

But here is the boat stopping opposite Mr. Roman's—Ex-governor of the State of Louisiana, and Ex-commissioner from the Confederate Government at Montgomery to the Government of the United States at Washington. Not very long ago he could boast of a very handsome garden—the French Creoles love gardens—Americans and English do not much affect them; when the Mississippi was low one fine day, levee and all slid down the bank into the maw of the river, and were carried off. This is what is called the "caving in" of a bank; when the levee is broken through at high water it is said that a "crevasse" has taken place. The governor, as he is called—once a captain always a captain—has still a handsome garden, however, though his house has been brought unpleasantly near the river.

His mansion and the out-offices stand in the shade of magnolias, green oaks, and other Southern trees. To the last Governor Roman was a Unionist, but when his State went he followed her, and now he is a secessionist for life and for death, not extravagant in his hopes, but calm and resolute, and fully persuaded that in the end the South must win. As he does not raise any cotton, the consequences for him will be extremely serious should sugar be greatly depreciated; but the consumption of that article in America is very large, and, though the markets in the North and West are cut off, it is hoped, as no imported sugar can find its way into the States, that the South will consume all its own produce at a fair rate. The governor is a very good type of the race, which is giving way a little before the encroachments of the Anglo-Saxons, and he possesses all the ease, candid manner, and suavity of the old French gentleman—of that school in which there are now few masters or scholars.

He invited me to visit the negro quarters. "Go where you like, do what you please, ask any questions. There is nothing we desire to conceal." As we passed the house, two or three young women flitted past in snow-white dresses with pink sashes, and no doubtful crinolines, but their head-dresses were not *en règle*—handkerchiefs of a gay colour. They were slaves going off to a dance at the sugar-house; but they were in-door servants, and therefore better off in the way of clothes than their fellow slaves who labour in the field.

On approaching a high paling at the rear of the house the scraping of fiddles was audible. It was Sunday, and Mr. Roman informed me that he gave his negroes leave to have a dance on that day. The planters who are not Catholics rarely give any such indulgence to their slaves, though they do not always make them work on that day, and sometimes let them enjoy themselves on the Saturday afternoon. Entering a wicket gate, a quadrangular enclosure, lined with negro huts, lay before us. The bare ground was covered with litter of various kinds, amid which pigs and poultry were pasturing. Dogs, puppies, and curs of low degree scampered about on all sides; and deep in a pond, swinking in the sun, stood some thirty or forty mules, enjoying their day of rest. The huts of the negroes, belonging to the personal service of the house, were separated from the negroes engaged in field labour by a close wooden paling; but there was no difference in the shape and size of their dwellings, which consisted generally of one large room, divided by a partition occasionally into two bedrooms.

Outside the whitewash gave them a cleanly appearance; inside they were dingy and squalid—no glass in the windows, swarms of flies, some clothes hanging on nails in the boards, dressers with broken crockery, a bedstead of rough carpentry; a fireplace in which, hot as was the day, a log lay in embers; a couple of tin cooking utensils; in the obscure, the occupant, male or female, awkward and shy before strangers, and silent till spoken to. Of course there were no books, for the slaves do not read. They all seemed respectful to their master.

We saw very old men and very old women, who were the canker-worms of the estate, and were dozing away into eternity mindful only of hominy, and pig, and molasses. Two negro fiddlers were working their bows with energy in front of one of the huts, and a crowd of little children were listening to the music, and a few grown-up persons of colour—some of them from the adjoining plantations. The children are generally dressed in a little sack of coarse calico, which answers all reasonable purposes, even if it be not very clean. It might be an interesting subject of inquiry to the natural philosophers who follow crinology to determine why it is that the hair of the infant negro, or of the child up to six or seven years of age, is generally a fine red russet, or even gamboge colour, and gradually darkens into dull ebon.

These little bodies were mostly large-stomached, well fed, and not less happy than free-born children, although much more valuable—for once they get over juvenile dangers, and advance towards nine or ten years of age, they rise in value to £100 or more, even in times when the market is low and money is scarce.

The women were not very well-favoured, except one yellow girl, whose child was quite white, with fair hair and light eyes; and the men were disguised in such strangely cut clothes, their hats and shoes and coats were so wonderfully made, that one could not tell what they were like. On all faces there was a gravity which must be the index to serene contentment and perfect comfort, for those who ought to know best declare they are the happiest race in the world. It struck me more and more, as I examined the expression of the faces of the slaves all over the South, that deep dejection is the prevailing, if not universal, characteristic of the race. Let a physiognomist go and see.

Here there were abundant evidences that they were well treated, for they had good clothing of its kind, good food, and a master who wittingly could do them no injustice, as he is, I am sure, incapable of it. Still, they all looked exceedingly sad, and even the old woman who boasted that she had held her old master in her arms when he was an infant, did not look cheerful, as the nurse at home would have done, at the sight of her ancient charge. The precincts of the huts were not clean, and the enclosure was full of weeds, in which poultry—the perquisites of the slaves—were in full possession. The negroes rear domestic birds of all kinds, and sell eggs and poultry to their masters. The money they spend in purchasing tobacco, molasses, clothes and flour—whiskey, their great delight, they must not have. Some seventy or eighty hands were quartered in this part of the estate. The silence which reigned in the huts as soon as the fiddlers had gone off to the sugar-house was profound.

Before leaving the quarter I was taken to the hospital, which was in charge of an old negress. The naked rooms contained several flock beds on rough stands, and five patients, three of whom were women. They sat listlessly on the beds, looking out into space; no books to amuse them, no conversation—nothing but their own dull thoughts, if they had any. They were suffering from pneumonia and swellings of the glands of the neck; one man had fever. Their medical attendant visits them regularly, and each plantation has a practitioner, who is engaged by the term for his services. Negroes have now only a nominal value in the market—that the price of a good field hand is as high as ever, but there is no one to buy him at present, and no money to pay for him, and the trade of the slave-dealers is very bad.

The menageries of the "Virginia negroes constantly on sale. Money advanced on all descriptions of property," &c., must be full—their pockets empty. This question of price is introduced incidentally in reference to the treatment of negroes. It has often been said to me that no one will ill-use a creature worth £300 or £400, but that is not a universal rule. Much depends on temper, and many a hunting-field could show that if value be a guarantee for good usage, the slave is more fortunate than his fellow chattel, the horse. If the growth of sugar-cane, cotton and corn, be the great end of man's mission on earth, and if all masters were like Governor Roman, Slavery might be defended as a natural and innocuous institution. Sugar and cotton are, assuredly, two great agencies in this latter world. The older got on well enough without them.

The scraping of the fiddles attracted us to the sugar-house, a large brick building with a factory-looking chimney, where the juice of the cane is expressed, boiled, granulated, and prepared for the refiner. In a space of the floor unoccupied by machinery some fifteen women and as many men were assembled, and four couples were dancing a kind of Irish jig to the music of the negro musicians—a double shuffle and thumping ecstasy, with loose elbows, pendulous paws, and angulated knees, heads thrown back, and backs arched inwards—a glazed eye, intense solemnity of mien, worthy of the minuet in *Don Giovanni*. At this time of year there is no work done in the sugar-house, but when the crushing and boiling are going on the labour is intense, and all the hands work in gangs night and day; and, if the heat of the fires be superadded to the temperature in September, it may be conceded that nothing but "involuntary servitude" could go through the toil and suffering required to produce sugar for us. This is not the place for an account of the processes and machinery used in the manufacture, which is a scientific operation, greatly improved by recent discoveries and apparatus.

In the afternoon the governor's son came in from the company which he commands. He has been camping out with them to accustom them to the duties of actual war, and he told me that all his men were most zealous and exceedingly proficient. They are all of the best families around,—planters, large and small, their sons and relatives, and a few of the Creole population, who are engaged as hoopers and stavemakers. One of the latter had just stained his hands with blood. He had reason to believe a culpable intimacy existed between his wife and his foreman. A circumstance occurred which appeared to confirm his worst suspicions. He took out his fire-lock, and, meeting the man, he shot him without uttering a word, and then delivered himself up to the authorities. It is probable his punishment will be exceedingly light, as divorce suits and actions for damages are not in favour in this part of the world.

Although the people are Roman Catholics, it is by no means unusual to permit relations within the degree of consanguinity forbidden by the Church to intermarry, and the elastic nature of the rules which are laid down by the priesthood in that respect would greatly astonish the orthodox in Ireland or Bavaria. The whole of the planters and their dependents along "the coast" are in arms. There is but one sentiment, as far as I can see, among them, and that is, "We will never submit to the North." In the evening, several officers of M. Alfred Roman's company and neighbours came in, and out under the shade of the trees, in the twilight, illuminated by the flashing fireflies, politics were discussed—all on one side, of course, with general conversation of a more agreeable character. The customary language of the Creoles is French, and several newspapers in French are published in the districts around us; but they speak English fluently.

Next morning, early, the governor was in the saddle and took me round to see his plantation. We rode through alleys formed by the tall stalks of the maze out to the wide, unbroken fields—hedgeless, unwalled, where the green cane was just learning to wave its long shoots in the wind. Along the margin in the distance there is an unbroken boundary of forest extending all along the swamp lands, and two miles in depth. From the river to the forest there is about one mile and a half or more of land of the very highest quality—unfathomable, and producing from one to one and a half hogshead an acre. Away in the midst of the crops were white-looking masses, reminding me of the *sepoys* and *sowars* as seen in Indian fields in the morning sun on many a march.

As we rode towards them we overtook a cart with a large cask, a number of tin vessels, a bucket of molasses, a pail of milk, and a tub full of hominy or boiled Indian corn. The cask contained water for the use of the negroes, and the other vessel held the materials for their breakfast, in addition to which they generally have each a dried fish. The food looked ample and wholesome, such as any labouring man would be well content with every day. There were three gangs at work in the fields. One of them with twenty mules and ploughs, was engaged in running through the furrows between the canes, cutting up the weeds and clearing away the grass, which is the enemy of the growing shoot.

The mules are of a fine, large, good-tempered kind, and understand their work almost as well as the drivers, who are usually the more intelligent hand on the plantation. The overseer, a sharp-looking Creole, on a lanky pony, whip in hand, superintended their labours, and, after a few directions and a salutation to the governor, rode off to another part of the farm. The negroes when spoken to saluted us and came forward to shake hands—a civility which must not be refused. With the exception of crying to their mules, however, they kept silence when at work. Another gang consisted of forty men, who were hoeing out the grass in Indian corn—easy work enough. The third gang was of thirty-six or thirty-seven women, who were engaged in hoeing out cane. Their clothing seemed heavy for the climate, their shoes ponderous and ill-made, so as to wear away the feet of their thick stockings. Coarse straw hats and bright cotton handkerchiefs protected their heads from the sun.

The silence which I have already alluded to prevailed among these gangs also—not a sound could be heard but the blows of the hoe on the heavy clods. In the rear of each gang stood a black overseer, with a heavy-thonged whip over his shoulder. If "Alcibiadev" or "Pompée" were called out, he came with outstretched hand to ask "how do you do," and then returned to his labour; but the ladies were coy, and scarcely looked up from under their flapping *chapeaux de paille* at their visitors. Those who are mothers leave their children in the charge of certain old women, unfit for anything else, and "suckers," as they are called, are permitted to go home to give their infants the breast at appointed periods in the day. I returned home *multa mecum revolens*.

After breakfast, in spite of a very fine sun, which was not unworthy of a January noon in Cawnpore, we drove forth to visit some planter friends of M. Roman, a few miles down the river. The levee road is dusty, but the gardens, white railings, and neat houses of the planters looked fresh and clean enough. There is a great difference in the appearance of the slaves' quarters. Some are neat, others are dilapidated and mean. As a general rule, it might be said that the goodness of the cottages was in proportion to the frontage of each plantation towards the river, which is a fair index to the size of the estate wherever the river bank is straight. The lines of the estate are drawn perpendicularly to the banks, so that the convexity or concavity of the bends determines the frontage of the plantation.

The absence of human beings in the fields and on the roads was remarkable. The gangs at work were hidden in the deep corn, and not a soul met us on the road for many miles except one planter in his gig. At one place we visited a very handsome garden, laid out with hot-houses and conservatories, ponds full of magnificent *Victoria Regia* in flower, orange trees, and many other tropical plants, native and foreign, date and other palms.

The proprietor owns an extensive sugar refinery. We visited his factory and mills, but the heat from the boilers, which seemed too much even for all but naked negroes who were at work, did not tempt us to make a very long sojourn inside. The ebony faces and polished black backs of the slaves were streaming with perspiration as they toiled over boiler, vat and centrifugal driers. The good refiner was not gaining much at present, for sugar has been falling rapidly in New Orleans, and the three hundred thousand barrels produced annually in the South will fall short in the yield of profit, which, on an average, may be taken at £11 a hogshead, without counting the molasses for the planter. All the planters hereabouts have sown an unusual quantity of Indian Corn, so as to have food for the negroes if the war lasts, without any distress from inland or sea blockade. The absurdity of supposing that blockade can injure them in the way of supply is a favourite theme to descant upon.

They may find out, however, that it is no contemptible means of warfare. At night, after our return, a large bonfire was lighted on the bank to attract the steamer to call for my luggage, which she was to leave at a point on the opposite shore, fourteen miles higher up, and I perceived that there are regular patrols and watchmen at night who look after levees and the negroes; a number of dogs are also loosed, but I am assured by a gentleman who has written me a long letter on the subject from Montgomery, that these dogs do not tear the negroes; they are taught merely to catch and mumble them, to treat them as a retriever well broken uses a wild duck. Next day I left the hospitable house of Governor Roman, full of regard for his personal character and of wishes for his happiness and prosperity, but assuredly in no degree satisfied that even with his care and kindness even the "domestic institution" can be rendered tolerable or defensible, if it be once conceded that the negro is a human being with a soul—or with the feelings of a man.

On those points there are ingenious hypotheses and subtle argumentations in print "down South," which do much to comfort the consciences of the anthropoproprietors. The negro skull won't hold as many ounces as that of the white man's. Can there be a more potent proof that the white man has a right to sell and to own a creature who carries a smaller charge of snipe dust in his head? He is plantigrade and curved as to the tibia! Cogent demonstration that he was made expressly to work for the arch-footed, straight-tibia'd Caucasian. He has a *rete mucosum* and a coloured pigment. Surely he cannot have a soul of the same colour as that of an Italian or a Spaniard, far less of a flaxen-haired Saxon! See these peculiarities in the frontal sinus—in *sinciput* or *occiput*! Can you doubt that the being with a head of that nature was made only to till, hoe, and dig for another race? Besides the Bible says that he is a son of Ham, and prophecy must be carried out in the rice swamps, sugar canes, and maize-fields of the Southern Confederation. It's flat blasphemy to set yourself against it.

Our Saviour sanctions slavery because he does not say a word against it, and it's very likely that St. Paul was a slave-owner. Had cotton and sugar been known, he might have been a planter! Besides, the negro is civilized by being carried away from Africa and set to work, instead of idling in native inutility. What hope is there of Christianizing the African races except by the agency of the apostles from New Orleans, Mobile, or Charleston, who sing the sweet songs of Zion with such vehemence, and clamour so fervently for baptism in the waters of the "Jawdam?" If these high, physical, metaphysical, moral and religious reasonings do not satisfy you, and you venture to be unconvinced and to say so, then I advise you not to come within reach of a mass meeting of our citizens, who may be able to find a rope and a tree in the neighbourhood.

As we jog along in an easy-rolling carriage drawn by a pair of stout horses, a number of white people met us coming from the Catholic chapel of the parish, where they had been attending a service for the repose of the soul of a lady much beloved in the neighbourhood. The black people are supposed to have very happy souls, or to be as utterly lost as Mr. Shandy's homuncule was under certain circumstances, for I have failed to find that any such services are ever considered necessary in their case, although they may have been very good— or where it would be most desirable—very bad Catholics. My good young friend, clever, amiable, accomplished, who had a dark cloud of sorrow weighing down his young life, that softened him to almost feminine tenderness, saw none of these things. He talked of foreign travel in days gone by—of Paris and poetry, of England and London hotels, of the great *Carême*, and of poor Alexis Soyer, of pictures, of politics—*de omne scibili.*

The storm gathered overhead, and the rain fell in torrents—the Mississippi flowed lifelessly by—not a boat on its broad surface. The road passed by plantations smaller and poorer than I have yet seen belonging to small planters, with only some ten or twelve slaves, all told. The houses were poor and ragged. At last we reached Governor Manning's place, and drove to the overseer's—a large, heavy-eyed old man, who asked us into his house from out of the rain till the boat was ready—and the river did not look inviting—full of drift trees, swirls, and mighty eddies. In the plain room in which we sat there was a volume of Spurgeon's Sermons and Baxter's works. "This rain will do good to our corn," said the overseer. "The niggers has had sceerce nothin' to do leetly, as they 'eve cleaned out the fields pretty well." We drove down to a poor shed on the levee called the Ferry-house, attended by one stout, young slave who was to row me over. Two flat-bottomed skiffs lay on the bank. The negro groped under the shed, and pulled out a piece of wood like a large spatula, some four feet long, and a small, round pole a little longer.

"What are those?" quoth I,

"Dem's oars, Massa," was my sable ferryman's brisk reply.

"I'm very sure they are not; if they were spliced they might make an oar between them."

"Golly, and dat's the trute, Massa."

"There, go and get oars, will you?"

While he was hunting about we entered the shed for shelter from the rain. We found "a solitary woman sitting" smoking a pipe by the ashes on the hearth, blear-eyed, low-browed, and morose—young as she was. She never said a word nor moved as we came in, sat and smoked, and looked through her gummy eyes at chickens about the size of sparrows, and at a cat no larger than a rat, which ran about on the dirty floor. A little girl some four years of age, not over-dressed—indeed, half-naked, "not to put too fine a point upon it"—crawled out from under the bed, where she had hid on our approach. As she seemed incapable of appreciating the uses of a small piece of silver presented to her—having no precise ideas on coinage or toffy—her parent took the *obolus* in charge with unmistakable decision; but, still, she would not stir a step to aid our Charon, who now insisted on the "key ov de oar-house." The little thing sidled off and hunted it out from the top of the bedstead, and I was not sorry to quit the company of the silent woman in black.

Charon pushed his skiff into the water—there was a good deal of rain in it—in shape a snuffer-dish, some ten feet long and a foot deep. I got in and the conscious waters immediately began vigorously spurting through the cotton wadding wherewith the craft was caulked. Had we gone out into the stream we should have had a swim for it, and they do say that the Mississippi is the most dangerous river for that healthful exercise in the known world.

"Why, deuce take you" (I said at least that, in my wrath), "don't you see that the boat is leaky?"

"See it now for true, Massa. Nobody able to tell dat till Massa get in, tho'."

Another skiff proved to be stanch. I bade goodbye to my friend, and sat down in my boat, which was soon forced up along the stream close to the bank, in order to get a good start across to the other side. The view, from my lonely position, was curious, but not at all picturesque. The landscape had disappeared at once. The world was bounded on both sides by a high bank, and was constituted by a broad river— just as if one were sailing down an open sewer of enormous length and breadth. Above the bank rose, however, the tops of tall trees and the chimneys of sugar-houses. A row of a quarter of an hour brought us to the levee on the other side. I ascended the bank and directly in front of me, across the road, appeared a carriage gateway, and wickets of wood, painted white, in a line of park palings of the same material, which extended up and down the road as far as the eye could follow, and guarded wide-spread fields of maize and sugar-cane.

An avenue of trees, with branches close set, drooping and over-arching a walk paved with red brick, led to the house, the porch of which was just visible at the extremity of the lawn, with clustering flowers, rose, jessamine, and creepers clinging to the pillars supporting the verandah. The proprietor, who had espied my approach, issued forth with a section of sable attendants in his rear, and gave me a hearty welcome. The house was larger and better than the residences even of the richest planters, though it was in need of some little repair, and had been built perhaps fifty years ago, but it had belonged to a wealthy family, who lived in the good old Irish fashion, and who built well, ate well, drank well, and—finally, paid very well.

The view from the Belvedere was one of the most striking of its kind in the world. If an English agriculturist could see 6,000 acres of the finest land in one field, unbroken by hedge or boundary, and covered with the most magnificent crops of tasselling Indian corn and sprouting sugar-cane, as level as a billiard table, he would surely doubt his senses. But here is literally such a sight. Six thousand acres, better tilled than the finest patch in all the Lothians, green as Meath pastures, which can be cultivated for a hundred years to come without requiring manure, of depth practically unlimited, and yielding an average profit on what is sold off it of at least £20 an acre at the old prices and usual yield of sugar. Rising up in the midst of the verdure are the white lines of the negro cottages and the plantation offices and sugar-houses, which look like large public edifices in the distance. And who is the lord of all this fair domain? The proprietor of Houmas and Orange-grove is a man, a self-made one, who has attained his apogee on the bright side of half a century, after twenty-five years of successful business.

When my eyes "uncurtained the early morning" I might have imagined myself in the magic garden of Cherry and Fair Star, so incessant and multifarious were the carols of the birds, which were the only happy coloured people I saw in my Southern tour, notwithstanding the assurances of the many ingenious and candid gentlemen who attempted to prove to me that the palm of terrestrial felicity must be awarded to their negroes. As I stepped through my window upon the verandah, a sharp chirp called my attention to a mocking-bird perched upon a rose-bush beneath, whom my presence seemed to annoy to such a degree that I retreated behind my curtain, whence I observed her flight to a nest cunningly hid in a creeping rose trailed around a neighbouring column of the house, where she imparted a breakfast of spiders and grasshoppers to her gaping and clamorous offspring.

While I was admiring the motherly grace of this melodious fly-catcher, a servant brought coffee, and announced that the horses were ready, and that I might have a three-hours' ride before breakfast. At Houmas *les jours se suivent et se ressemblent*, and an epitome of the first will serve as a type for all, with the exception of such variations in the kitchen and cellar produce as the ingenuity and exhaustless hospitality of my host were never tired of framing.

If I regretted the absence of our English agriculturist when I beheld the 6,000 acres of cane and 1,600 of maize unfolded from the Belvedere the day previous, I longed for his presence still more, when I saw those evidences of luxuriant fertility attained without the aid of phosphates or guano. The rich Mississippi bottoms need no manure, a rotation of maize with cane affords them the necessary recuperative action. The cane of last year's plant is left in stubble, and renews its growth this spring under the title of *ratoons*. When the maize is in tassel, cow-peas are dropped between the rows, and when the lordly stalk, of which I measured many twelve and even fifteen feet in height—bearing three and sometimes four ears—is topped to admit the ripening sun, the pea vine twines itself around the trunk, with a profusion of leaf and tendril that supplies the planter with the most desirable fodder for his mules in "rolling time," which is their season of trial.

Besides this, the corn blades are culled and cured. These are the best meals of the Southern race-horse, and constitute nutritious hay without dust. The cow-pea is said to strengthen the system of the earth for the digestion of a new crop of sugar-cane. A sufficient quantity of the cane of last season is reserved from the mill and laid in pits, where the ends of the stalk are carefully closed with earth until spring. After the ground has been ploughed into ridges these canes are laid in the endless tumuli, and not long after their interment a fresh sprout springs at each joint of these interminable flutes.

As we ride through the wagon roads, of which there are not less than thirty miles in this confederation of four plantations, held together by the purse and the life of our host, the unwavering exactitude of the rows of cane, which run without deviation at right angles with the river down to the cane-brake, two miles off, proves that the negro would be a formidable rival in a ploughing match. The cane has been "laid by"—that is, it requires no more labour—and will "lap," or close up, though the rows are seven feet apart. It feathers like a palm top; a stalk which was cut measured six feet, although from the ridges it was but waist high. On dissecting it near the root, we find five nascent joints, not a quarter of an inch apart. In a few weeks more these will shoot up like a spy-glass pulled out to its focus.

There are four lordly sugar-houses, as the grinding mills and boiling and crystallizing buildings are called, and near each is to be found the negro village, or "quarter," of that section of the plantation. A wide avenue, generally lined with trees, runs through these hamlets, which consist of twenty or thirty white cottages, single storied and divided into four rooms. They are whitewashed, and at no great distance might be mistaken for New England villages, with a town-hall which often serves in the latter for a "meeting-house," with, occasionally, a row of stores on the ground floor.

The people, or "hands," are in the field, and the only inhabitants of the settlements are scores of *"picaninnies,"* who seem a jolly congregation, under the care of crones, who here, as in an Indian village, act as nurses to the rising generation destined from their births to the limits of a social Procrustean bed. The increase of property on the estate is about 5 *per cent. per annum* by the birth of children.

We ride an hour before coming upon any "hands" at work in the fields. There is an air of fertile desolation that prevails in no other cultivated land. The regularity of the cane, its garden-like freedom from grass or weeds, and the *ad unguem* finish and evenness of the furrows would seem the work of nocturnal fairies, did we not realize the system of "gang-labour" exemplified in a field we at length reach, where some thirty men and women were giving with the hoe the last polish to the earth around the cane, which would not be molested again until gathered for the autumnal banquet of the rolling-mills.

Small drains and larger ditches occur at almost every step. All these flow into a channel, some fifteen feet wide, which runs between the plantations and the uncleared forest, and carries off the water to a "bayou" still more remote. There are twenty miles of deep ditching before the plantation, exclusive of the canal, and as this is the contract work of "Irish navvies," the sigh with which our host alluded to this heavy item in plantation expenses, was expressive. The work is too severe for African thews, and experience has shown it a bad economy to overtask the slave.

The sugar-planter lives in apprehension of four enemies. These are the river when rising, drought, too much or unseasonable rain, and frost. The last calls into play all his energies, and tasks his utmost composure. In Louisiana the cane never ripens as it does in Cuba, and they begin to grind as early in October as the amount of juices will permit. The question of a crop is one of early or late frost. With two months' exemption they rely, in a fair season, upon a hogshead of 1,200 pounds to the acre, and if they can run their mills until January, the increase is more than proportionate, each of its latter days in the earth adding saccharine virtue to the cane.

At an average of a hogshead to the acre, each working hand is good for seven hogsheads a year, which, at last year's prices, 8 cents per pound for ordinary qualities, would be a yield of £140 *per annum* for each full field hand.

Two hogsheads to the acre are not unfrequently, and even three have been, produced upon rich lands in a good season. Estimating the sugar at 70 *per cent.*, and the refuse, *bagasse*, at 30 *per cent.*, the latter would give us two tuns and a quarter to the acre, which open one's eyes to the tireless activity of nature in this semi-tropical region.

From the records of Houmas I find that, in 1857, the year of its purchase at about £300,000, it yielded a gross of $304,000, say £63,000, upon the investment.

In the rear of this great plantation there are 18,000 additional acres of cane-brake which are being slowly reclaimed, like the fields now rejoicing in crops, as fast as the furnace of the sugar-house calls for fuel. Were it desirable to accelerate the preparation of this reserve for planting, it might be put in tolerable order in three years at a cost of £15 per acre. We extended our ride into this jungle on the borders of which, in the unfinished clearing, I saw plantations of "negro corn," the sable cultivators of which seem to have disregarded the symmetry practised in the fields of their master, who allows them from Saturday noon until Monday's cockcrow for the care of their private interests, and in addition to this, whatever hours in the week they can economize by the brisk fulfilment of their allotted tasks. Some of these patches are sown broadcast, and the corn has sprung up like Zouave *tirailleurs* in their most fantastic vagaries, rather than like the steady regimental drill of the cane and maize we have been traversing.

Corn, chickens, and eggs, are from time immemorial the perquisites of the negro, who has the monopoly of the two last named articles in all well ordered Louisiana plantations. Indeed, the white man cannot compete with them in raising poultry, and our host was evidently delighted when one of his negroes, who had brought a dozen Muscovy ducks to the mansion, refused to sell them to him except for cash.

"But Louis, won't you trust me? Am I not good for three dollars?"

"Good enough, Massa; but dis nigger want de money to buy flour and coffee for him young family. Folks at Donaldsonville will trust Massa—won't trust nigger."

The money was paid, and, as the negro left us, his master observed, with a sly, humorous twinkle, "That fellow sold forty dollars worth of corn last year, and all of them feed their chickens with my corn, and sell their own."

There are three overseers at Houmas, one of whom superintends the whole plantation, and likewise looks after another estate of 8,000 acres, some twelve miles down the river, which our host added to his possession two years since, at a cost of £150,000. In any part of the world, and in any calling, Mr. S—— (I do not know if he would like to see his name in print) would be considered an able man. Mr. S.

attends to most of the practice requiring immediate attention. We visited one of those hospitals, and found half a dozen patients ill of fever, rheumatism, and indigestion, and apparently well cared for by a couple of stout nurses. The truckle bedsteads were garnished with mosquito bars, and I was told that the hospital is a favourite resort, which its inmates leave with reluctance. The pharmaceutical department was largely supplied with a variety of medicines, quinine and preparations of sulphites of iron."Poor drugs," said Mr. S., "are a poor economy."

I have mentioned engineering as one of the requisites of a competent overseer. To explain this I must observe that Houmas is esteemed very high land, and that in its cultivated breadth there is only a fall of eight feet to carry off its surplus water. In the plantation of Governor Manning, which adjoins it, an expensive steam draining machine is employed to relieve his fields of this encumbrance, which is effected by the revolutions of a far-wheel some twenty feet in diameter, which laps up the water from a narrow trough into which all the drainage fows, and tosses it into an adjoining bayou.

On Governor Manning's plantation we saw the process of clearing the primitive forest, of which 150 acres were sown in corn and cotton beneath the tall girdled trees that awaited the axe, while an equal breadth on the other side of a broad and deep canal was reluctantly yielding its tufted and fibrous soil, from which the jungle had just been removed, to the ploughs of some fifty negroes, drawn by two mules each. Another season of lustration by maize or cotton, and the rank soil will be ready for the cane.

The cultivation of sugar differs from that of cotton in requiring a much larger outlay of capital. There is little required for the latter besides negroes and land, which may be bought on credit, and a year's clothing and provisions. There is a gambling spice in the chances of a season which may bring wealth or ruin—a bale to the acre, which may produce 7d. per pound. In a fair year the cotton planter reckons upon ten or twelve bales to the hand, in which case the annual yield of a negro varies from £90 to £120. His enemies are drought, excessive rains, the ball worm, and the army worm; his best friend "a long picking season."

There is more steadiness in the price of sugar, and a greater certainty of an average crop. But the cost of a sugar-house, with its mill, boilers, vacuum pans, centrifugal and drying apparatus, cannot be less than £10,000, and the consumption of fuel—thousands of cords of which are cut by the "hands"—is enormous. There were cases of large fortunes earned by planting sugar with large beginnings, but these had chiefly occurred among early settlers, who had obtained their lands for a song. A Creole, who recently died at the age of fifty-five, in the neighbourhood, and who began with only a few thousand dollars, had amassed more than $1,000,000 in twenty-five years, and two of his sons—skilful planters—were likely to die each richer than his father.

This year the prospects of sugar are dreary enough, at least while the civil war lasts, and my host, with a certainty of 6,500 hogsheads upon his various plantations, has none of a market. In this respect cotton has the advantage of keeping longer than sugar. At last year's prices, and with the United States protective tariff of 20 *per cent* to shield him from foreign competition, his crop would have yielded him over £100,000. But all the sweet teeth of the Confederate States army can hardly "make a hole" in the 450,000 hogsheads which this year is expected to yield in Louisiana and Texas. Under the new tariff of the Seceding States the loss of protection to Louisiana alone may be stated, within bounds, at $8,000,000 *per annum*—which is making the planters pay pretty dear for their Secession whistle.

When I arrived at Houmas there was the greatest anxiety for rain, and over the vast, level plateau every cloud was scanned with avidity. Now, a shower seemed bearing right down upon us, when it would break, like a flying soap-bubble, and scatter its treasures short of the parched fields in which we felt interested. The wind shifted and hopes were raised that the next thunder-cloud would prove less illusory. But no!"Kenner" has got it all. On the fifth day, however, the hearts of all the planters and their parched fields were gladdened by half a day of general and generous rain, beneath which our host's cane fairly reeled and revelled. It was now safe for the season, and so was the corn. But "*one man's meat is another's poison*," and we heard more than one "Jeremiad" from those whose fields had not been placed in the condition which enabled those of our friend to carry off a potation of twelve hours of tropical rain with the ease of an alderman or a Lord Chancellor made happier or wiser by his three bottles of port.

What is termed *hacienda* in Cuba, *rancho* in Mexico, and "plantation" elsewhere, is styled "habitation" by the Creoles of Louisiana, whose ancestors began more than a century ago to reclaim its jungles.

At last "*venit summa dies et inetuctabile tempus.*" I had seen as much as might be the best phase of the great institution—less than I could desire of a most exemplary, kind-hearted, clear-headed, honest man.

In the calm of a glorious summer evening, arrayed in all the splendor of scenery that belongs to dramas in Cloudland, where mountains of snow, peopled by "*gorgons, and hydras, and chimæras dire*," rise from seas of fire that bear black barks, freighted with thunder, before the breeze of battle, we crossed the Father of Waters, waving an *adieu* to the good friend who stood on the shore, and turning our back to the home we had left behind us.

It was dark when the boat reached Donaldsonville, on the opposite "coast." I should not be surprised to hear that the founder of this remarkable city, which once contained the archives of the State, now transferred to Baton Rouge, was a North Briton. There is a simplicity and economy in the plan of the place not unfavourable to that view, but the motives which induced the Donaldson to found his Rome on the west of Bayou La Fourche from Mississippi must be a secret to all time. Much must the worthy Scot have been perplexed by his neighbors, a long-reaching colony of Spanish Creoles, who toil not and spin nothing but fishing-nets, and who live better than Solomon, and are probably as well dressed, *minus* the barbaric pearl and gold of the Hebrew potentate.

Take the odd little, retiring, modest houses which grow in the hollows of Scarborough, add to them the least imposing mansions in the natural town of Folkestone, cast them broad-sown over the surface of the Essex marshes, plant a few trees in front of them, then open a few "*café billiards*" of the camp sort along the main street, and you have done a very good Donaldsonville. A policeman welcomes us on landing, and does the honours of the market, which has a beggarly account of empty benches, the Texan bull gone into beef, and a coffee-shop. The policeman is a tall, lean, west country man; his story is simple, and he has it to tell. He was one of Dan Rice's company—a travelling Astley. He came to Donaldsonville, saw, and was conquered by one of the Spanish beauties, married her, became tavern keeper, failed, learned French, and was now constable of the parish. There was, however, a weight on his mind. He had studied the matter profoundly, but he was not near the bottom. How did the friends, relatives, and tribe of his wife live? No one could say. They reared chickens, and they caught fish; when there was a pressure on the planters, they turned out to work for 6s. 6d. a day, but those were rare occasions.

The policeman had become quite gray with excogitating the matter, and he had "nary notion of how they did it." Donaldsonville has done one fine thing. It has furnished two companies of soldiers—all

Irishmen—to the wars, and a third is in the course of formation. Not much hedging, ditching, or hard work these times for Paddy? The blacksmith, a huge tower of muscle, claims exemption on the ground that "the divil a bit of him comes from Oireland; he nivir hird av it, barrin' from the buks he rid," and is doing his best to remain behind, but popular opinion is against him. As the steamer would not be up till toward dawn, or later, it was a relief to saunter through Donaldson-ville to see society, which consisted of several gentlemen and various Jews playing games unknown to Hoyle, in oaken bar-rooms flanked by billiard tables.

My good friend the doctor, whom I had met at Houmas, who had crossed the river to see patients suffering from an attack of *Euchre*, took us round to a little club, where I was introduced to a number of gentlemen, who expressed great pleasure at seeing me, shook hands violently, and walked away; and finally we melted off into a cloud of mosquitoes by the river bank, in a box prepared for them, which was called a bedroom. These rooms were built in wood on the stage close to the river.

"Why can't I have one of these rooms?" asked I, pointing to a larger mosquito-box.

"It's engaged by ladies."

"How do you know?"

"*Parceque elles ont envoyes leur butin.*"

It was delicious to meet the French "plunder" for baggage—an old phrase so nicely rendered in the mouth of the Mississippi boatman. Having passed a night of extreme discomfiture with the winged de-mons of the box, I was aroused toward dawn by the booming of the steam drum of the boat, dipped my head in water among drowned mosquitoes, and went forth upon the landing. The policeman had just arrived. His eagle eye lighted on a large flat, on the stern of which was inscribed, "Pork, corn, butter, beef," &c. Several spry citizens were also on the platform. After salutations and compliments, policeman speaks: "When did *she* come in?" (meaning flat).

First Citizen—"In the night, I guess."

Second Citizen—"There's a lot of whiskey aboard, too."

Policeman (with pleased surprise)—"You never mean it?"

First Citizen—"Yes, Sir; one hundred and twenty gallons!"

Policeman (inspired by a bright aspiration of patriotism)—"It's a West country boat; why *don't* the citizens seize it? And whiskey rising from 17 cents to 35 cents a gallon!"

Citizens murmur approval, and I feel the whiskey part of the cargo is not safe.

"Yes, Sir," says Citizen Three, "they seize all our property at Cairey (Cairo), and I'm for making an example of this cargo."

Further reasons for the seizure of the article were adduced, and it is probable they were as strong as the whiskey, which has, no doubt, been drunk long ago on the very purest principles. In course of conversation with the Committee of Taste which had assembled, it was revealed to me that there was a strict watch kept over those boats which are freighted with whiskey forbidden to the slaves, and with principles, when they come from the West country, equally objectionable.

"Did you hear, Sir, of the chap over at Duncan Kenner's as was caught the other day?"

"No, Sir, what was it?"

"Well, Sir, he was a man that came here and went over among the niggers at Kenner's to buy their chickens from them. He was took up, and they found he'd a lot of money about him."

"Well, of course, he had money to buy the chickens."

"Yes, Sir, but it looked suspicious. He was a West country fellow, tew, and he might have meant tamperin' with 'em. Lucky he was not taken in the arternoon."

"Why so?"

"Because if the citizens had been drunk they'd have hung him on the spot."

The *Acadia* was now alongside, and in the early morning Donaldsonville receded rapidly into trees and clouds. To bed, and make amends for mosquito visits. On awaking, find that I am in the same place I started from; at least, the river looks just the same. It is difficult to believe that we have been going eleven miles an hour against the turbid river, which is of the same appearance as it was below, the same banks, bends, driftwood and trees.

Beyond the levees there were occasionally large clearings and plantations of corn and cane, of which the former predominated. The houses of the planters were not so large or so good as those on the lower banks. Large timber rafts, navigated by a couple of men, who stood in the shade of a couple of upright boards, were encountered at long intervals. The river was otherwise dead. White egrets and blue herons rose from the marshes where the banks had been bored through by crayfish, or crevasses had been formed by the waters. The fields were not much more lively, but at every landing the whites who came down were in some sort of uniform, and a few negroes were in attendance to take in or deliver goods.

There were two blacks on board in irons—captured runaways—and very miserable they looked at the thought of being restored to the bosom of the patriarchal family from which they had, no doubt, so prodigally eloped. I feared the fatted calf-skin would not be applied to their backs. The river is about half a mile wide here and is upward of one hundred feet deep. The planters' houses in groves of pecan and magnolias, with verandah and belvedere, became more frequent as the steamer approached Baton Rouge, already visible in the distance over a high bank or bluff on the right-hand side.

Before noon the steamer hauled alongside a stationary hulk, which once "walked the waters" by the aid of machinery, but which was now used as a floating hotel, depot, and storehouse—three hundred and fifteen feet long, and fully thirty feet on the upper deck above the level of the river. Here were my quarters till the boat for Natchez should arrive. The proprietor was somewhat excited on my arrival because my servants was away. "Where have you been, you ——?"

"Away to buy de newspaper, Massa."

"For who, you ——?"

"Me buy 'em for no one, Massa; me sell 'um agin, Massa."

"See now, you ——, if ever you goes aboard to meddle with newspapers, I'm —— but I'll kill you, mind that!"

Baton Rouge is the capital of the State of Louisiana, and the State House is a quaint and very new example of bad taste. The Deaf and Dumb Asylum near it is in a much better style. It was my intention to visit the State Prison and Penitentiary, but the day was too hot, and the distance too great, and so I dined at the oddest little Creole restaurant, with the funniest old hostess and the strangest company in the world. On returning to the boat hotel, Mr. Conrad, one of the citizens of the place, and Mr. W. Avery, a Judge of the Court, were good enough to call to invite me to visit them, but I was obliged to decline. The old gentlemen were both members of the Home Guard, and drilled assiduously every evening. Of the one thousand three hundred voters at Baton Rouge, more than seven hundred and fifty are already off to the wars, and another company is being formed to follow them. Mr. Conrad has three sons in the field already.

The waiter who served our drinks in the bar wore a uniform, and his musket lay in the corner among the brandy bottles. At night a patriotic meeting of citizen soldiery took place in the bow, in which song and whiskey had much to do, so that sleep was difficult; but at seven o'clock on Wednesday morning the *Mary T.* came alongside, and soon afterward bore me on to Natchez through scenery which became wilder and less cultivated as she got upward. Of the one thousand five hundred steamers on the river not a tithe are now in employment, and the owners are in a bad way. It was late at night when the steamer arrived at Natchez, and next morning early I took shelter in another engineless steamer, which was thought to be an hotel by its owners.

Old negress on board, however, said, "There was nothing for breakfast; go to Curry's on shore. Walk up hill to Curry's—a bar-room, a waiter and flies."

"Can I have any breakfast?"

"No, Sir-ree; it's over half an hour ago."

"Nothing to eat at all?"

"No, Sir."

"Can I get something anywhere else?"

"I guess not."

It had been my belief that a man with money in his pocket could not starve in any country *soi-disant* civilized life. Exceptions prove rules, but they are disagreeable things. I chewed the cud of fancy *faute de mieux*, and became the centre of attraction to citizens, from whose conversation I learned that this was "Jeff. Davis's fast day."

Observed one, "It quite puts me in mind of Sunday: all the stores closed."

Said another, "We'll soon have Sunday every day, then, for I 'spect it won't be worthwhile for most shops to keep open any longer."

Natchez, a place of much trade and cotton export in the season, is now as dull—let us say as Harwich without a regatta. But it is ultra-secessionist, *nil obstante*. My hunger was assuaged by a friend who drove me up to his comfortable mansion through a country not unlike the wooded parts of Sussex, abounding in fine trees, and in the only lawns and park-like fields I have yet seen in America. In the evening, after dinner, my host drove me over to visit a small encampment under a wealthy planter, who has raised, equipped, and armed his company at his own expense.

We were obliged to get out at a narrow lane and walk toward the encampment on foot; a sentry stopped us, and we observed that there was a semblance of military method in the camp. The captain was walking up and down in the verandah of the poor, deserted hut for which he had abandoned his splendid home. *A Book of Tactics* (Hardee's)—which is, in part, a translation of the French *Manual*—lay on the table. Our friend was full of fight, and said he would give all he had in the world to the cause. But the day before, and a party of horse, composed of sixty gentlemen in the district, with from £20,000 to £50,000 each, had started for the war in Virginia. Everything to be seen or heard testifies to the great zeal and resolution with which the South have entered upon the quarrel. But they hold the power of the United States and the loyalty of the North to the Union at far too cheap a rate.

Next day was passed in a delightful drive through cotton fields, Indian corn, and undulating woodlands, amid which were some charming residences. I crossed the river at Natchez, and saw one fine plantation in which the corn, however, was by no means so fine as I have often seen. The cotton looks well, and some had already burst into flower—bloom, as it is called—which had turned to a flagrant pink, and seemed saucily conscious that its boll would play an important part in the world. In this part of Mississippi the secessionist feeling was not so overpowering at first as it has been since the majority declared itself, but the expression of feeling is now all one way. The rage of Southern sentiment is to me inexplicable, making every allowance for Southern exaggeration. It is sudden, hot, and apparently causeless as summer lightning.

From every place I touched at along the Mississippi, a large proportion of the population has gone forth to fight, or is preparing to do so. The whispers which rise through the storm are few and feeble. Some there are who sigh for the peace and happiness they have seen in England. But they cannot seek those things; they must look after their property. Each man maddens his neighbour by desperate resolves, and threats, and vows. Their faith is in Jefferson Davis's strength, and in the necessities and weakness of France and England. The inhabitants of the tracts which lie on the banks of the Mississippi, and on the inland regions hereabout, ought to be, in the natural order of things, a people almost nomadic, living by the chase and by a sparse agriculture, in the freedom which tempted their ancestors to leave Europe.

But the Old World has been working for them. All its trials have been theirs; the fruits of its experience, its labours, its research, its discoveries, are theirs. Steam has enabled them to turn their rivers into highways, to open primeval forests to the light of day and to man. All these, however, would have availed them little had not the demands of manufacture abroad, and the increasing luxury and population of the North and West at home, enabled them to find in these swamps and uplands sources of wealth richer and more certain than all the gold mines of the world. But there must be gnomes to work those mines. Slavery was an institution ready to their hands. In its development there lay every material means for securing the prosperity which Manchester opened to them, and in supplying their own countrymen with sugar. The small, struggling, deeply mortgaged proprietors of swamp and forest set their negroes to work to raise levees, to cut down trees, to plant and sow.

As the negro became valuable by his produce, the Irish emigrant took his place in the severer labours of the plantation, and ditched and dug, and cut into the waste land. Cotton at ten cents a pound gave a nugget in every boll. Land could be had for a few dollars an acre. Negroes were cheap in proportion. Men who made a few thousand dollars, invested them in more negroes and more land, and borrowed as much again for the same purpose. They waxed fat and rich—there seemed no bounds to their fortune. But threatening voices came from the North—the echoes of the sentiments of the civilized world repenting of its evil pierced their ears, and they found their feet were of clay, and that they were nodding to their fall in the midst of their power. Ruin inevitable awaited them if they did not shut out these sounds and stop the fatal utterances.

The issue is to them one of life and death. Whoever raises it hereafter, if it be not decided now, must expect to meet the deadly animosity which is displayed toward the North. The success of the South—if it can succeed—must lead to complications and results in other parts of the world for which neither it nor Europe is now prepared. Of one thing there can be no doubt—a Slave State cannot long exist without a slave-trade. The poor whites who will have won the fight will demand their share of the spoils. The land is abundant, and all that is wanted to give them fortunes is a supply of slaves. They will have them in spite of their masters, unless a stronger power prevents the accomplishment of their wishes.

Letter 14

Cairo, Ill., June 20, 1861.

My last letter was dated from Natchez, but it will probably accompany this communication, as there are no mails now between the North and the South, or *vice versa*. Tolerably confident in my calculations that nothing of much importance could take place in the field till some time after I had reached my post, it appeared to me desirable to see as much of the South as I could, and to form an estimate of the strength of the Confederation, although it could not be done at this time of the year without considerable inconvenience, arising from the heat, which renders it almost impossible to write in the day, and from the mosquitoes, which come out when the sun goes down, and raise a blister at every stroke of the pen. On several days lately the thermometer has risen to ninety-eight degrees—on one day to one hundred and five degrees—in the shade.

On Friday evening, June 14, I started from Natchez for Vicksburg on board the steamer *General Quitman*, up the Mississippi. These long yellow rivers are very fine for patriots to talk about, for poets to write about, for buffalo fish to live in, and for steamers to navigate when there are no snags, but I confess the Father of Waters is extremely tiresome. Even the good cheer and the comfort of the *General Quitman* could not reconcile me to the eternal beating of steam drums, blowing whistles, bumpings at landings, and the general oppression of levees, clearings, and plantations, which marked the course of the river, and I was not sorry next morning when Vicksburg came in sight on the left bank of the giant stream—a city on a hill, not very large, besteepled, becupolaed, large-hoteled.

Here lives a man who has been the pioneer of hotels in the West, and who has now established himself in a big caravanserai, which he rules in a curious fashion. M'Makin has, he tells us, been rendered

176

famous by Sir Charles Lyell. The large dining room—a stall, *à manger*, as a friend of mine called it—is filled with small tables covered with parti-coloured cloths. At the end is a long deal table, heavy with dishes of meat and vegetables, presided over by negresses and gentlemen of uncertain hue. In the centre of the room stood my host, shouting out at the top of his voice the names of the joints, and recommending his guests to particular dishes, very much as the chronicler tells us was the wont of the taverners in old London. Many little negroes ran about in attendance, driven hither and thither by the command of their white Soulouque—white-teethed, pensive-eyed, but sad as memory.

"Are you happy here " asked I of one of them who stood by my chair. He looked uneasy and frightened. "Why don't you answer?"

"I'se feared to tell dat to massa."

"Why, your master is kind to you?"

"Berry good man, sir, when he not angry wid me!" And the little fellow's eyes filled with tears at some recollection which pained him. I asked no more.

Vicksburg is secessionist. There were hundreds of soldiers in the streets, many in the hotel, and my host said some hundreds of Irish had gone off to the wars, to fight for the good cause. If Mr. O'Connell were alive, he would surely be pained to see the course taken by so many of his countrymen on this question. After dinner I was invited to attend a meeting of some of the citizens at the railway station, where the time passed very agreeably till four o'clock, when the train started for Jackson, the capital of Mississippi; and after a passage of two hours through a poor, clay country, seared with water-courses and gullies, with scanty crops of Indian corn and very backward cotton, we were deposited in that city. It must be called a city.

It is the State capital, but otherwise there is no reason why, in strict nomenclature, it should be designated by any such title. It is in the usual style of the "cities" which spring up in the course of a few years amid the stumps of half-cleared fields in the wilderness— wooden houses, stores kept by Germans, French, Irish, Italians; a large hotel swarming with people, with a noisy billiard-room and a noisier bar, the arena and the cause of "difficulties;" wooden houses, with portentous and pretentious white porticoes, and pillars of all the Grecian orders: a cupola or two, and two or three steeples, too large for the feeble bodies beneath—hydrocephalic architecture; a State house, looking well at a distance, ragged, dirty, and mean within; groups of idlers in front of "Exchange," where the business transacted consists of a barter between money or credit and "drinks" of various stimulants; a secluded telegraph office round a corner; a forward newspaper office in the street, and a population of negroes shuffling through the thick dust which forms the streets.

I called on Mr. Pettus, the governor of the State of Mississippi, according to invitation, and found him in the State House in a very poor room, with broken windows and ragged carpets and dilapidated furniture. He is a grim, silent man, tobacco-ruminant, abrupt-speeched, firmly believing that the state of society in which he exists, wherein there are monthly foul murders perpetrated at the very seat of government, is the most free and civilized in the world. He is easy of access to all, and men sauntered in and out of his office just as they would walk into a public house. Once on a time, indeed, the governor was a deer hunter in the forest, and lived far away from the haunts of men, and he is proud of the fact. He is a strenuous seceder, and has done high-handed things in his way—simple apparently, honest probably, fierce certainly—and he lives, while he is governor, on his salary of $4,000 a year in the house provided for him by the State. There was not much to say on either side. I can answer for one.

Next day being Sunday I remained at rest in the house of a friend listening to local stories—not *couleur de rose*, but of a deeper tint—blood-red—how such a man shot another, and was afterwards stabbed by a third; how this fellow and his friends hunted down in broad day and murdered one obnoxious to them—tale after tale such as I have heard through the South and seen daily narratives of in the papers. Aceldama! No security for life! Property is quite safe. Its proprietor is in imminent danger, were it only from stray bullets when he turns a corner. The "bar," the "drink," the savage practice of walking about with pistol and poniard—ungovernable passions ungoverned because there is no law to punish the deeds to which they lead—these are the causes of acts which would not be tolerated in the worst days of Corsican *vendette*, and which must be put down, or the countries in which they are unpunished will become as barbarous as jungles of wild beasts. In the evening I started by railroad for the city of Memphis, in Mississippi.

There was a sleeping car on the train, but the flying bug and the creature less volatile, more pungent and persistent, which bears its name, murdered sleep, and when Monday morning came I was glad to arise and get into one of the carriages, although it was full of noisy soldiers bound to the camp at Corinth, in the State of Mississippi,

who had been drinking whiskey all night, and were now scream-
ing for water and howling like demons. At Holly Spring, where a
rude breakfast awaited us, the warriors got out on the top of the carriages and performed a war dance to the music of their band, which
was highly creditable to the carriage-maker's workmanship. Along the
road at all the settlements and clearings the white people cheered, and
the women waved white things, and secession flags floated. There is no
doubt of the state of feeling in this part of the country; and yet it does
not look much worth fighting for—an arid soil, dry water-courses,
clay ravines, light crops. Perhaps it will be better a month hence, and
negroes may make it pay. There were many in the fields, and it struck
me they looked better than those who work in gangs on the larger
and richer plantations.

Among our passengers were gentlemen from Texas going to Richmond to offer services to Mr. Davis. They declared the feeling in their
State was almost without exception in favour of secession. It is as
astonishing how positive all these people are that England is in absolute dependence on cotton for her national existence. They are at
once savage and childish. If England does not recognize the Southern
Confederacy pretty quick, they will pass a resolution not to let her
have any cotton, except, &c. Suppose England does ever recognize a
Confederation based on the principles of the South, what guarantee is
there that in her absolute dependence, if it exists, similar coercive steps
may not be taken against her? "Oh! we shall be friends, you know;"
and so on.

On the train before us there had just passed on a company armed
with large bowie-knives and rifled pistols, who called themselves the
"Toothpick Company." They carried a coffin along with them, on
which was a plate with "Abe Lincoln" inscribed on it, and they amused
themselves with the childish conceit of telling the people as they went
along that "they were bound" to bring his body back in it. At Grand
Junction Station the troops got out and were mustered preparatory to
their transfer to a train for Richmond, in Virginia. The first company,
about seventy strong, consisted exclusively of Irish, who were armed
with rifles without bayonets. The second consisted of fifty-six Irish,
armed mostly with muskets; the third were of Americans, who were
well uniformed, but had no arms with them. The fourth, clad in green,
were nearly all Irish; they wore all sorts of clothing, and had no pre-
tensions to be regarded as disciplined soldiers.

I am led to believe that the great number of Irish who have enlisted for service indicates a total suspension of all the works on which they are ordinarily engaged in the South. They were not very orderly. "Fix bayonets," elicited a wonderful amount of controversy in the ranks. "Whar are yer dhrivin to?" "Sullivan, don't yer hear we're to fix beenits." "Ayse the strap of mee baynit, sargint, jewel!" "If ye prod me wid that agin, I'll let dayloite into ye." Officer, reading muster—"No. 23, James Phelan." No reply. Voice from the ranks—"Faith Phelan's gone; sure he wint at the last dipot."

Old men and boys were mixed together, but the mass of the rank and file were strong, full-grown men. In one of the carriages were some women dressed as "*vivandieres*," minus the *coquet* air and the trousers and boots of those ladies. They looked sad, sorry, dirty, and foolish. There was a great want of water along the line, and the dust and heat were very great and disagreeable. When they have to march many of the men will break down, owing to bad shoes and the weight of clothes and trash of various kinds they sling on their shoulders. They moved off amid much whooping, and our journey was continued through a country in which the railroad engineer had made the only opening for miles at a time.

When a clearing was reached, however, there were signs that the soil was not without richness, and all the wheat was already cut and in sheaf. The passengers said it was fine and early, and that it averaged from forty to sixty bushels to the acre (more than it looked). Very little ground here is under cotton. It was past one o'clock on Monday when the train reached Memphis, in Tennessee, which is situated on a high bluff overhanging the Mississippi. Here is one of the strategic positions of the Confederates. It is now occupied by a force of the Tennesseans, which is commanded by Major-General Pillow, whom I found quartered in Gayoso House, a large hotel, named after one of the old Spanish rulers here, and as he was just starting to inspect his batteries and the camp at Randolph, sixty odd miles higher up the river, I could not resist his pressing invitations, tired as I was, to accompany him and his staff on board the *Ingomar*, to see what they were really like.

First we visited the bluff on the edge of which is constructed a breastwork of cotton bales, which no infantry could get at, and which would offer no resistance to vertical and but little to horizontal fire. It is placed so close to the edge of the bluff at various places that shell and shot would knock away the bank from under it. The river rolls below deep and strong, and across the roads or water-courses leading to it are feeble barricades of plank, which a howitzer would shiver to pieces in a few rounds. Higher up the bank, on a commanding plateau, there is a breastwork and parapet, within which are six guns, and the general informed me he intended to mount thirteen guns at this part of the river which would certainly prove very formidable to such steamers as they had on these waters, if any attempt were made to move from Cairo.

In the course of the day I was introduced to exactly seventeen colonels and one captain. My happiness was further increased by an introduction to a youth of some twenty-three years of age, with tender feet if I may judge from prunella slippers, dressed in a green cutaway, jean pants, and a tremendous *sombrero* with a plume of ostrich feathers, and gold tassels looped at the side, who had the air and look of an apothecary's errand boy. This was "General" Maggles (let us say) of Arkansas. Freighted deeply with the brave, the *Ingomar* started for her voyage, and we came alongside the bank at Chickasaw Bluffs, too late to visit the camp, as it was near midnight before we arrived. I forgot to say that a large number of steamers were lying at Memphis, which had been seized by General Pillow, and he has forbidden all traffic in boats to Cairo. Passengers must go round by rail to Columbus.

June 18.—I have just returned from a visit to the works and batteries at the intrenched camp at Randolph's Point, sixty miles above Memphis, by which it is intended to destroy any flotilla coming down the river from Cairo, and to oppose any force coming by land to cover its flank, and clear the left bank of the Mississippi. The *Ingomar* is lying under the rugged bank, or bluff, about 150 feet high, which recedes in rugged tumuli and watercourses filled with brushwood from the margin of the river, some half mile up and down the stream at this point, and Brigadier-General Pillow is still riding round his well-beloved earthworks and his quaint battalions, while I, anxious to make the most of my time now that I am fairly on the run for my base of operations, have come on board, and am now writing in the cabin, a long-roofed room, with berths on each side, which runs from stem to stern of the American boats over the main deck. This saloon presents a curious scene.

Over the bow, at one side, there is an office for the sale of tickets, now destitute of business, for the *Ingomar* belongs to the State of Tennessee; at the other side is a bar, where thirsty souls, who have hastened on board from the camp for a *julep*, a smash, or a cocktail, learn with disgust that the only article to be had is fine Mississippi water with ice in it. Lying on the deck in all attitudes are numbers of men asleep, whose plumed felt hats are the only indications that they are soldiers, except in the rare case of those who have rude uniforms, and buttons and stripes of coloured cloth on the legs of their pantaloons.

A sentry is sitting on a chair smoking a cigar. He is on guard over the after part of the deck, called the ladies' saloon, and sacred to the general and his staff and attendants. He is a tall, good-looking young fellow, in a gray flannel shirt, a black wide-awake, gray trowsers, fastened by a belt, on which is a brass buckle inscribed "U. S." His rifle is an Enfield, and the bayonet-sheath is fastened to the belt by a thong of leather. That youthful patriot is intent on the ups and downs of fortune as exemplified in the pleasing game of *euchre*, or *euker*, which is exercising the faculties of several of his comrades, who, in their shirt-sleeves, are employing the finest faculties of their nature in that national institution; but he is not indifferent to his duties, and he forbids your correspondent's entrance until he has explained what he wants, and who he is, and the second is more easy to do than the first.

The sentry tells his captain, who is an *euchreist*, that "It's all right," and resumes his seat and his cigar, and the work goes bravely on. Indeed, it went on last night at the same table, which is within a few yards of the general's chair; and now that I have got a scrap of paper and a moment of quiet, let me say what I have to say of this position, and of what I saw—pleasant things they would be to the Federalist general up at Cairo, if he could hear them in time, unless he is as little prepared as his antagonist. On looking out of my cabin this morning, I saw the high and rugged bluff of which I have spoken on the left bank of the river. A few ridge-poled tents, pitched under the shade of some trees, on a small spur of the slope, was the only indication immediately visible of a martial character. But a close inspection in front enabled me to detect two earthworks mounted with guns, on the side of the bank, considerably higher than the river, and three heavy guns, possibly 42-pounders, lay in the dust close to the landing-place, with very rude carriages and bullock-poles to carry them to the batteries.

A few men, ten or twelve in number, were digging at an encampment on the face of the slope. Others were lounging about the beach, and others, under the same infatuation as that which makes little boys disport in the Thames under the notion that they are washing themselves, were bathing in the Mississippi. A dusty cart track wound up to the brow of the bluff, and there disappeared. Some carts toiled up and down between the boat and the crest of the hill. We went on shore. There was no ostentation of any kind about the reception of the general and his staff. A few horses were waiting impatiently in the sun, for the flies will have their way, and heavy men are not so unbearable as small mosquitoes.

With a cloud of colonels—one late United Statesman, who was readily distinguishable by his air from the volunteers—the general proceeded to visit his batteries and his men. The first work inspected was a plain parapet of earth, placed some fifty feet above the river, and protected very slightly by two small flanking parapets. Six guns, 32-pounders, and howitzers of an old pattern were mounted *en barbette*, without any traverses whatever. The carriages rested on rough platforms, and the wheels ran on a traversing semicircle of plank, as the iron rails were not yet ready. The gunners, a plain looking body of men, very like railway labourers and mechanics without uniform, were engaged at drill. It was neither quick nor good work—about equal to the average of a squad after a couple of days' exercise; but the men worked earnestly, and I have no doubt, if the Federalists give them time, they will prove artillerymen in the end. The general ordered practice to be made with round shot.

After some delay, a kind of hybrid ship's carronade was loaded. The target was a tree, about two thousand five hundred yards distant, I was told. It appeared to me about one thousand seven hundred yards off. Everyone was desirous of seeing the shot; but we were at the wrong side for the wind, and I ventured to say so. However, the general thought and said otherwise. The word "Fire!" was given. Alas? the friction-tube would not explode. It was one of a new sort, which the Tennesseans are trying their 'prentice hand at. A second ball answered better. The gun went off, but where the ball went to no one could say, as the smoke came into our eyes. The party moved to windward, and, after another fuse had missed, the gun was again discharged at some five degrees elevation, and the shot fell in good line, two hundred yards short of the target, and did not ricochet.

Gun No. 2 was then discharged, and off went the ball, at no particular mark, down the river; but if it did go off, so did the gun also, for it gave a frantic leap and jumped with the carriage off the platform; nor was this wonderful, for it was an old-fashioned chamber carronade or howitzer, which had been loaded with a full charge, and solid shot enough to make it burst with indignation. Turning from this battery, we visited another nearer the water, with four guns (32-

pounders), which were well placed to sweep the channel with greater chance of ricochet; and higher on the bank, toward a high peak commanding the Mississippi, here about seven hundred yards broad, and a small confluent which runs into it, was another battery of two guns, with a very great command, but only fit for shell, as the fire must be plunging.

All these batteries were very ill constructed, and in only one was the magazine under decent cover. In the first it was in rear of the battery, up the hill behind it. The parapets were of sand or soft earth, unprovided with merlons. The last had a few sand-bags between the guns. Riding up a steep road, we came to the camps of the men on the wooded and undulating plateau over the river, which is broken by water-courses into ravines covered with brushwood and forest trees. For five weeks the Tennessee troops under General Pillow, who is at the head of the forces of the State, have been working at a series of curious intrenchments which are supposed to represent an intrenched camp, and which look like an assemblage of mud beaver dams. In a word, they are so complicated that they would prove exceedingly troublesome to the troops engaged in their defence, and it would require very steady, experienced regulars to man them so as to give proper support to each other.

The maze of breastworks, of flanking parapets, of parapets for field-pieces, is overdone. Several of them might prove useful to an attacking force. In some places the wood was cut down in front, so as to form a formidable natural abattis; but generally here, as in the batteries below, timber and brushwood were left uncut up to easy musket shot of the works, so as to screen an advance of riflemen, and to expose the defending force to considerable annoyance. In small camps of fifteen or twenty tents each the Tennessee troops were scattered, for health sake, over the plateau, and on the level ground a few companies were engaged at drill. The men were dressed and looked like labouring people—small farmers, mechanics, with some small, undersized lads. The majority were in their shirt sleeves, and the awkwardness with which they handled their arms showed that, however good they might be as shots, they were by no means proficients in manual exercise. Indeed, they could not be, as they have been only five weeks in the service of the State called out in anticipation of the secession vote, and since then they have been employed by General Pillow on his fortifications.

They have complained more than once of their hard work, particularly when it was accompanied by hard fare, and one end of General Pillow's visit, was to inform them that they would soon be relieved from their labours by negroes and hired labourers. Their tents, small ridge-poles, are very bad, but suited, perhaps, to the transport. Each contains six men. I could get no accurate account of their rations even from the quartermaster-general, and commissary-general there was none present; but I was told that they had "a sufficiency—from ¾ lb. to 1¼ lb. of meat, of bread, of sugar, coffee, and rice, daily." Neither spirits nor tobacco is served out to these terrible chewers and not unaccomplished drinkers

Their pay "will be" the same as in the United States Army or the Confederate States Army—probably paid in the circulating medium of the latter. Seven or eight hundred men were formed in line for inspection. There were few of the soldiers in any kind of uniform, and such uniforms as I saw were in very bad taste, and consisted of gaudy facings and stripes on very strange garments. They were armed with old-pattern percussion muskets, and their ammunition pouches were of diverse sorts. Shoes often bad, knapsacks scarce, head-pieces of every kind of shape—badges worked on the front or sides, tinsel in much request. Every man had a tin water-flask and a blanket. The general addressed the men, who were in line two deep (many of them unmistakably Irishmen), and said what generals usually say on such occasions—compliments for the past, encouragement for the future. "When the hour of danger comes I will be with you."

They did not seem to care much whether he was or not; and, indeed, General Pillow, in a round hat, dusty black frock coat, and ordinary "unstriped" trowsers, did not look like one who could give any great material accession to the physical means of resistance, although he is a very energetic man. The major-general, in fact, is an attorney-at-law, or has been so, and was partner with Mr. Polk, who, probably from some of the reasons which determine the actions of partners to each other, sent Mr. Pillow to the Mexican war, where he nearly lost him, owing to severe wounds received in action. The general has made his entrenchments as if he were framing an indictment. There is not a flaw for an enemy to get through. but he has bound up his own men in inexorable lines also.

At one of the works a proof of the freedom of "citizen soldiery" was afforded in a little hilarity on the part of one of the privates. The men had lined the parapet, and had listened to the pleasant assurances of their commander, that they would knock off the shovel and the hoe very soon, and be replaced by the eternal gentlemen of colour. "Three cheers for General Pillow" were called for, and were responded to by the whooping and screeching sounds that pass muster in this part of the world for cheers. As they ended, a stentorian voice shouted out, "Who cares for General Pillow?" and, as no one answered, it might be unfairly inferred that gallant officer was not the object of the favour or solicitude of his troops; probably a temporary unpopularity connected with the hard work, found expression in the daring question.

Randolph's Point is, no doubt, a very strong position. The edges of the plateau command the rear of the batteries below; the ravines in the bluff would give cover to a large force of riflemen, who could render the batteries untenable if taken from the river face, unless the camp in their rear on the top of the plateau was carried. Great loss of life, and probable failure, would result from any attack on the works from the river merely. But a flotilla might get past the guns without any serious loss in the present state of their service and equipment; and there is nothing I saw to prevent the landing of a force on the banks of the river, which, with a combined action on the part of an adequate force of gunboats, could carry the position.

As the river falls the round-shot fire from the guns will be even less effective. The general is providing water for the camps by means of large cisterns dug in the ground, which will be filled with water from the river by steam power. The officers of the Army of Tennessee with whom I spoke were plain, farmerly planters, merchants, and lawyers; and the heads of the department were in no respect better than their inferiors by reason of any military acquirements, but were shrewd, energetic, common-sense men. The officer in command of the works, however, understood his business, apparently, and was well supported by the artillery officer. There were, I was told, eight pieces of field artillery disposable for the defence of the camp.

Having returned to the steamer, the party proceeded up the river to another small camp in defence of a battery of four guns, or rather of a small parallelogram of soft sand covering a man a little higher than the knee, with four guns mounted in it on the river face. No communication exists through the woods between the two camps, which must be six or seven miles apart. The force stationed here was composed principally of gentlemen. They were all in uniform. A detachment worked one of the guns, which the general wished to see fired with round shot.

In five or six minutes after the order was given the gun was loaded, and the word given, "Fire." The gunner pulled the lanyard hard, but the tube did not explode. Another was tried. A strong jerk pulled it out bent and incombustible. A third was inserted, which came out broken. The fourth time was the charm, and the ball was projected about 60 yards to the right, and 100 yards short of the mark—a stump, some 1,200 yards distant, in the river. It must be remembered that there are no disparts, tangents, or elevating screws to the guns; the officer was obliged to lay it by the eye with a plain chock of wood. The general explained that the friction tubes were the results of an experiment he was making to manufacture them; but I agreed with one of the officers, who muttered in my ear, "The old linstock and portfire are a darned deal better."

There were no shells, I could see, in the battery, and, on inquiry, I learned the fuses were made of wood at Memphis, and were not considered by the officers at all trustworthy. Powder is so scarce that all salutes are interdicted, except to the governor of the State. In the two camps there were, I was informed, about 4,000 men. My eyesight, so far as I went, confirmed me of the existence of some 1,800, but I did not visit all the outlying tents. On landing the band had played "God Save the Queen" and "Dixie's Land;" on returning we had the "*Marseillaise*" and the national anthem of the Southern Confederation; and, by way of parenthesis, it may be added, if you do not already know the fact, that "Dixie's Land" is a synonym for Heaven.

It appears that there was once a good planter, named "Dixie," who died at some period unknown, to the intense grief of his animated property. They found expression for their sorrow in song, and consoled themselves by clamouring in verse for their removal to the land to which Dixie had departed, and where probably the revered spirit would be greatly surprised to find himself in their company. Whether they were ill-treated after he died, and thus had reason to deplore his removal, or merely desired Heaven in the abstract, nothing known enables me to assert. But Dixie's Land is now generally taken to mean the Seceded States, where Mr. Dixie certainly is not at this present writing. The song and air are the composition of the organized African Association for the advancement of music and their own profit, which sings in New York, and it may be as well to add, that in all my tour in the South I heard little melody from lips black or white, and only once heard negroes singing in the fields.

Several sick men were put on board the steamer, and were laid on mattresses on deck. I spoke to them, and found they were nearly all suffering from diarrheal, and that they had no medical attendance in camp. All the doctors went to fight, and the Medical Service of the Tennessee troops is very defective. As I was going down the river I had some interesting conversation with General Clark, who commands about 5,000 troops of the Confederate States, at present quartered in two camps at Tennessee on these points. He told me the commissariat and the Medical Service had given him great annoyance, and confesses some desertions and courts-martial had occurred.

Guard-mounting and its accessory duties were performed in a most slovenly manner, and the German troops from the Southern parts were particularly disorderly. It was late in the afternoon when I reached Memphis. I may mention, *obiter*, that the captain of the steamer, talking of arms, gave me a notion of the sense of security he felt on board his vessel. From under his pillow he pulled one of his two Derringer pistols, and out of his clothes-press he produced a long heavy rifle and a double gun, which was, he said, capital with ball and buckshot.

June 19.—Up at 3 o'clock, a. m., to get ready for the train at 5, which will take me out of Dixie's Land to Cairo. If the owners of the old hostelries in the Egyptian city were at all like their Tennessean fellow craftsmen in the upstart institution which takes its name, I wonder how Herodotus managed to pay his way. My sable attendant quite entered into our feelings, and was rewarded accordingly. At 5 a. m., covered with dust, contracted in a drive through the streets which seem *"paved with waves of mud,"* to use the phrase of a Hibernian gentlemen connected with the baggage department of the omnibus, *"only the mud was all dust,"* to use my own, I started in the cars along with some Confederate officers and several bottles of whiskey, which at that early hour was considered by my unknown companions as a highly efficient prophylactic against the morning dews; but it appeared that these dews are of such a deadly character that, in order to guard against their effects, one must become dead drunk.

The same remedy, I am assured, is sovereign against rattlesnake bites. I can assure the friends of these gentlemen that they were amply fortified against any amount of dew or of rattlesnake poison before they got to the end of their whiskey, so great was the supply. By the Memphis papers it seems as if the institution of blood prevailed there as in New Orleans, for I read in my paper as I went along of two murders and one shooting as the incidents of the previous day, contributed by "the local." To contrast with this low state of social existence, there must be a high condition of moral feeling, for the journal I was reading contained a very elaborate article to show the wickedness of any one paying his debts, and of any State acknowledging its liabilities, which would constitute an invaluable *vade mecum* for Basinghall Street.

At Humboldt, there was what was called a change of cars—a process that all the philosophy of the Baron could not have enabled him to endure without some loss of temper, for there was a whole Kosmos of Southern patriotism assembled at the station, burning with the fires of Liberty, and bent on going to the camp at Union City, forty-six miles away, where the Confederate forces of Tennessee, aided by Mississippi regiments, are out under the greenwood tree. Their force was irresistible, particularly as there were numbers of relentless citizenesses—what the American papers call "quite a crowd"—as the advanced guard of the invading army. While the original occupants were being compressed or expelled by crinoline—that all-absorbing, defensive, and aggressive article of feminine war reigns here in widespread, iron-bound circles—I took refuge on the platform, where I made, in an involuntary way, a good many acquaintances in this sort: "Sir, my name is Jones—Judge Jones of Pumpkin County. I am happy to know you, Sir." We shake hands affectionately.

"Colonel," (Jones *loquitur*) "allow me to introduce you to my friend Mr. Scribble! Colonel Maggs, Mr. Scribble."

The colonel shakes hands, and immediately darts off to a circle of his friends, whom he introduces, and they each introduce someone else to me, and, finally, I am introduced to the engine-driver, who is really an acquaintance of value, for he is good enough to give me a seat on his engine, and the bell tolls, the steam-trumpet bellows, and we move from the station an hour behind time, and with twice the number of passengers the cars were meant to contain. Our engineer did his best to overcome his difficulties, and we rushed rapidly, if not steadily, through a wilderness of forest and tangled brakes, through which the rail, without the smallest justification, performed curves and twists, indicative of a desire on the part of the engineer to consume the greatest amount of rail on the shortest extent of line.

My companion was a very intelligent Southern gentlemen, formerly editor of a newspaper. We talked of the crime of the country, of the brutal shootings and stabbings which disgraced it. He admitted their existence with regret but he could advise and suggest no remedy. "The rowdies have rushed in upon us, so that we can't master them."

"Is the law powerless?"

"Well, Sir, you see these men got hold of those who should administer the law, or they are too powerful or too reckless to be kept down."

"That is a reign of terror—of mob-ruffianism!"

"It don't hurt respectable people much, but I agree with you it must be put down."

"When—how?"

"Well, Sir, when things are settled we'll just take the law into our own hands. Not a man shall have a vote unless he's American born, and by degrees we'll get rid of these men who disgrace us.?"

"Are not many of your regiments composed of Germans and Irish—of foreigners, in fact?"

"Yes, Sir."

I did not suggest to him the thought which rose in my mind, that these gentlemen, if successful, would be very little inclined to abandon their rights while they had arms in their hands, but it occurred to me as well that this would be rather a poor reward for the men who were engaged in establishing the Southern Confederacy. The attempt may fail, but assuredly I have heard it expressed too often to doubt that there is a determination on the part of the leaders in the movement to take away the suffrage from the men whom they do not scruple to employ in fighting their battles. If they cut the throats of the enemy they will stifle their own sweet voices at the same time, or soon afterward—a capital recompense to their emigrant soldiers!

The portion of Tennessee traversed by the railroad is not very attractive, for it is nearly uncleared. In the sparse clearings were fields of Indian corn, growing amid blackened stumps of trees and rude log shanties, and the white population which looked out on us was poorly housed, at least, if not badly clad. At last we reached Corinth. It would have been scarcely recognizable by Mummius—even if he had ruined his old handiwork over again. This proudly-named spot consisted apparently of a grog-shop in wood, and three shanties of a similar material, with out-offices to match, and the Acro-Corinth was a grocery store, of which the proprietors had no doubt gone to the wars, as it was shut up, and their names were suspiciously Milesian. But, if Corinth was not imposing, Troy, which we reached after a long run through a forest of virgin timber, was still simpler in architecture and general design. It was too new for "*Troja fuit*," and the general "fixins" would scarcely authorize one to say to hope *Troja fuerit*.

The Dardanian Towers were represented by a timber-house, and Helen the Second—whom we may take on this occasion to have been simulated by an old lady smoking a pipe, whom I saw in the verandah—could have set them on fire much more readily than did her interesting prototype ignite the City of Priam. The rest of the place and of the inhabitants, as I saw it and them, might be considered as an agglomerate of three or four sheds, a few log huts, a saw-mill, and some twenty negroes sitting on a log and looking at the train. From Troy the road led to a cypress swamp, over which the engines bustled, rattled, tumbled, and hopped at a perilous rate along a high trestlework, and at last we came to "Union City," which seemed to be formed by great aggregate meetings of discontented shavings which had been whiled into heaps out of the forest hard by. But here was the camp of the Confederates, which so many of our fellow-passengers were coming out into the wilderness to see.

Their white tents and plank huts gleamed through the green of oak and elm, and hundreds of men came out to the platform to greet their friends, and to inquire for baskets, boxes, and hampers, which put me in mind of the quartermaster's store at Balaklava. We have all heard of the unhappy medical officer who exhausted his resources to get up a large chest from that store to the camp, and who on opening it, in the hope of finding inside the articles he was most in need of, discovered that it contained an elegant assortment of wooden legs; but he could not have been so much disgusted as a youthful warrior here who was handed a wicker-covered jar from the luggage van, which he "tapped" on the spot, expecting to find it full of Bourbon whiskey, or something equally good. He raised the ponderous vessel aloft, and took a long pull, to the envy of his comrades, and then spirting out the fluid, with a hideous face, exclaimed, "D——, &c. Why, if the old woman has not sent me sirup!"Evidently no joke, for the crowd around him never laughed and gravely dispersed.

It was fully two hours before the train got away from the camp, leaving a vast quantity of good things and many ladies, who had come on in the excursion train, behind them. There were about 6,600 men there, it was said—rude, big, rough fellows, with sprinklings of odd companies, composed of gentlemen of fortune exclusively. The soldiers who were only entitled to the name in virtue of their carrying arms, their duty, and possibly their fighting qualities, lay under the trees playing cards, cooking, smoking, or reading the papers; but the camp was guarded by sentries, some of whom carried their firelocks under their arms like umbrellas, others by the muzzle with the butt over the shoulder; one for ease, had stuck his, with the bayonet in the ground, upright before him; others laid their arms against the trees, and preferred a sitting to an upright posture. In front of one camp there were two brass fieldpieces, seemingly in good order. Many of the men had sporting rifles or plain muskets.

There were several boys of fifteen and sixteen years of age among the men, who could scarcely carry their arms for a long day's march; but the Tennessee and Mississippi infantry were generally the materials of good soldiers. The camps were not regularly pitched, with one exception; the tents were too close together; the water is bad, and the result that a good deal of measles, fever, diarrheal, and dysentery prevailed. One man who came on the train was a specimen of many of the classes which fill the ranks—a tall, very muscular, handsome man, with a hunter's eye, about thirty-five years of age, brawny-shouldered, brown-faced, black-bearded, hairy-handed; he had once owned one hundred and ten negroes—equal, say, to £20,000—but he had been a patriot, a lover of freedom, a filibuster. First, he had gone off with Lopez to Cuba, where he was taken, put in prison, and included among the number who received grace; next he had gone off with Walker to Nicaragua, but in his last expedition he fell into the hands of the enemy, and was only restored to liberty by the British officer who was afterward assaulted in New Orleans for the part he took in the affair.

These little adventures had reduced his stock to five negroes, and to defend them he took up arms, and he looked like one who could use them. When he came from Nicaragua he weighed only one hundred and ten pounds—now he was over two hundred pounds—a splendid *bete fauve*; and, without wishing him harm, may I be permitted to congratulate American society on its chance of getting rid of a considerable number of those of whom he is a representative man. We learned incidentally that the district wherein these troops are quartered was distinguished by its attachment to the Union. By its last vote Tennessee proved that there are at least forty thousand voters in the State who are attached to the United States Government.

At Columbus the passengers were transferred to a steamer, which in an hour and a half made its way against the stream of the Mississippi to Cairo. There, in the clear light of the summer's eve, were floating the Stars and Stripes—the first time I had seen the flag, with the exception of a glimpse of it at Fort Pickens, for two months. Cairo is in

Illinois, on the spur of land which is formed by the junction of the Ohio River with the Mississippi, and its name is probably well known to certain speculators in England, who believed in the fortunes of a place so appropriately named and situated. Here is the camp of Illinois troops under General Prentiss, which watches the shores of the Missouri on the one hand, and of Kentucky on the other.

Of them, and of what may be interesting to readers in England, I shall speak in my next letter. I find there is a general expression of satisfaction at the sentiments expressed by Lord John Russell, in the speech which has just been made down here, and that the animosity excited by what a portion of the American press called the hostility of the Foreign Minister to the United States has been considerably abated, although much has been done to fan the anger of the people into a flame, because England had acknowledged the Confederate States have *limited* belligerent rights.

LEONAUR

ALSO FROM LEONAUR
AVAILABLE IN SOFTCOVER OR HARDCOVER WITH DUST JACKET

AN APACHE CAMPAIGN IN THE SIERRA MADRE by John G. Bourke—An Account of the Expedition in Pursuit of the Chiricahua Apaches in Arizona, 1883.

BILLY DIXON & ADOBE WALLS by Billy Dixon and Edward Campbell Little—Scout, Plainsman & Buffalo Hunter, *Life and Adventures of "Billy" Dixon* by Billy Dixon and *The Battle of Adobe Walls* by Edward Campbell Little (*Pearson's Magazine*).

WITH THE CALIFORNIA COLUMN by George H. Petis—Against Confederates and Hostile Indians During the American Civil War on the South Western Frontier, *The California Column, Frontier Service During the Rebellion* and *Kit Carson's Fight With the Comanche and Kiowa Indians.*

THRILLING DAYS IN ARMY LIFE by George Alexander Forsyth—Experiences of the Beecher's Island Battle 1868, the Apache Campaign of 1882, and the American Civil War.

INDIAN FIGHTS AND FIGHTERS by Cyrus Townsend Brady—Indian Fights and Fighters of the American Western Frontier of the 19th Century.

THE NEZ PERCÉ CAMPAIGN, 1877 by G. O. Shields & Edmond Stephen Meany—Two Accounts of Chief Joseph and the Defeat of the Nez Percé, *The Battle of Big Hole* by G. O. Shields and *Chief Joseph, the Nez Percé* by Edmond Stephen Meany.

CAPTAIN JEFF OF THE TEXAS RANGERS by W. J. Maltby—Fighting Comanche & Kiowa Indians on the South Western Frontier 1863-1874.

SHERIDAN'S TROOPERS ON THE BORDERS by De Benneville Randolph Keim—The Winter Campaign of the U. S. Army Against the Indian Tribes of the Southern Plains, 1868-9.

WILD LIFE IN THE FAR WEST by James Hobbs—The Adventures of a Hunter, Trapper, Guide, Prospector and Soldier.

THE OLD SANTA FE TRAIL by Henry Inman—The Story of a Great Highway.

LIFE IN THE FAR WEST by George F. Ruxton—The Experiences of a British Officer in America and Mexico During the 1840's.

ADVENTURES IN MEXICO AND THE ROCKY MOUNTAINS by George F. Ruxton—Experiences of Mexico and the South West During the 1840's.

9 781782 820338